D0576499

Praise for

SHADOWBOSSES

"With impressive detail, Mallory Factor uncovers how government employee unions have saddled the American taxpayer with billions of dollars of crushing debt and sapped efficiency from our government. Even the Department of Defense has come under the influence of unions that have erased pay-for-performance in the civilian workforce. This is a story that needed to be told, and Factor tells it with force."
—**Donald H. Rumsfeld**, Former U.S. Secretary of Defense

"SHADOWBOSSES shows how government unions are driving us down the road to serfdom, increasing the role of government in our lives, and putting into place an endless, expensive bureaucracy that will be difficult to dismantle. By explaining the complex problem of government unions in plain and simple terms, Factor shows us how these unions and their political supporters are endangering America and what we must do to restore faith in our republic. SHADOWBOSSES is a must read for anyone who cares about America." —**Newt Gingrich**, Former Speaker of the House

"This book is a must-read for anyone who stands for truth and transparency in government. SHADOWBOSSES masterfully exposes the cozy relationship between public sector unions and the Democratic Party, and the unethical misuse of compulsory union dues to elect those who cater to the special interests of union bosses. Step one: read this book. Step two: Get out there and find more Gov. Scott Walkers who can help us get this country back on the road to economic recovery!"
—**Dick Armey**, Former House Majority Leader
and Chairman, FreedomWorks

"If you care about the future of America, read Shadowbosses. In this often amusing and always compelling book, Mallory Factor gives us the simple truth about how government employee unions are driving our country down the wrong path—towards the poor house instead of towards prosperity. Shadowbosses is a vital wake up call for all American taxpayers and workers, and shows us how we can turn our ship around before it is too late." —**Herman Cain**

"If you want to discover how labor unions have stolen the liberty and property of their members, and of American taxpayers as well, and gotten away with it, read SHADOWBOSSES. With his witty and take-no-prisoners style, Professor Mallory Factor uses hair raising tales to demonstrate the age old truism that when your partner is the government, you can get away with anything.
—**Judge Andrew P. Napolitano**, Senior Judicial Analyst, Fox News Channel

"In *SHADOWBOSSES*, Mallory Factor has written a compelling and alarming account of the growing power of these radical leviathans, and of the heroic efforts of individuals, like Wisconsin governor Scott Walker, to oppose them. This is a disturbing book, and an indispensable one."

—**David Horowitz**, Author, Founder of Freedom Center

"In *Atlas Shrugged* Ayn Rand described what happens when the looters and moochers gain control of society and of government: destruction. In *SHADOWBOSSES*, Mallory Factor shows in frightening and dramatic detail how one group of looters is coming to dominate our political lives—the government employee unions. *SHADOWBOSSES* uncovers one of today's most dangerous threats to our liberty—and it shows us how to stop that threat before it's too late."

—**Yaron Brook**, President and Executive Director, The Ayn Rand Institute

"Witty, insightful and timely, Mallory Factor's *SHADOWBOSSES* exposes the venality of today's government union leaders. Their lust for power threatens the very foundations of our democracy."   —**Colin A. Hanna**, President, Let Freedom Ring

"In *SHADOWBOSSES*, Mallory Factor provides a chilling expose of the power of unions and their tremendous influence on government and politicians....This country can no longer afford the outrageous salaries, health, and pension benefits of government employees that far exceed those paid to employees in the private sector. If you are concerned about the future of our country, this book is must reading."

—**Sally C. Pipes**, President & CEO, Pacific Research Institute

"*SHADOWBOSSES* is the first book to explore and expose the secret, sometimes violent, world of government unions and the way they run our democracy. The mainstream media is afraid to cover this story. You should be afraid _not_ to read this book. Buy it now and give extra copies to your friends, family, neighbors and countrymen. It is just that important."

—**Richard Miniter**, Forbes.com Columnist, Bestselling Author of
Losing bin Laden and *Shadow War*

"Mallory Factor's *SHADOWBOSSES* puts the torch to the political keg of dynamite beneath the Democratic Party. No better book has ever been written on the unions. No more important book has ever been written for the American taxpayer."

—**Ben Shapiro**, Breitbart News Editor-At-Large, Bestselling Author of
Primetime Propaganda

"Wonder how the anti-capitalist Obama administration brought rampant socialism to the White House? *SHADOWBOSSES* reveals the real power behind the Obama throne—the government employee unions and their bosses. *SHADOWBOSSES* is a game changer."   —**Mark W. Smith**, Bestselling Author and Constitutional Lawyer

SHADOWBOSSES

Government Unions Control America and Rob Taxpayers Blind

MALLORY FACTOR
with ELIZABETH FACTOR

CENTER
STREET

NEW YORK   BOSTON   NASHVILLE

Center Street
Hachette Book Group
237 Park Avenue
New York, NY 10017

www.CenterStreet.com

Printed in the United States of America

RRD-C

First Edition: August 2012
10 9 8 7 6 5 4 3 2

Center Street is a division of Hachette Book Group, Inc.
The Center Street name and logo are trademarks of Hachette Book Group, Inc.

The Hachette Speakers Bureau provides a wide range of authors for speaking events. To find out more, go to www.HachetteSpeakersBureau.com or call (866) 376-6591.

The publisher is not responsible for websites (or their content) that are not owned by the publisher.

Library of Congress Cataloging-in-Publication Data
Factor, Mallory.
    Shadowbosses : government unions control America and rob taxpayers blind / Mallory Factor, with Elizabeth Factor. — 1st ed.
        p. cm.
    ISBN 978-1-4555-2274-3
    1. Government employee unions—United States. 2. Government employee unions—Political activity—United States. I. Factor, Elizabeth. II. Title.
    HD8005.2.U5F33 2012
    331.88'1135173—dc23

                                                                    2012015934

*To our beloved parents: my mother, Sylvia,
and Elizabeth's parents, Karen and Jim*

Contents

Introduction

They sat around the table together in a carefully guarded ceremonial meeting room in the capital city. The government was represented by the political leader of the country, a tall and stately figurehead for the nation. Across the table sat those who had put him in power: his Shadowbosses.

The leader and the Shadowbosses had come to a standoff. Their stated positions on an important public matter were at odds with one another. And so, the meeting was called to harmonize their positions.

By the time the meeting was over, the parties were close to a deal; the details would be worked out in the coming days. But the deal would send the country in a new, more radical direction. And the people would never understand that they had been sold out by their leader and his Shadowbosses. Until now.

THIS meeting did *not* take place in Soviet-era Moscow with the Communist Party dictating terms to an Eastern European political leader. Nor did it take place today in a former Soviet republic with the oligarchs telling the government leader what to do.

This meeting actually took place on January 11, 2010. *At the White House.*

The Smoke-Filled Room

At that table sat President Barack Obama and the most important labor union bosses in America. Many of the powerful labor officials that we will meet in this book were at the meeting:

- Dennis Van Roekel, boss of America's largest labor union, the National Education Association (NEA);
- Richard Trumka, former mine worker and fabled strongman of the American Federation of Labor and Congress of Industrial Organizations (AFL-CIO);
- Andy Stern, the elegant, Ivy League–educated head of the Service Employees International Union (SEIU), now retired;
- Gerald McEntee, the thirty-year head of the American Federation of State, County and Municipal Employees (AFSCME);
- James P. Hoffa Jr., head of the International Brotherhood of Teamsters and son of the thug/legend Jimmy Hoffa; and
- Randi Weingarten, firebrand president of the American Federation of Teachers (AFT).[1]

What could be so important to bring together all these powerful labor bosses at the White House? The President needed their help to pass Obamacare, and the labor unions were threatening to tank his legislation. Why? Because Obama had proposed to tax union members' extremely expensive health-care plans, the so-called Cadillac plans, to pay some of the cost of Obamacare.

Before the meeting, Richard Trumka of the AFL-CIO spoke at the National Press Club, where he condemned Obama's proposal to tax the Cadillac plans.[2] The *New York Times* reported, "Mr. Trumka and other union leaders said before Monday's meeting that they intended to tell Mr. Obama that the tax would be economically and politically unwise."[3] The head of the International Association of Fire Fighters was even more direct, "The President's support for the excise tax is a huge disappointment and cannot be ignored. If President Obama continues to support it and signs a bill that includes the excise tax on workers, we will hold him accountable."[4]

After the White House meeting, the union bosses' tone changed. Trumka emerged from the meeting sounding satisfied. "It was a frank and productive meeting between friends about moving forward with health-care reform," Trumka announced to the press. "Meeting between friends" wasn't precise enough—it was really a meeting between our country's elected leader and the union officials who got him into office and who hold him accountable—his Shadowbosses.

The White House meeting was closed to the press and even to White House staff. Obama, as a candidate, had promised that all health-care negotiations would be broadcast on C-SPAN in an open forum. Obama, as President, broke his promise of transparency to satisfy the unions' demands out of the public eye and to get Obamacare enacted.

Two days after the meeting with Obama, the union bosses met with Vice President Joe Biden and Secretary of Health and Human Services Kathleen Sebelius to hammer out details of the deal. When the meeting ended, the Obama Administration announced that it would give labor unions a seven-year moratorium on taxing Cadillac plans. It was a victory for the unions, but not for the taxpayers who are stuck paying an additional $120 billion for this concession to the unions—on top of the other costs of Obamacare.[5] Even the *New York Times* emphasized in an editorial, "The agreement treats unionized workers far more favorably than nonunion workers, the price for the support of important Democratic constituencies."[6] But actually, the government unions got even

WHAT IS A SHADOWBOSS?

In our own lives, our Shadowbosses are the people we really work for: the people who hold us accountable for the decisions we make in our lives. It's our fathers, telling us to study harder so we will have the chance for a bright future. It's our mothers, pressing us to stay out of trouble. It's our football coaches, standing on the sidelines and sending in the plays. For some of us, God is our Shadowboss, giving us a plan for action we ought to take and consequences if we don't.

For many of our political leaders, though, their Shadowbosses are the government employee unions. These unions tell them what to do, which legislation to support, and when to bend to the demands of the unions in contract negotiations. The Shadowbosses are there to pat politicians on the back when they support the interests of government employee unions, and they're there to tear them down if they go against those interests.

more in the deal—Obama opened up enormous new opportunities for the unions which you will learn about later in this book.

This story is frustrating for most Americans. It shows us that we've lost control of our government, and our politicians ignore us in favor of influential union bosses. It suggests that our republic is in some kind of peril.

But we're not just in some kind of peril. We're Kate Winslet and Leonardo DiCaprio travelling aboard the *Titanic*. President Obama is steering the ship. And the union bosses are the only ones with lifeboats.

Our government is no longer answering to the American people; it has new masters. Behind taxpayers' backs, our country is controlled by a group of movers and shakers who manipulate the system for their own advantage. These are the heads of the government employee unions: the Shadowbosses.

A Different Type of Union

This all may seem like antiunion paranoia. After all, when we think of unions, we may remember impoverished Norma Rae striking for livable working conditions, or Bud Fox at the end of the movie *Wall Street* fighting corporate titans to help Bluestar Airlines employees keep their jobs. We may think of coal miners fighting for safer working conditions so that they can avoid black lung and of ladies' garment workers demanding improvements to their sweatshop working environments.

Government employee unions, which the unions themselves usually call "public sector unions" or "public worker unions," aren't those kinds of unions. Government employee unions remind us more of Norma Rae's bosses than Norma Rae; they make us think more about Gordon Gekko than the employees of Bluestar Airlines. These unions act more like bosses of government employees than their representatives.

Unlike private sector unions, government employee unions grow our government at the expense of the taxpayers. These unions are cynical exploiters of the taxpayer buck for their own advantage. When these unions win, all taxpayers lose—including members of private sector unions, who suffer higher taxes along with the rest of us when government grows.

The labor movement is now focused on government employees for its future growth. In recent decades, government employees have swelled union ranks—and government employees now represent the majority of all union members in our nation. The teachers unions, the Service Employees International Union (SEIU), and the American Federation of State, County and Municipal Employees (AFSCME), just to name several government employee unions, represent millions of government workers. Even unions like the United Auto Workers and the Teamsters, which used to represent only private sector workers, represent tens of thousands of government employees. Government employees now actually have a rate of unionization that is *five times greater* than private sector workers, which is why government employee unions are so important to today's union movement.

But government employee unions are a completely different animal from the private sector unions with which we may be more familiar. And the ramifications for America of having a unionized government workforce is completely different and far worse for our nation than having unionized workers in American businesses. To see why, we need to look first at the role of labor unions in the private sector.

Private Sector Unions

Private sector unions represent workers who make and run things in our country—workers in businesses. For example, private sector union workers make cars, airplanes, clothing, equipment, and steel. They work in a wide range of fields including mining, transportation, construction, telecommunications, and the movie and television industries.

In private companies with unionized workers, management and unions negotiate at arm's length against each other over workers' wages, working conditions, and benefits. The party on each side of the negotiating table is beholden to its own master. Management represents the owners or stockholders of the company, and the union represents the workers. But in a certain way, the managers, owners, union, and workers all share similar goals—making sure that the company stays in business.

When a unionized business grows and thrives, there is more profit to share and more workers to hire, leading to more union members and more union dues. With American businesses facing intense competition, many union officials realize that if their demands are too great, businesses will lose out to competitors and have to shutter their doors.

But in many cases, the unions demand too much, and as a result, unionized businesses are less competitive and go out of business. The percentage of private sector workers in labor unions has been declining since the 1950s, both because unionized businesses have been failing and because workers in new businesses don't choose to unionize. Basically, private sector unions have been driving themselves out of business for sixty years.

Government Employee Unions

Government employee unions are a totally different animal. Government employee unions use politics as the central plank of their business plans—unlike private sector unions, which have far less need for politics to maintain their bottom line.

> *Government employee unions use politics to elect their own bosses—the government officials, like mayors and governors, who will be the actual bosses of the union members. And unions get to fire bosses who don't perform for them.*

Today, government employee unions, including many hybrid private sector–government employee unions like the United Steelworkers and the Teamsters, represent 37 percent of all government workers. These unions represent over 8.3 million government workers: federal government workers in Washington, state workers in our state capitals, and municipal workers in our cities. Unions represent almost every type of government worker including postal carriers, federal border control agents, Treasury Department workers, public school teachers, university professors and graduate student teaching assistants at public universities, secretaries in city hall, police, firefighters, prison guards, to name just a few types. Government is a growth area for unions, compared with the private sector. There are now *twice* as many government post office workers represented by labor unions as union members in the entire domestic auto industry.[7]

Government employee unions use politics to elect their own bosses—the government officials, like mayors and governors, who will be the actual bosses of the union members. And unions get to fire bosses who don't perform for them. How does that work? The unions use political spending to help pro-union politicians get elected to office. These politicians become government officials who make decisions about union contracts and legislators who pass laws important to unions. And, if these politicians don't support the unions' agenda, the unions throw them out and elect other politicians in their place. Government employee unions are great at getting their allies reelected and punishing at the polls any politicians who fight their power.

In theory, when unions negotiate contracts for their members, unions sit on one side of the bargaining table, and government officials representing the taxpayers sit on the other side of the bargaining table. In reality, though, the government officials on the other side of the table may be beholden to the same unions against which they are negotiating. Unions effectively end up sitting on both sides of the negotiating table. The only party not represented at the table is you, the American taxpayer.

"In the private sector, the capitalist knows that when he negotiates with the union, if he gives away the store, he loses his shirt," writes *Washington Post* columnist Charles Krauthammer. In contrast, in the government sector, "the politicians who approve any deal have none of their own money at stake." It's the "perfect cozy setup" for politicians, he explains; the more a politician favors the union, the more the union will favor him for reelection.[8] The system is perfect for union bosses, great for pro-union politicians, also, but terrible for taxpayers.

But isn't that essentially bribing government officials to take your view in negotiations—and isn't it illegal? You would think so. But then you have to consider who makes the laws and who benefits from union political spending—the answer in both cases is government officials. Remember, when the fox is guarding the hen house, it's not illegal to eat the hens. For example, insider trading on financial information is illegal on Wall Street, but until just this year, insider trading on political information by members of Congress was perfectly legal.[9] If legal bribery benefits government officials, is it really any surprise that it is legal?

Legal bribery is just part of the "unholy alliance between unions and the Democratic Party," explains Fox News host Sean Hannity. "Unions give hundreds of millions [of] dollars, help elect Democrats, they get sweetheart deals that have to be paid for down the road."[10] Don't these sweetheart deals that government officials give the unions cost a

NOT YOUR FATHER'S UNION

Union membership among workers in American business—the private sector—has declined dramatically from a high of 35 percent of private sector workers in the 1950s to its current low of less than 7 percent. Faced with this declining market for their services, the unions of yesteryear found a new market—government workers. United Auto Workers represents auto workers of course, but it also represents more than fifty thousand government workers including firefighters, zookeepers, and academic workers at public universities like the University of California. Teamsters represents truckers, but the union also represents over two hundred thousand government workers including police officers, parole officers, public works employees, school bus drivers, and transit workers. United Steelworkers represents steel and aluminum workers, but it also represents government employees including university professors, health-care workers, and law enforcement workers. Government is the driver for the future growth for unions—and unions drive future growth of our government.

bundle? Sure, but here's the beauty of being a government worker: you don't have to care. Outrageous concessions to the unions don't drive the government out of business and make you lose your job, like they do in the private sector. The government will *always* be in business. Unwieldy union contracts just make the government immensely bigger and more expensive—and more burdensome to the taxpayers.

Taxpayers versus Tax Receivers

Government employee unions have figured out that in America today, there are just two groups of people: the "net taxpayers" and the "net tax receivers." You're probably in the first category. You, the taxpayer, are the kind of person who has a productive job. Maybe you are a member of a private sector union. But in any case, you make our nation's "pie."

While you are working hard making pie, government employee unions are busy taking pie and redistributing it to themselves and government employees.[11] They eat the pie that you make. And they're not the only ones. More than 50 percent of the American population now receives more from the government than they pay in, and the percentage of these "net tax receivers" is growing every day. Net tax receivers naturally tend to favor the growth of government because they benefit from it; taxpayers tend to oppose it because it costs them when government grows. Our nation doesn't have much of a problem when a small percentage of people in our nation are net tax receivers; the problem arises when the percentage of people who draw their support from government, including government employees, is so high that it imperils our nation's economic growth. That is where we are heading.

Those of us who make the pie are not organized into a group battling the growth of government. We have our own lives to live. We're just trying to keep enough pie to feed our families. We don't have time to march against those who want to steal our pie, even while government employee unions tell their members to rally against greedy pie makers, particularly big companies and the so-called "1 percent."

Many government employee union bosses, though, are the true 1 percent, living off the rest of us. Many union bosses receive salaries and benefits approaching or exceeding half a million dollars. Countless other union officials make generous salaries that are multiple times what their union members make. For example, at the national headquarters of America's largest labor union, the National Education Association, over half of the employees make over $75,000 in salary a year, and thirty-one employees make over $200,000 in salary a year, not including generous benefit packages.[12] It's good to be a pie eater.

New Tammany Hall

Government employee unions aren't just bankrupting our economy— they're also compromising our system of free elections. Unlike the private sector unions that came before them, government employee unions use bought-and-paid-for politicians to help create legislation granting them unending benefits.

Together, government employee unions and their paid-for politicians destroy all semblance of transparent and open government. Want to know what happened to your country? It was bargained away by our elected representatives, who were paid for lock, stock, and barrel by those government employee unions. Government employee unions are the "new Tammany Hall."[13] Senator Jim DeMint (R-SC) is even more to the point: "The unions are the most powerful political group in the country today. Their power in politics is unprecedented. And without the unions, the Democrat Party fades away."[14]

> *"People think that the labor movement is a subsidiary of the Democrat Party. They are wrong. Today, the Democrat Party is a subsidiary of the labor movement."*

As a former Labor Department official told us, "People think that the labor movement is a subsidiary of the Democrat Party. They are wrong. Today, the Democrat Party is a subsidiary of the labor movement." And the power and money in today's labor movement is centered on the government employee unions. These unions will do anything in their power to elect politicians who will serve their interests: they'll spend huge amounts on politics, send in political ground troops to get out the vote, flood the airways with negative advertising to destroy their opponents—whatever it takes to win elections. And as government employee unions rise in power, the Democrat Party gets closer to becoming the permanent party in power.

It's not as though nobody saw this coming. Not so long ago, even liberals agreed that it was illegal and inappropriate to give labor unions the power to act as "exclusive" bargaining agents for government workers against our government.

Even *union bosses* thought government employee unions were a nonstarter. "It is impossible to bargain collectively with the government," wrote George Meany, the newly installed chief of the AFL-CIO—the federation of labor unions—in 1955. A few years later, the governing council of the AFL-CIO affirmed that government workers have no right to bargain collectively with the government "beyond the ability to petition Congress—a right available to every citizen."[15]

The point was obvious to everyone at that time: no organization

COLLECTIVE BARGAINING AGAINST THE GOVERNMENT

The federal government and forty-three states allow unions to be recognized as the exclusive bargaining agent for some or all government workers. A union will be appointed as the exclusive bargaining representative of a group of workers if the union receives more than half of the votes cast in a union election. Thereafter, the union will have collective, monopoly bargaining power over all workers in the group, even those who voted against the union or didn't cast their votes, in almost all matters relating to their job.

The union will have the power to negotiate for all these workers against their government employer over working conditions, salary, and benefits (unless set by law), and to represent these workers in grievances against their employer. Whether they join the union or not, all future workers will also be represented by the union without any additional vote being required. Government workers subject to collective bargaining include almost all types of federal, state, and local government workers—office workers, mail carriers, police, firefighters, prison guards, sanitation workers, teachers, university workers, and other government workers.

should have special rights to demand government cash for a certain group of Americans. To grant such special rights to one interest group would be to compromise the integrity of our republic.

Money now flows from government employee unions to politicians and back again to the same unions in a never-ending cycle of greed and corruption. Now, virtually all Democrats and even a few Republicans in Congress and legislatures across the country promote legislation giving unions more and more power over our government and its employees. All the while, the politicians know that union money will cycle right back to them in return for their pro-union votes.

"So," you say, "I get it. The government employee unions spend huge dollars on politics to get favors from government officials—but so does the oil industry, the banks, and nearly every other industry lobby. Why are government employee unions any worse for America than these groups?"

No question about it—crony capitalism is terrible, but crony unionism is far more pernicious. Let's look at just three major differences between how government employee unions and corporate America operate. First, government employee unions trample the rights of workers by forcing them to pay dues as a condition of their employment and to support political causes that they don't believe in. As economist Arthur Laffer recently wrote, "Most high-school civics students would agree that no American worker should either be prohibited from joining a union or required to join one as a condition of employment. And no union member—or anyone else for that matter—should be required to contribute to political causes they oppose."[16] Yet, that is exactly what unions do to workers when they forcibly unionize them. Corporations don't do that, nor are many private sector workers forcibly unionized anymore.

Second, government employee unions imperil our communities by having the power to call essential workers on strike, and doing this even if such strikes are technically illegal, as we will see. If private sector workers are called out on strike by their union, some people may be inconvenienced. If essential public safety workers like policemen or firefighters, or even our unionized border patrol agents for example, go on strike, whether legally or illegally, communities suffer far worse fates.

Third, while corporations may hire lobbyists to represent their interests before our government, at least the corporations actually contribute to the growth of our economy by making products and providing services that make the pie bigger and make America more competitive. When government employee unions lobby our government, they are really just lobbying to make our government bigger, which weighs down our economy as a whole. Unions partner with government officials to grow the size of government, to hire more government employees, and to grant them more compensation. Then, these unions keep our government inefficient by preventing it from reorganizing, streamlining, and privatizing government services, because a more efficient government would mean less union dues revenue. There will be a tipping point when our government gets so big that the last remaining taxpayers in

America will no longer be able to support the enormous cost of running our government. And we are rapidly approaching this point.

Private Organizations for Private Benefit

It is important to realize that government employee unions, like all unions, are private organizations. Unions feed off the largesse of government for the benefit of their members and union bosses. Government employee unions get their business directly from our government but are not themselves a part of the government. Unions represent government employees because that is their business.

Albert Shanker, who served as the head of the American Federation of Teachers from 1974 to 1997, is credited with saying: "When schoolchildren start paying union dues, that's when I'll start representing the interests of schoolchildren."[17] Although it is hotly disputed whether or not he actually said this, the quote hammers home the point that the

FORCED DUES

Once a union acquires collective bargaining power over a group of workers, the union will try to get as many workers as possible to join the union. Government workers in the federal government and the twenty-three right-to-work states have an actual choice as to whether to join and support the union, including unions that have been appointed to represent them in collective bargaining. But in twenty-seven states, workers can be required to pay union dues and fees whether they actually join the union or not, and they can be fired if they don't pay them. Unions call the forced fees that nonunion members have to pay "agency fees" or "fair share fees." Because forced fees are generally set at about the same level as union dues, most workers decide to join the union to avoid pressure from the union officials in their workplace and to get the small amount of insurance coverage that comes with union membership. Unions make the vast majority of their dues income from these forced-dues states.

unions' sole function is to represent their members, not to work toward goals that may be in our nation's interest. Unions act in the interest of the unions themselves, not the public good. We must never forget that unions are run for the benefit of union bosses and their members and are not benevolent organizations.

Rebel States

Twenty-three states are "right-to-work" states, meaning that these states have right-to-work laws that protect most private sector workers against being fired if they don't join a union or pay dues. Government workers in these states are generally also given right-to-work protections, but not all workers in these states are protected against being forced to pay union dues. For example, airline and railroad employees are not protected by right-to-work laws no matter where they live or work. This is because the federal Railway Labor Act governs these workers and trumps state right-to-work laws.[18] So pilots at United and American Airlines, for example, are unionized and are forced to pay union dues even if they live and work in right-to-work states.

In right-to-work states, though, most workers have a choice as to whether or not to financially support a union. Not so in the other states, the "forced dues" states that don't protect this important right. In forced-dues states, a union that controls a group of workers under a collective bargaining contract can force *every last one* of those workers to pay union dues or be fired, including state and local government employees.[19] And because so many workers are forced to pay union dues in forced-dues states, unions earn most of their dues income in these states.

Just because right-to-work states don't generate much dues income for unions, it doesn't mean that unions leave these states alone. The Shadowbosses have long tentacles. Unions spend considerable money, earned in the forced-dues states, to influence politics and policy in the right-to-work states. And government employee unions maintain a web of paid political organizers in every congressional district in America to make sure that their reach covers our entire nation. Unions are far more involved in politics and policy in right-to-work states than most people believe.

Union Tribbles

Government employee unions are always working to expand their membership and to organize new groups of workers. They're like the tribbles in *Star Trek*—they seem harmless until they clog up the essential functions of the ship—in this case, our government.

To keep their dues business growing, government employee unions are reaching beyond merely representing government workers. Unions have been working to organize new groups of workers who are not employees of the government or any company but who receive subsidies from the government. In a number of states, government employee unions have already forced parents who care for their disabled children and people who care for their aging parents into unions and made them pay dues. The next step is to expand this organizing model to new groups of Americans—Social Security recipients, disability recipients, veterans, welfare moms, food stamp recipients, and other groups that receive government funds and benefits.[20]

Think about it—there are 3.5 million civilian employees who work for the federal government, making it the largest single employer in America, and around 17 million people working for our state and local governments.[21] The unions are already representing 8.3 million of them. But there are also tens of millions of Americans who receive some benefits or entitlements from the government who could also be unionized with a few tweaks to existing laws. Imagine how much more income unions could generate by representing them as well.

What does all this mean in practical terms? The unbridled growth of crony unionism and government corruption will destroy the United States as we know it. Not just crazy deficits or nutty benefits packages—utter ruin. We're almost there already.

Bankrupting America

The enormous costs of paying state and local government employees is tearing through state and local budgets. It's bad in every state in the nation—though, of course, it's much worse in states with heavily unionized government employees and where unions are permitted to extract forced dues from workers.

HOW MUCH POWER DO UNIONS HAVE IN YOUR STATE?

This Chart Shows How *Labor Union Friendly* or *Taxpayer Friendly* Each State Is Based on Its Laws, Regulations, Court Decisions, and Union Density.

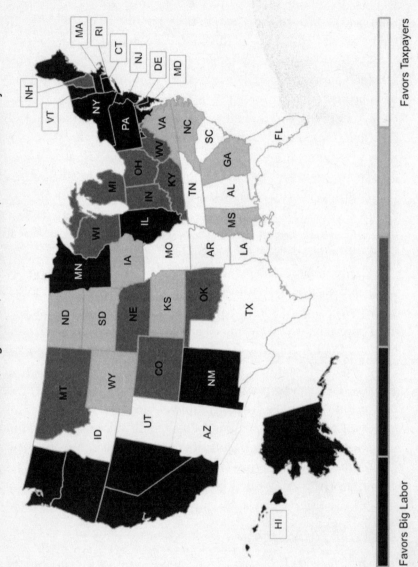

Favors Big Labor

Favors Taxpayers

Courtesy: F. Vincent Vernuccio, Competitive Enterprise Institute, www.workplacechoice.org

Government employee costs—generous salaries, benefits, and pensions—have grown exponentially and in union controlled states, these costs can't be reduced without the consent of the unions. Union-negotiated contracts make it nearly impossible for union-controlled states to bring their budgets into line, putting them in a far more precarious financial condition than less unionized states, which have more flexibility to "right-size" as needed.

Not coincidentally, states with the longest and strongest history of government employee unions are also the states with the worst budget crises. Of the ten states with the highest debt per capita in 2010, all of them are heavily unionized and none of them are right-to-work states.[22] Congress has even heard testimony that identified government employee unions as a "major contributing factor—perhaps *the* major contributing factor" to our state and local budgetary crises.[23]

Why Johnny Can't Read

Another crisis in America is our failing K–12 education system. The blame for this problem can be laid at the feet of the two teachers unions, the National Education Association (NEA) and the American Federation of Teachers (AFT). That's because the unions negotiate the teachers' contracts that determine who gets hired, who gets fired, what teachers teach, how they are trained, and ultimately whether American students are competitive with the rest of the world.

Let's be honest—if you were to imagine an ideal K–12 program for the twenty-first century, would you select a nine-and-a-half-month program that breaks for ten weeks in the summer? Would you choose a 170- to 180-day school year, when America's competitors have a school year of 220 days or more? Would you need to spend an average of nearly $11,000 a year per school child, not including the cost of school buildings and infrastructure?[24] Would you build extensive infrastructure that is only used seven to eight hours a day, for only part of the year?

Our school schedule made sense when we lived according to the agrarian calendar and we needed our kids to help us in the fields during planting and harvest. But now we are competing with China and India and many other nations whose children go to school for more hours a day and more days a year than ours do. We need a school calendar that is optimized for student learning.

There's something standing in the way of improving the competitiveness of our students—the teachers unions. The teachers unions control the school calendar, prevent us from paying better teachers more, stop principals from firing bad teachers, and even control what our teachers are allowed to teach our children.

The teachers unions insist that it is your fault that our K–12 system is failing—you, the greedy taxpayer. Of course, they tell us everything would be better if we just spent *more* money on education. But throwing more money at the problem isn't really the answer. In fact, Microsoft founder Bill Gates recently admitted to the *Wall Street Journal* that the $5 billion he spent trying to improve K–12 education in America yielded very few measurable improvements at all.[25] And Apple's immortal entrepreneur Steve Jobs reportedly told President Obama shortly before his death that until the teachers unions can be "broken," there is "almost no hope for educational reform."[26]

But at least we're getting the best teachers, right? Well, no. Just ask the young middle school teacher who won the "teacher of the year" award at the end of her second year teaching in New Jersey. After she received the award, she was fired. Why fire the teacher of the year? Because union rules dictate that the most recently hired teachers must be laid off first—which is known as "last in, first out."[27] The teachers unions set the rules that dictate that if a school district wants to keep great new teachers, it has to keep all the teachers who were hired before them—regardless of quality or performance. Under virtually all union contracts, school principals can't lay off their worst performers while keeping their best ones.

The National Education Association, which is America's largest labor union and the smaller American Federation of Teachers, which together control so much of our education system, put out the message that education is underfunded in America and our teachers are underpaid. In reality, we spend more than almost any other nation on our children's education. And the average salary for our public school teachers is significantly higher than the median average personal income in the United States, not even taking into account the extensive vacation time and the better-than-average benefits that teachers receive. By asking us all for more money for education, the teachers unions try to shift the blame for our failing K–12 education system from their shoulders to our own.

Final Frontier

This is an America run by the government employee unions. And it's only getting worse.

After World War II, over 35 percent of workers in the private sector were union members. Today, private sector union membership clocks in below 7 percent.[28] To keep the money flowing and their coffers full, labor unions have had to seek out new frontiers.

They've found their frontier—it's our government.[29] In this book, you'll learn how unions now hold power over our government workers at the federal, state, and local levels. You'll learn how these unions are destroying our rule of law and free elections, you'll find out why Obama is the perfect partner for government employee unions, and you'll learn how the teachers unions control America's classrooms in all fifty states. You'll discover what it's like to be a member of a government employee union—what the union does *for you* and what it does *to you*. You'll also learn why government employee unions spend so much of their dues income on politics and about the corruption and coercion within the unions themselves. You'll find out what's coming next—how their ultimate goal is to make *you* a member of a government employee union, with or without your permission, and how they intend to stop any politicians or groups that oppose them.

You may recall the philosopher's stone, the elusive substance that was believed by the ancients to be able to turn metal into gold. For the labor unions, it's no myth: government employee unions are the philosopher's stone, turning government employees into gold for the labor union movement. All they have to do is continue to mobilize the net "pie" recipients to support their agenda and elect their candidates.

For the past half century, they've been winning. Unions' power and privilege has always ratcheted up, never down—"toward greater union power, never less."[30]

Our job is to reverse that pattern.

As President Ronald Reagan wrote in 1985, "Someone must *stand up* to those who say, 'Here's the key, there's the Treasury, just take as many of those hard-earned tax dollars as you want.'"[31] If there has ever been a time in our history to stand up for the American taxpayer against government employee unions, it is now.

Let's get started.

CHAPTER 1

Meet the Shadowbosses

The scorpion wanted to cross a river, but he was a poor swimmer. So he begged a nearby frog for a ride across the river.

"Why would I let you ride on my back?" the frog responded. "You are a scorpion and surely will sting me."

"If I were to sting you," the scorpion replied haughtily, "we'd both drown, since I can't swim."

The frog saw the logic of the situation and agreed. The scorpion crawled aboard the frog's back, and they started across the river.

Halfway across, the scorpion stung the frog.

As the paralyzed frog began to sink, he turned to the scorpion, bewildered. "Why would you do that?" he asked. "You fool! Now we'll both drown."

"I am a scorpion," the scorpion answered. "It is my nature to sting."

And they both drowned.

TODAY, we're the frog. Government employee unions are the scorpions. If we allow them to stay on our backs much longer, they will sting us and we will all drown. And, like the trusting frog, we're letting them.

Government employee unions should be expected to do what these unions do—demand more and more from our government until they bankrupt our nation and us. And our job is to refuse them. It is up to us to save our poor nation from the scorpion's sting that we all know is coming in the middle of the river.

Public Servants Become Public Masters

Two generations ago, there were public-minded government servants. Most government employees took real pride in their work. Their common goal was to build and staff a government that served the people well.

Before government employee unions came on the scene, government employees understood that service meant sacrifice in terms of pay. Sure, you wouldn't get rich working a government job, but you'd have a lifetime job with a good pension at the end, and you'd get to make a difference. Working for the government was a privilege, and you were really working for your fellow citizens. But now far fewer government employees approach their jobs as a privilege to serve. What changed?

Labor unions came along, unionized many government employees, and drastically increased what a government employee could expect to receive in pay and benefits. Now most forms of "public service" are more profitable than working in the private sector. The government employee unions also trained government employees to demand ever higher pay and never-ending benefits, all funded by their fellow citizens.[1]

To be clear, we shouldn't begrudge individual government employees for what they get in pay and benefits from the government. As we wrote this book, we even thought more than a few times that we should go out and apply for government jobs ourselves. We understand that government workers don't make the system, they just benefit from it. But make no mistake, the culture of "public service" has changed from a focus on giving back to a focus on getting. And through their incessant focus on extracting more from the employer, unions have encouraged government workers to consider their jobs as an entitlement, not a privilege.

Many Americans, including Tea Party supporters, are angered by the decline of true public service. According to Tea Party advocate Donna Wiesner Keene, "Tea Party members are loyal tax-paying citizens, but their anger begins with the lack of value received for taxes—the transformation of government worker from asset to liability, of the people's government to the union's government."[2] With this crucial change, government employee unions have been able to unite all net tax receivers into a huge special interest group that is focused on growing the government. Net tax receivers are those Americans whose income comes from the government one way or another—as salary, welfare benefits, and subsidies. Don't government employees pay taxes? Of course they do. But it isn't close to the amount they receive in salary and benefits—and, after all, they're really just paying back tax dollars they already received from you. They give the government a cut of the pie they just took from your stove. This doesn't make government employees bad people, and many government workers surely give good service in exchange for their salary. But whether government workers work hard for their money or not, it doesn't change the fact that they are dependent on government to earn their living and are paid with taxpayer dollars.

This mammoth special interest group of net tax receivers is represented by the Democrat Party. Whether individual net tax receivers are liberal or conservative, it is the Democrat Party that supports their personal interests in keeping government large and growing it bigger.

On the other side is a dwindling group of people who actually pay the taxes that keep the other group afloat. How much longer are taxpayers going to be able to support the weight of net tax receivers?

You Should Work for the Government

Once unions organized government workers, the earlier pay gap between government and private sector workers closed. Then, the gap expanded in the other direction. Government service is now far more lucrative than private sector work ever has been or probably ever will be. If you get a government job, you can be set for the rest of your life— above market salary, great health benefits, and virtually unlimited job security while you are working, followed by early retirement and a generous and steady guaranteed pension until your death.

The smartest among you who didn't know this before reading this book will put the book down right now and go apply for a government job. Michelle Obama, our First Lady, says: "Don't go into corporate

America. You know, become teachers. Work for the community. Be social workers. Be a nurse. Those are the careers that we need, and we're encouraging our young people to do that."[3] Michelle Obama captures the message that we are all given about government service—that America needs more government workers to serve our nation. But is it really true anymore? How much "service" does our nation really need? And are we paying our government employees too much?

Paying Government Employees

Economists have shown that government workers are overpaid compared with private sector workers, but it still remains a much debated question. Unions and some liberals argue that government employees still are not paid enough because they are so much more "qualified" than private sector workers.

Federal government workers averaged over *twice* the salary and benefits that an average private sector worker makes. Federal government employees average a stunning $126,141 annually in salary and benefits.[4] And how many federal government workers do you think make more than $100,000 in salary alone, before overtime and benefits? Ten thousand? Twenty thousand? Fifty thousand? No, actually there were 459,016 federal workers making more than $100,000 in salary alone, *over one in five of all federal civil service workers.*[5] We can't possibly need that many highly paid government workers to run our federal government, even if they are über-qualified.

One of the best detailed comparisons of full-time federal government workers and private-sector workers was undertaken by James Sherk of the Heritage Foundation. His report shows that federal workers earn an average of 22 percent more in cash salary than a comparable private sector worker, controlling for the major factors like age, education, race, and location.[6] Pile on all the other retirement, health, and other benefits federal workers receive and you have a huge gap between federal government and private workers. Federal workers receive total compensation of "30 percent to 40 percent...above and beyond their observable skills," Sherk found.[7] Other reports have shown that federal government workers at the low end of the pay scale experience the greatest premium over private sector workers.[8] Chris Edwards of the

Cato Institute shows that state and local government workers made on average 34 percent more in salary and 70 percent more in benefits than private sector workers.[9] With that knowledge, why would anyone want to make the sacrifice required to work in the private sector?

Job for Life

And then there is the job security that comes with being a government worker. Ronald Reagan once stated, "A government bureau is the nearest thing to eternal life we'll ever see on this earth." He was making the important point that once our government creates a new government program, it is very hard to get rid of it. The same could be said of hiring a government employee—once hired, they are rarely, if ever, fired.

At almost all government jobs, you would have to work pretty hard to be fired—drug use on the property, embezzlement, murder, that kind of thing. Businesses fire their workers three times as often as the federal government.[10] Once you have been on the job with the government a few years, there is almost no chance that you will be fired or laid off. In fact, there is really only one way that you will be separated from your apparently God-given right to continue holding your federal job—death. At many federal agencies, death is more common than getting fired.[11] The corpse from *Weekend at Bernie's* is probably still sitting at his desk, drawing federal pay.

Here's an easy, impartial test to determine whether working for the government is a good deal: how often do government workers voluntarily quit their jobs compared to the private sector?[12] If government workers are underpaid, they'd probably quit their jobs more than private sector workers; but if they are overpaid, they would probably hold on to those valuable jobs more than people in the private sector.

So, do government workers quit? Sure, but not very often. Government workers practically never quit their jobs—once employed by the government, state and local workers quit at one-third the rate of private sector workers.[13] Federal government workers quit even less often—at only one-eighth the rate of private sector workers.[14] Government workers seem to either die at their government-issued desks—or, more frequently, on the links in Florida living off their guaranteed pensions. Why would anyone in their right mind ever give up a deal that good?

READY TO BE A PUBLIC SERVANT?

Here's one real federal government job that you might consider. Go be an "invitation coordinator" for the new Consumer Financial Protection Bureau.[15] You'll send out invitations, handle RSVPs, and be like a government wedding planner. Applicants must be highly qualified to "serve as expert on calendar issues"—after all, mixing up Mondays and Tuesdays is a challenge too many Americans have to face every day, especially consumers invited to parties at the Consumer Financial Protection Bureau.

So, what can you expect to receive as compensation for your in-demand invitation coordinating service? Try a starting salary of up to $103,000, plus five weeks of vacation. Your local stationery store isn't likely to give you that. Plus, with government employment, the government will pick up 75 percent of your health insurance premiums with "coverage for preexisting conditions, and no waiting periods," not to mention a cushy retirement program. Are you ready to enter "public service" yet?

Pension Jackpot

Retirement is where the real payoff comes—and it comes quicker for government workers than for the rest of us. Government workers are generally able to retire with thirty years of service at age fifty-five, or even earlier, at a full pension for life.[16] In contrast, only 20 percent of private sector workers get this type of traditional defined benefit pension from their employer.[17] Almost all business workers have to depend on a retirement plan based on their own contributions and modest contributions from their employer, their Social Security payments, and any other savings to fund their retirement.[18] And to receive full Social Security benefits, these workers now have to wait until they are sixty-six or sixty-seven (depending on their year of birth). Retirement security is very difficult to achieve for most American workers, except for the most successful and, of course, except for government workers.

The average New York City police officer, for example, can retire after only twenty-two years of service—often in his early forties.[19] An officer who retires as a captain can expect to receive upwards of $92,000 per year in retirement benefits, costing the city nearly $3 million during his retirement. Of course, we appreciate our police officers—they put their lives at risk to keep us safe. But no matter how much we appreciate them, we also have to realize that retired government workers in all areas of service are bringing our government's house down and foisting huge burdens on the next generation of Americans.

Now, how many Americans do you think have the $3 million in retirement savings it would take to fund that police officer's pension we were just discussing? Unfortunately, not too many. If you want to see how much you'd collect in pension if you were a government employee, the Manhattan Institute has a handy calculator at CalculateYourPublicPension.com which shows you how much you would collect on a state-by-state basis. Try it—you'll be so shocked you might actually consider trading in your corporate job or your small business for the benefits of government work.[20]

Although there are differences between pensions available at the federal, state, and local levels, most government workers get a pension based on at least 60 percent of their last working salary. Since pension income is generally based on average salary from the last three working years of his career, the government worker can jack up his overtime in his last years on the job to boost, even double, the amount of his pension.[21] And it gets even better—in some states, government workers who have hit retirement age can retire and get hired back at their same job and earn another government salary on top of their pension.[22] It's one for the price of two!

Government Service Lifestyle

Government workers must work harder than workers in the private sector for all that extra pay and benefits, right? You decide. A news team investigation in Pittsburgh tracked edits to Wikipedia, the open-source website where anyone can log in to change facts about events, people, and objects. The news team found "thousands of edits done by government employees on government time using government computers.

And few of those edits have anything to do with government business." What were these intrepid scholars up to? They were editing the Wikipedia pages for Steelers quarterback Ben Roethlisberger, singer Beyoncé, and James Bond. One employee edited the profile for Lurch, the butler on *The Addams Family*—he added the valuable information that Lurch didn't actually play the harpsichord. Another employee wrote a full plot summary for a *Star Wars* TV series. Overall, the news team found 1,536 edits by state employees and 5,542 edits by federal offices. And, as the news team pointed out, "Wikipedia is just one Web site."[23]

Even if these wiki-employees are an aberration, we do know that government employees tend to be in the office less often than workers in businesses. Federal employees get a whopping 13 days of sick leave, 10 federal holidays, and up to 26 additional days of vacation for a total of up to 49 days of paid time off per year. Because unions encourage their workers to use all their "sick" days as holidays instead of just when they are actually sick, government workers get the equivalent of up to ten paid weeks of vacation per year—that's equal to working a four-day workweek every week![24] How would your business do with you gone that much?

There are lots of other benefits of working for the government, too. According to Steven Greenhut in his book *Plunder!* "Drivers of one out of every 22 cars on California roads have special license plates whereby their addresses are kept secret from toll agencies and parking enforcement agencies. When an officer pulls over someone with one of these plates, the addresses are in a special database that alerts the officer that the driver is a government worker, or fellow police officer, or a family member of someone in law enforcement or government work. The result is a de facto pass on many, if not most traffic laws by the drivers."[25] If working for the government can get you out of speeding tickets, what can't it do?

On the downside, though, most union contracts prevent government workers from getting paid extra for good performance, although some government employees do get extra bonuses in the form of performance awards.[26] So if you don't feel like having your performance evaluated but still want to earn good pay and retire early with great benefits, the government sector is for you. But if you want to be paid based on your performance, try the private sector.

This may explain why you have a harder and harder time getting people at the Social Security bureau or the Department of Motor Vehicles to hustle to serve you. After all, they understand what you may not—they don't work for you; you work for them. Your job is to keep making the pie so that the government employee unions and their "net tax receiver team" can eat more of it. Now, get back to work!

Government Unions Rising

Unions were on the endangered species list by the 1960s and 1970s. Then, like most real-life endangered species, they found their great protector: the government. Now unions are flourishing, and they are threatening all the other species in our political ecosystem.

Of the 125 million people working in America, only about 13 percent are represented by a union. But of the 20.5 million people working for our government, 41 percent are represented by a government employee union. One in three federal workers, 35 percent of state government work-

> *Of the 125 million people working in America, only about 13 percent are represented by a union. But of the 20.5 million people working for our government, 41 percent are represented by a government employee union.*

ers, and almost 47 percent of local government workers are represented by a government employee union.[27] In the more heavily unionized states, government employee unionization rates can be as high as 60 to 70 percent. More than two in three public school teachers are unionized, about two in three police officers and firefighters are unionized, and one in two corrections officers are unionized.[28]

In the private sector, unions are still on the endangered list and still declining every year—less than 7 percent of all private sector workers are union members.[29] Workers in America's businesses seem to have decided that whatever benefits unions bring, they are not worth the cost. But in the government sector, unions are flourishing.

Millions of government employees join unions. Of course, many government employees in forced-dues states join the union because they have to pay union dues anyway. But over a million federal employees are members of a government employee union, even though these workers can't be compelled to financially support a union.[30] And to a much lesser extent, some government employees in right-to-work states who also can't be forced to pay union dues still join a union.

All government employees rushing into the unions must be getting something important for the expensive dues that they pay their union, but what? They're keeping their lucrative jobs even when common sense would dictate that these jobs should be cut. The unions are protecting them from being displaced by technology and greater efficiency in the workplace.

Protecting the Dinosaurs

Unions protect government workers against their own obsolescence. To see how, look at the U.S. Postal Service, a branch of our government that employs about 750,000 workers,[31] including 574,000 heavily unionized career postal workers.[32] The Postal Service has far more employees than any corporation in America except Walmart.[33] A public relations pamphlet from the post office boasts, "If it were a private sector company, the U.S. Postal Service would rank 29th in the 2010 Fortune 500," a ranking based on gross revenue.[34] Of course, if the Postal Service were really a private sector company, it would have been out of business a long time ago.[35]

Despite investing up to $2.7 billion annually in capital investments on new mail processing equipment and other equipment designed to increase efficiency,[36] your mail service is not getting more efficient. Perhaps this is because postal managers sometimes keep "using [obsolete] mechanical equipment even when automatic equipment was available, just to keep workers from standing around idle."[37] Or it may be because postal union contracts prohibit the Postal Service from reassigning idle workers to facilities that actually need them.[38] Even as the Postal Service was losing $8.5 billion in 2010 (with that much cash, you could actually buy Chrysler), the confident president of the American Postal Workers Union still said that he was fighting for "more—more control over activities at work, more money, better benefits—we want more."[39] More, more, more.

Similarly, while many countries in the world transformed their air traffic control system using Global Positioning System (GPS) technology over a decade ago, our air traffic controllers union is still resisting this "new" technology.[40] "Wait!" you protest. "Air traffic controllers union? Didn't President Reagan hand those guys their heads in the early '80s?" Yes. But, like a zombie buried prematurely, the union hand reached out from the grave. Just a few years later, air traffic controllers re-unionized and elected the National Air Traffic Controllers Association (NATCA) as their exclusive representative. Why? Because they needed the union to protect their jobs against improved technology making many air traffic control jobs obsolete.[41]

We all rely on GPS today to find the best route, even to keep a virtual eye on where our friends are via Facebook and collect badges at our favorite coffee bar via foursquare. Why is our air traffic control system ignoring GPS and still handing off aircraft from tower to tower across the country using radar, more or less the same way we did when John F. Kennedy was president?[42] It's because a GPS-based system requires significantly fewer controllers to do the same job, and union bosses prefer to stick with the old system. So long as unions have friends in high places in our government, flying in the United States will be more expensive and less efficient than in all those other countries that use GPS.

And how did the union handle it when national news media reported incidences of air traffic controllers falling asleep on the job, putting planes and passengers' lives in jeopardy? The union negotiated with the Federal Aviation Administration (FAA) for the perfect solution—for each shift, it required that another air traffic controller be placed on duty to make sure that the first air traffic controller doesn't fall asleep, and actually allowed controllers to listen to the radio and read on the job to help keep themselves awake.[43] If that doesn't work, undoubtedly the unions can propose an air traffic controller watcher watcher. And so on.

In government, we all know who the dinosaurs are—some postal workers, air traffic controllers, and pencil pushers. These are the people who would lose if the unions were kicked out and the government streamlined itself. And the winners would be us, the taxpayers. But we are dispersed and not fully aware of what the unions and our government are up to. Most of us still believe that we're flying pretty safe and getting our mail more or less on time. By the same token, when we *really* need a package delivered quickly, we bypass the U.S. Postal Service and take a stroll down to nonunionized FedEx instead.

Buying the Government

Government employee unions use campaign contributions and political support to influence government decision makers at all levels of government. Using this very friendly and effective method of persuasion, the government employee unions can get Congress to give them more federal workers to unionize, persuade states to force more workers to pay dues to them, and ensure that other elected officials go easy on them in contract negotiations.

Political activity was not as important to the private sector unions because politicians couldn't generally affect the unions' bottom line as directly. But buying political influence—legal bribery—works perfectly for government employee unions. After all, it is the government that determines whether these unions will be able to represent new groups of government employees, so it makes sense for unions to invest their money in putting their friends in government. These unions run like smoothly oiled machines, and they argue that nobody gets hurt by their political influence. Except the American pie maker, that is.

The Real 1%

What do government employee unions do with all that dues money that they earn off the backs of government workers and American taxpayers? They pay the Shadowbosses first, of course. While former SEIU president Andy Stern lamented the fact that people "sometimes think being a union leader is a right or an inheritance,"[44] the truth is that the Shadowbosses themselves think that being a union boss is a right. Stern himself drew $306,388 in compensation in 2009 before stepping down in 2010.[45] Being a Shadowboss is like being a dictator of a third-world country—once you've got power, you don't step down willingly and you take as much as you can while you are in office.

Gerald McEntee, the president of the American Federation of State, County and Municipal Employees (AFSCME), makes $555,367.[46] AFSCME's former international secretary-treasurer William Lucy took home $847,810 in salary alone in 2010. AFSCME had sixteen executives at the national headquarters who made in excess of $200,000 per year, and almost half its headquarters employees made over $75,000 in 2010. There are many more union officials earning high salaries at the state and local level, although this information is much harder to come by. In contrast, the average AFSCME member makes less than $45,000 per year.[47]

Dennis Van Roekel, president of the National Education Association, makes almost $400,000; Randi Weingarten, president of the American Federation of Teachers, makes over $425,000 in salary annually, almost ten times what an average teacher earns.[48] And over half the union officials at the headquarters of the two teachers unions make over $75,000 a year. Even a pro-labor commentator complained about bloated union boss salaries, "With union members everywhere getting squeezed by employers, fat salaries for top officials only widen the gap between elected leaders and the rank and file."[49] The left—including the unions—proclaims that it's unfair for Wall Street executives to make huge salaries, and that the 1 percent are living off the rest of us. But the true 1 percent includes the union bosses, who rake in the money, dine at the White House, and live it up on the backs of their members. By any measure, workers should be striking against the union bosses themselves!

> *The left—including the unions— proclaims that it's unfair for Wall Street executives to make huge salaries, and that the 1 percent are living off the rest of us. But the true 1 percent includes the union bosses, who rake in the money, dine at the White House, and live it up on the backs of their members. By any measure, workers should be striking against the union bosses themselves!*

Government's where it's at, and the government employee unions have one goal: grow government, unionize more government workers, and charge the bill to the taxpayers. And that's just what's happened. Anytime you see potential government growth, you should suspect that the government employee unions are behind it.

UNION BOSSES' SALARIES AT THE LARGEST GOVERNMENT EMPLOYEE UNIONS AND FEDERATIONS

Union or Federation	Top Officials and their salaries	Union Officials making over $75,000 at national union headquarters out of total employees*	Membership
AFL–CIO Federation	Richard Trumka (compensation $283,340); Previously John Sweeney (1995–2009)	206 of 404	Total membership of affiliated unions is 11.7 million
National Education Association (NEA)	Dennis Van Roekel (compensation $397,721)	532 of 992	Almost 3.3 million members including teachers, school support staff, school administrators, and higher education staff
Service Employees International Union (SEIU)	Mary Kay Henry (compensation $253,660); Previously Andy Stern (1996–2010) and John Sweeney (1980–1995)	340 of 892	1.9 million members including one million government employees, public school employees, bus drivers, and child care providers
American Federation of State, County and Municipal Employees (AFSCME)	Gerald McEntee, President, (compensation $555,367); Previously Jerry Wurf (1964–1981)	292 of 662	Almost 1.5 million members including law enforcement, home care providers, EMTs, sanitation workers, social workers, government office workers

International Brotherhood of Teamsters	James P. Hoffa Jr. (compensation $368,000); Previously Jimmy Hoffa (1958–1971)	190 of 630	1.3 million members including 239,000 government workers in law enforcement, prisons, public works, schools
American Federation of Teachers (AFT)	Randi Weingarten (compensation $428,284); Previously Al Shanker (1974–1997)	256 of 412	887,567 members including teachers, district employees, bus drivers, cafeteria employees
International Association of Fire Fighters (IAFF)	Harold Schaitberger (compensation $324,903)	107 of 144	296,186 members
American Federation of Government Employees (AFGE)	John Gage (compensation $214,097)	151 of 339	280,292 members—AFGE is the largest union for civilian, non-postal federal employees
Postal Unions	Various	Various	Postal unions include the National Association of Letter Carriers (285,592 members), the American Postal Workers Union (248,012 members), and Postal Mail Handlers (198,042 members)

Many other unions also represent government workers, including National Treasury Employees Union, United Steelworkers, International Brotherhood of Electrical Workers, International Association of Machinists, United Auto Workers, Communications Workers of America, and others.

* These unions have many additional employees at the state and/or local level with salaries over $75,000 but only the employees of the national union are given here.

All union official compensation and membership numbers from union reports to Office of Labor-Management Standards (OLMS), Center for Union Fact, and official union websites.

Where Do Government Employee Unions Come From?

If you were hired today as a police officer in California, a teacher in New York, or as a government bureaucrat in Illinois, you would be told that there is a specific union that will represent you in matters with your employer. You will also be told that you will be paying dues or fees to that union for the privilege of representation.[50] And if you refuse to pay these union tithes, you will be fired. Simple enough.

But how did that union get all this power? Clearly, *you* have no say in the matter, but what about Old Joe, who's been here for the last twenty years? It turns out he doesn't know how the union got there, either. It was here when he was hired. Old Joe never voted to bring in the union or to keep it there. It just seems that the union has always been there since the dawn of time.

Actually, most government employee unions gained control over government workers sometime in the 1960s or early 1970s, when many states passed laws allowing monopoly collective bargaining over government workers. A state might have done this because it was a trend sweeping the nation at the time—all the cool states were doing it. Or, more likely, the unions had made enough pro–labor union "friends" in the legislature and had supported the governor in his election to make it happen. Now, unions exercise collective bargaining power over at least some state and local government workers in forty-three states, plus the District of Columbia.[51]

In any case, when these laws were first passed, a bunch of different labor unions made a beeline for your state, like flies to honey, and tried to unionize every group of government workers in sight. First, the unions as a group would have had to convince at least 30 percent of the workers in a bargaining group, say the police officers in San Diego County, to sign cards asking the state to hold a union election. Once the unions had collected enough cards, the state held a secret-ballot election. That is when it got ugly. For a few weeks or months, the various unions fought tooth and nail—and kneecap—for every last worker, spending hundreds of dollars per worker trying to get their vote. When the election was held, whichever union won the majority of votes from police officers voting in the election was certified as the representative for *all* police officers in the county. The other unions licked their wounds and went away to organize other workers in other jurisdictions.

What if you voted against the union because you wanted to be able to negotiate your own pay and benefits individually with the department? Too bad. The union became your exclusive representative, too.

Union Contracts

The newly installed union would now negotiate detailed contracts with the county or locality. The first contract would be a "union security contract" giving the union power to represent workers and collect dues; the second contract would cover employment terms for the officers.

The union's highest priority in negotiating its own contract is always a "forced dues" provision that allows the union to collect dues and fees from every worker it represents, union member or not. This is the gold mine that fuels the government employee union movement. The represented workers aren't forced to actually join the union—but even if they don't join, they are forced to pay "agency fees" to the union, which unions more gently call "fair-share" fees. Because the nonmember fees are the same or almost the same as union dues, most workers join the union. With union membership, you get some extra insurance coverage, some other benefits—and most of all, the union thug outside your office door or hovering over your cubicle will go away. So if you can't beat 'em, you might as well join 'em.

For unions, forced-dues contracts are a home run—they get to extract money from your wallet without your permission or say-so. Forced-dues provisions are permitted in twenty-seven states and in union contracts in at least twenty-two states.[52] Generally, more than three-quarters of the dues income that government worker unions collect is from forced-dues states. In fact, over half the unions' total dues income comes from just six states: California, New York, Illinois, Pennsylvania, Ohio, and New Jersey.[53]

So, what services does the union provide you in exchange for your dues? The union gets between you and your employer in matters involving your job. Your union negotiates an employment contract that controls every aspect of your working life—from how much salary you get (where permitted by law) to how early you can retire, from how much vacation you can get every year to how many bathroom breaks you can take every day.[54] Union representatives will also handle any complaints that you have against your employer, or your employer may have against you, and on and on. You will not generally deal with your employer on matters concerning your employment—only via the union representative. If you have a fight with your boss, instead of sitting down with your boss directly, you get your union representative, your boss gets his lawyer, and they have a chat.

And the union gets some goodies, too—the government must pay union officials for the time that they spend on union matters—called "official time" or "release time"—and give the union the right to be present physically in your government workplace, to keep other unions out of your workplace, to use your workplace mail system, to keep other unions from using your mail system, and other benefits. It's a great deal for the union.

When contracts are renegotiated, the members of your union get to decide whether or not to accept the union contract, which is generally coupled with automatic recertification of the union until the next contract is put into place.[55] Very few members vote in these matters—very often, less than 10 percent—probably because union members realize that this is just rubber-stamping. And so life goes on, with the union having a virtual lock on a group of workers until the end of time.

So you get a government job forty years after the union was certified in your workplace. You don't get to decide whether you want this particular union to represent you—or whether you want a union to represent you at all. And you don't get to decide whether you want to pay union dues. You just get to decide whether you want to take the job—isn't that just a whole lot simpler?

Official Time

One of the craziest things that our government does is actually pay union officials to work for the union *during their paid workday*—called "official time" (or "release time"). Union officials and "volunteers" are actually paid for time that they spend at work on union matters. And some government employees can even work on union matters all the time for decades, without performing any actual work for the government, and still get paid their government salary, benefits, and longevity raises.

Official time is one of those key provisions that unions demand in their collective bargaining agreement with the government. As James Sherk of the Heritage Foundation explains, "Official time is a public subsidy for private matters. If federal employees value their union representation, then they should pay for it with their dues. If they do not value that representation enough to pay for it, taxpayers should not subsidize it."[56] But we do.

One of the craziest things that our government does is actually pay union officials to work for the union during their paid workday—called "official time" (or "release time"). Union officials and "volunteers" are actually paid for time that they spend at work on union matters. And some government employees can even work on union matters all the time for decades, without performing any actual work for the government, and still get paid their government salary, benefits, and longevity raises.

The federal government permits official time under federal law, but is not required to keep track of how much it costs taxpayers. But the past few years, they checked on it for chuckles, and found out that federal employees spent over 3 million hours in 2010 on official time, representing over 1,700 man-years of work and costing taxpayers about $137 million.[57] Our federal, state, and local governments combined pay for over 23 million hours of official time annually, representing around 13,000 man-years of work and costing taxpayers over $1 billion per year.[58] One commentator cleverly noted, "Official time allows union representatives to conduct routine union affairs and file frivolous grievances during working hours. Like an open bar at a wedding, there's no cost to the guest (the union) but great cumulative cost to the bride's father (the taxpayers)."[59]

Monopoly Bargaining over Government Workers

In most private businesses, you bargain for yourself—no group has the monopoly power to bargain for you. If you get an offer to be an insurance broker at a business on Main Street, you will negotiate with the owner of the business over your starting salary, relocation expenses, health insurance contributions, company car, and other benefits. Then, a year after you have taken the job, when a rival firm makes you an offer to jump ship and go work for them, you renegotiate with your original employer for better terms. You're responsible for setting your working conditions with your employer. Nobody does it for you.

Now, imagine instead that you decide to take that job we have been talking about as a policeman in San Diego. When you are hired for that job, you are given the union-negotiated contract that specifies your pay, benefits, and nearly every aspect of your job. The union is your exclusive bargaining representative in almost all matters involving your job. This is not a service that they perform for you—it is a power that they hold over you. You are not even allowed to speak with your employer about any matter involving your job without the union doing the speaking for you. To the union, you are not an individual but a member of a bargaining unit—a group of employees that are represented by the same union and bound by the same union-negotiated contract. Whether you like it or not, you are part of a collective, a group of people that are dealt with only as a group. The union bargains for all of you as though you're identical widgets.

Collective Bargaining Burdens

Unions like to talk about the right to collective bargaining, but it is no right. Collective bargaining is what happens to you when your actual right to sell your own labor is taken away from you and given instead to a government employee union.

There is nothing wrong with individual workers deciding that they want to be members of a labor union. Free association is the essence of American republicanism. Workers have the right to join a union, a church, or any lawful assembly, as do all Americans. But with government employee unions, usually an earlier group of workers selected the union and made the choice to unionize. This election may have taken place forty or fifty years ago, but the union still has the power to represent all current and future workers—until the union is decertified, which rarely happens. The unions' collective bargaining power tramples the worker's right to sell his own labor.

Current workers didn't choose to bargain with their employers collectively—the union is already representing them whether they want it to or not. When it comes to employment, your relationship with the employer *is supposed to be consensual.* The Thirteenth Amendment to the Constitution bars slavery and involuntary servitude. If you're being forced to work for a union—which in essence is what happens when you take a job at a unionized employer and are forced to pay union dues—you're not giving your consent to that relationship. You should not have to pay a middleman at a private organization like a union just to get or keep your government job.

With collective bargaining, the union also inserts itself between the government employer and its employees, and sours the relationship. The union sets up an "us versus them" mind-set by casting its demands as a fight for employees' "rights" against the employer.[60] As a result, employees tend to be more connected to their union than to their employer. The government has transferred part of its "boss" function over its own employees to the union, while retaining its full responsibility to pay their salaries.

One of the arguments against privatizing a lot of government functions like the police, jails, and schools is that these functions are too important to be subject to market forces. But if these critical functions shouldn't be subject to Adam Smith's "invisible hand" of the market, they certainly should not be subject to the "iron fist" of the labor unions. The market— in contrast to the union—would keep salaries, benefits, and retirement packages for government workers at market norms, would increase productivity, and would improve the fiscal health of our nation significantly.

> *One of the arguments against privatizing a lot of government functions like the police, jails, and schools is that these functions are too important to be subject to market forces. But if these critical functions shouldn't be subject to Adam Smith's "invisible hand" of the market, they certainly should not be subject to the "iron fist" of the labor unions.*

Good Faith Leads to Bad Bargains

Another important right that the government gives up when it lets the union fox into its hen house is its right to walk away from the table in negotiations with the union. The terms of the collective bargaining agreement compel the government to bargain with the union in good faith.[61] So, the government employer cannot walk away from the bargaining table, but must continue bargaining with the union until agreement is reached, or in most cases, face binding arbitration. This means unelected arbitrators can get the final decision on the terms of employment contracts between our government and its employees.

Unlike the government's own negotiators, the arbitrators make the decision based on what they consider fair, regardless of its cost and how the state will pay for it. This means arbitrators actually have the power to force a state or municipality to raise taxes by granting costly concessions to the unions and government employees.[62] As economist Charles Baird explains, "An arbitrator in government-sector labor disputes is unelected but has power unilaterally to determine the size of government payrolls and thus significantly affect state fiscal priorities. Some states have been forced to raise taxes to pay arbitrators' awards."[63] Baird calls this a form of "taxation without representation."

Once the arbitrator approves a concession, the state or locality is left to figure out how to pay for it.[64] But politicians may not mind arbitration because they can blame the arbitrator for overly generous terms in union contracts, giving politicians political cover against criticism from other constituents.

Strike!

The biggest problem with unionization of government workers is strikes. In theory, organizing workers into labor unions is supposed to promote "labor peace" because there is an organized procedure for workers and employers to work out their differences. In reality, unionizing workers increases the number of work stoppages and strikes, whether legal or illegal. A frequently quoted labor truism is "The only illegal strike is an unsuccessful one."[65] When strikes are successful, the strikers negotiate for amnesty for their illegal strike activity. So, no-strike clauses don't have the teeth needed to actually prevent strikes.

Strikes are not only a problem for our nation, but also for the workers themselves. Union members don't have any rights to vote on whether or not their union calls a strike. Unions themselves decide how to call a strike which may include a vote by union members, but may just involve a decision by union officers. And of course, if the union calls a strike, union members lose their pay and receive only "strike pay" from the union, which is generally a lot less, so a prolonged strike can cause members significant financial hardship.[66]

Strikes are more pernicious when undertaken by government workers than in the private sector. If workers in a toothpaste factory go on strike, using one of President Reagan's favorite examples, people can just buy a different type of toothpaste. The business owner loses, but the community doesn't suffer much. But what happens when the police or firefighters in your city go on strike? Other than a few private security firms out there, the government has a monopoly on protecting citizens from crime and fire. If the police or firefighters in your community go on strike—whether their union-negotiated contract permits them to do so or not—who are the citizens in that community going to call?

The power given to the labor unions over government workers is far more ominous for public safety workers than for mere pencil pushers. As one commentator put it, collective bargaining is less of a problem when "the maintenance men of a public zoo are authorized to compel public bargaining than when soldiers, policemen, firefighters, public-school teachers, and garbagemen have such authority."[67]

If government workers who provide essential services to our nation are organized and can strike, whether legally or illegally, the community faces a real threat. This is one of the reasons that Congress prohibited collective bargaining over certain national security employees—the FBI, the CIA, and the Secret Service.[68] We just can't have the men and women who are responsible for our national security called off the job for a strike. But as we will see in Chapter 4, the Obama Administration permitted the Transportation Security Administration (TSA) to unionize, creating a big chink in our national security armor.[69] Other national security employees and civilian military employees have been unionized as well, which could leave our nation defenseless and exposed in case of strikes.

Problems with Right-to-Work States

If you are lucky enough to live in a right-to-work state, you probably don't think these points really apply to your state. *After all*, you think, *we don't even have unions in our state.*

RIGHT-TO-WORK AND FORCED-UNIONISM STATES

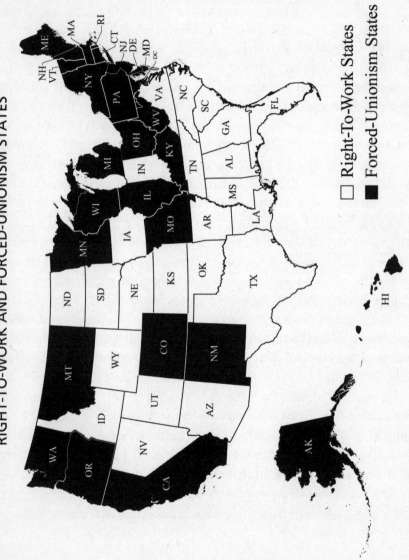

☐ Right-To-Work States

■ Forced-Unionism States

Courtesy: National Right to Work Committee

Wrong. As you will see in nearly every chapter of this book, right-to-work laws protect most workers in your state from the worst union ill—forcing workers to pay union dues to get or keep their job.[70] But government employee unions are still operating in every state in America and affecting policy and elections there. Right-to-work laws are good, but we must do better if we are going to defeat the government employee union menace that is plaguing our nation.

Right-to-work laws are a significant step in the right direction. The greatest goal of unions, as we've explained, is to increase the number of workers from whom it can forcibly collect dues. Nothing else impacts the bottom line of the unions more than forced-dues collection, so the unions are constantly trying to find new pockets of workers that they can force into this type of economic servitude. If more states passed right-to-work laws and made union membership truly voluntary, union bosses would stop being the Shadowbosses that they are today. It is that simple.

Government workers in right-to-work states do join unions, but far fewer join than in the forced-dues states, where the workers are forced to pay union dues whether they join the union or not.

Right-to-work laws, which are on the books in twenty-three states, protect most workers only against being forced to pay dues to a union—not against being forced to accept representation by a union. Hard as it is to believe, sixteen of the twenty-three right-to-work states can and do permit unions to exercise collective bargaining power over government workers at the state or local level. Collective bargaining gives unions considerable influence over government in these states.

To prevent union control over government workers, states must actually prevent the state government and its localities from giving unions collective bargaining power over workers, as seven states do: Arizona, Georgia, Mississippi, North Carolina, South Carolina, Texas, and Virginia. Only these states come close to adequately protecting workers' rights and, correspondingly, have among the lowest unionization rates of government workers in the nation. But even prohibiting collective bargaining doesn't prevent the government employee unions from reaching into almost every state and local election, as we'll show.

RIGHT-TO-WORK STATES THAT FORBID UNION BARGAINING FOR GOVERNMENT EMPLOYEES

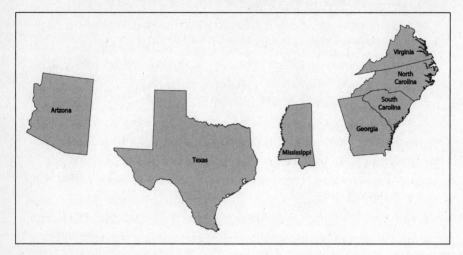

Courtesy: National Right to Work Committee

Conclusion

This sad tale began when government employee unions and elected officials realized that they could do more together than apart. With the unions backing them, elected officials didn't have to eat so many corn dogs and kiss so many babies at so many state fairs. Rather than having to please thousands of voters, politicians found it far easier just to gratify their Shadowbosses, the government employee union officials. And union officials realized that rather than trying to organize all those businesses, they could get the government to let them unionize huge numbers of government employees, more or less with the stroke of a pen. Of course, none of the government officials who sign exorbitant union contracts actually have to pay for them—that is your job as an American taxpayer.

The scam was on.

Not surprisingly, the transformation to union control of our government didn't happen all at once. There's an old saying about how to cook a frog. If you put a frog in a pot of boiling water, the frog will jump out. But if you put a frog in a pot of cold water and gradually heat the water, the frog will stay in the pot, trying to adapt until it's too late and he is cooked.

You, dear taxpayer, are the frog.

In the next chapter, we will tell you how you got in the pot, who turned up the heat, and why you're starting to feel more than a little woozy.

Chapter 1 Summary Points

- Union bosses pay themselves rich salaries by getting you to foot the bill.
- Of the 125 million people working in America, only about 13 percent are represented by a union. For private sector workers, less than 7 percent are members of a union. But of the 20.5 million people working for our government, 41 percent are represented by a government employee union.
- One in three federal workers is represented by a union. Thirty-five percent of state workers and almost 47 percent of local workers are unionized, and as much as 60 to 70 percent of government employees are unionized in certain heavily unionized states.
- Two in three teachers, police officers, and firefighters are unionized.
- Government service is now more lucrative than the private sector. Federal workers can earn 30 to 40 percent more in salary and benefits and 22 percent more in cash salary than they would earn in the private sector with the same skills.
- There are over 459,016 federal workers making over $100,000 in salary—over one in five of all federal civil service workers. Federal employees get up to ten weeks of paid leave per year, or almost the equivalent of working only four days a week.
- Government workers retire at full pension substantially earlier than private sector workers retire (usually only with their savings and Social Security).
- The key to union wealth and power is forced-dues contract provisions, which are permitted in twenty-seven states and practiced in at least twenty-two states.

- Federal, state, and local government employees work on union matters for about 23 million hours annually—while being paid by the government. This "official time" costs American taxpayers over $1 billion per year.
- Government employee unions can cripple America's economy, communities, and national security via strikes.
- Right-to-work laws protect workers against being forced to pay dues to a union in twenty-three states, but in sixteen of these states, government workers can still be forced under union collective bargaining control.

HOW DOES YOUR STATE RANK?

States Ranked by Percent of Government Employees in a Labor Union (Right-to-Work States in Bold)

Rank	State	Government Employees in a Union (percent)	Government Employees in a Union or Represented by a Union (percent)
1	New York	72.2	75.3
2	Connecticut	64.5	66.3
3	Massachusetts	62.9	64.2
4	Rhode Island	62.6	63.7
5	Minnesota	60.0	61.8
6	Oregon	59.4	62.9
7	New Jersey	58.9	60.4
8	California	56.9	60.0
9	Alaska	53.2	56.0
10	Washington	52.4	56.5
11	Illinois	52.0	54.1
12	Michigan	52.0	55.0
13	Pennsylvania	51.8	56.6
14	Hawaii	50.7	53.4
15	Wisconsin	50.3	53.4

Rank	State	Government Employees in a Union (percent)	Government Employees in a Union or Represented by a Union (percent)
16	New Hampshire	48.8	54.6
17	Vermont	48.7	52.2
18	Maine	45.8	55.5
19	Ohio	42.6	45.6
20	**Nevada**	40.9	47.1
21	Montana	38.4	41.9
22	Delaware	36.7	39.5
23	**Iowa**	35.9	46.0
24	Maryland	31.0	34.8
25	**Indiana**	28.3	31.4
26	West Virginia	26.9	30.2
27	Colorado	26.4	29.8
28	**Florida**	26.4	31.8
29	**Nebraska**	25.4	32.6
30	**Alabama**	24.8	26.8
31	Missouri	21.4	28.1
32	Kentucky	19.9	24.6
33	**Kansas**	19.7	27.8
34	**Utah**	17.6	22.2
35	D.C.	17.5	19.7
36	New Mexico	17.4	23.8
37	**Texas**	17.1	21.1
38	**Arizona**	16.6	21.2
39	**Oklahoma**	16.6	21.1
40	**North Dakota**	16.5	21.2
41	**South Dakota**	16.3	21.9
42	**Tennessee**	15.3	20.0
43	**Idaho**	14.9	17.1
44	**Virginia**	14.1	17.1
45	**Wyoming**	13.5	16.2

Continued

Rank	State	Government Employees in a Union (percent)	Government Employees in a Union or Represented by a Union (percent)
46	Arkansas	12.2	13.9
47	South Carolina	11.8	15.4
48	Mississippi	10.4	15.3
49	Georgia	9.9	12.4
50	Louisiana	9.8	13.9
51	North Carolina	9.1	13.3

Based on data provided by Unionstats.com.

Data Sources: Current Population Survey (CPS) Outgoing Rotation Group (ORG) Earnings Files, 2011. Sample includes employed wage and salary workers, ages 16 and over.

© 2012 by Barry T. Hirsch and David A. Macpherson. The use of data requires citation.

CHAPTER 2

The Union Fist

IN a small city in upstate New York, near Buffalo, the bosses of a local union are on trial. They are charged with federal racketeering and extortion conspiracy in their efforts to *encourage* local companies to sign labor contracts with the union. What did they do? They allegedly threw boiling coffee at nonunion workers and committed $1 million in vandalism of company property.[1] Court documents also charge them with sending threatening letters to company officials at their homes, stabbing a company president in the neck, and telling another company executive that they were going to his home to sexually assault his wife.[2]

But the most unbelievable part of the case was an alleged conversation between a union boss and a company president. The president allegedly asked the union boss why he should sign a collective bargaining agreement with the union: "You guys slash my tires, stab me in the neck, try to beat me up in a bar. What are the positives to signing? There are only negatives."

"The positives," the union boss allegedly replied, "are that the negatives you are complaining about would go away."[3]

This story sounds like it has to be a joke, but it is taken directly from the grand jury indictment in the case.

How did the unions get so brazen about their power over companies—and now our government? Unions have a long history of thuggery, and the rise of government employee unions is likewise mired in corruption and deceit. It involves egregious threats of violence and high-level manipulation. But it started, as most awful things do, with good intentions.

Labor Unions Rising

In the mid-1800s, labor unions started out as voluntary organizations of workers in particular trades. Workers joined unions of their own free will, and the unions bargained for better salaries, benefits, and working conditions on behalf of their members. In some cases, labor unions helped workers improve dangerous and unhealthy working conditions. The meatpackers unions, for example, were backed by the public thanks to the muckraking work of Upton Sinclair, author of the 1906 novel *The Jungle*. In that book, he depicted meat workers toiling under terrible working conditions; some stumbled into rendering tanks and were made into lard, which went on grocery shelves nonetheless.

In many cases, labor unions coerced workers to join their unions and brought violent, bloody strikes to their industries. Bashing heads and breaking kneecaps were accepted weapons in the union arsenal. But the important point is that unions started out as *voluntary* associations—even if those associations became less voluntary over time. So how did forced unionism begin and then spread to the government sector?

It started during World War I, when President Woodrow Wilson relied on labor unions to organize workers for the war effort, as an emergency measure to increase productivity and preserve labor peace.[4] But it took the Great Depression to truly legitimize labor unions. The Depression—and President Franklin Delano Roosevelt's class-warfare rhetoric—made people believe that the rich were making their money on the backs of poor workers. These people also came to believe that labor unions would rebalance the power between workers and business owners.

President Roosevelt was one of the biggest proponents of labor unions and redistribution of wealth. Despite being an immensely rich white fellow, FDR despised the so-called moneyed class. The rich, he claimed, were trying to take excess profits from their businesses and, in the process, cheating workers out of what was rightfully theirs. Thus, laws needed to be changed to give labor unions more power to grab a bigger chunk of the profits.

Fighting against excess profits by businesses was a popular rallying cry of the time, mainly because of its populist message: soak the rich.

In a way, FDR was the first member of the broad Occupy Wall Street coalition.

End of Voluntarism

The father of the American labor union movement, Samuel Gompers, had opposed forcing workers into labor unions when he led the American Federation of Labor through 1924. "No lasting gain has ever come from compulsion," he said.[5] Furthermore, Gompers believed that man's ownership of his own labor is a precious right: "The only difference between a free man and a slave is the right to sell or withhold his labor power. This precious right must be cherished and guarded against all invasions."[6] Gompers had articulated a very important principle of workers' rights—everyone has the right to sell or refuse to sell his labor in the marketplace. If workers decide to sell their labor collectively, that is fine as long as it is their choice to do so and they are not forced into collective bargaining.

But FDR wasn't concerned with preserving voluntarism in the labor movement. In 1935, Congress passed and FDR signed the National Labor Relations Act (NLRA). The chief Senate sponsor of the NLRA was New York Democrat Robert Wagner—which is why the law is still commonly referred to as the Wagner Act. Wagner was a member of Roosevelt's "Brain Trust," and a true believer in the "excess profits" line of reasoning. The Wagner Act gave labor unions extensive powers to unionize workers in American businesses. Those powers would be extended to allow unions to organize government workers around a quarter century later.

After the Wagner Act passed, workers could be forced to join a union and forced to pay union dues to get or keep their jobs. So, if you worked in a factory and a majority of workers decided to accept a union as their representative, you'd now be represented by the union, and you'd have to pay dues. Only later, in 1947, did the Labor-Management Relations Act (also known as the Taft-Hartley Act) allow individual states to pass right-to-work laws giving workers protection against being fired for not paying union dues, and there are now twenty-three right-to-work states with these laws on the books.

After passage of the Wagner Act, businesses had a much harder time resisting labor unions who came in to unionize their workforce. As historian Burton Folsom explains, "The Wagner Act certainly weighted the scales toward labor."[7] The Wagner Act requires employers to bargain collectively with unions. It also forbids employers from using certain "unfair labor practices" to prevent employees from unionizing. The Act also put into place a watchdog organization to make sure that businesses were abiding by the new restrictions: the National Labor Relations Board (NLRB). As you'd expect, the NLRB is usually used as a pro-union club against businesses. (In 2011, the NLRB brought suit against Boeing for opening a new factory in right-to-work South Carolina instead of expanding its operations in union-dominated Washington State, which NLRB dropped when Boeing reached an agreement with the union in its Washington plant to expand production there.)[8]

For nearly two years after the Wagner Act was adopted, it had relatively little impact because employees and businesses expected the law would be overturned by the U.S. Supreme Court as unconstitutional— as it should have been. In April 1937, the Court, under intense pressure from FDR, who threatened to pack the Court with additional justices to get the decision that he wanted,[9] upheld the constitutionality of the Wagner Act in a 5–4 decision. Once approved by the Court, the Wagner Act accomplished what Wagner and FDR had intended it to do— increase unionization. Membership in labor unions soared—the United Auto Workers actually experienced a *tenfold* increase in membership in the year the case was decided.[10]

The other corollary was that within just a few months after the Supreme Court's decision upholding the Wagner Act, business profits fell dramatically. After job growth of almost 7 million jobs over the previous five years, the economy turned downward again in 1937, and *1.9 million jobs* were lost from the economy. Private sector employment didn't reach its pre-Depression level until 1941, as industry mobilized for World War II.[11]

With the labor unions owing their prominence to FDR, an unshakable alliance was formed between unions and Democrats. FDR and other politicians had pushed for the Wagner Act based on their progressive worldview, of course—but their support also had something to do with their campaign coffers, which were increasingly full of labor union cash.[12] As the unions prospered, so did their favored politicians.

Meanwhile, labor unions were focused on growing their membership and their bottom lines. "We are in business to make money," said thug-boss Jimmy Hoffa of the Teamsters, who would disappear mysteriously in 1975. "We are out for every quarter we can get." James Peirce, the president of the National Federation of Federal Employees, agreed: "We all need more members, greater representation, more money for our political funds."[13] William W. Winpisinger, the International Association of Machinists president, focused on socialist goals: "I am convinced the only way organized labor can repel the armies of right-wing radicalism is by fighting for total redistribution of this nation's income and wealth."[14] The mission hasn't changed. Unions are still pushing for forced redistribution of income—from everyone else to them.

Even FDR felt that extending collective bargaining to government workers would be disastrous because it could lead to government workers striking against the government, which would be "unthinkable and intolerable."[15] The unthinkable and intolerable, however, would soon become the law of the land.

From FDR to JFK

A little more than a quarter of a century later, another friend of labor would open the gate to government workers unions. In January 1962, President John F. Kennedy signed Executive Order No. 10,988, granting unions monopoly bargaining power over federal employees.[16] The Executive Order was supposed to promote the idea that "orderly and constructive relationships be maintained between employee organizations and management officials."[17] And for Kennedy, this meant interposing unions between government workers and their employer through collective bargaining.

By extending collective bargaining to federal government workers, the Executive Order would prove to be a win-win for the unions and Democrats. And more union power meant getting a little closer to the permanent establishment of a dominant Democrat Party.

Before Kennedy's Executive Order, many federal employees, like private workers, had the *right* to join a union. The National Treasury

Employees Union was founded in 1938;[18] the American Federation of Government Employees (AFGE), now the largest union representing federal workers,[19] was founded in 1932. And our foreign service employees could join the American Foreign Service Association as early as 1924.[20]

But JFK's Executive Order changed everything. For the first time, federal employees could be *forced* to accept a union as their "exclusive" bargaining representative, just like in the private sector.

Not a big deal, right? Wrong. Having unions represent private workers in their dealings with business owners is vastly different from having unions represent government workers in their dealings with their government employer, as we've explained. "You know," F. Scott Fitzgerald is said to have told Ernest Hemingway, "the rich are different from you and me." "Yes," Hemingway replied. "They have more money." The government is different from the rest of us, too. It can hand out as much cash as it wants to anybody and never has to face any real consequences. No bankruptcy. When government employee unions wrest concessions from the government, the cost comes right out of the taxpayers' pockets— the government officials supposedly negotiating for the taxpayers don't feel a thing. It's good to be the government. But it's even better to be the union bargaining against the government.

Now, JFK didn't go so far as to allow unions to collect dues from every federal worker that they represent. He actually carved out a provision allowing employees to decide whether or not to join a union and pay union dues. Those federal right-to-work protections have now become a critical right for federal workers.[21] In the federal government and the right-to-work states, unions cannot force the workers that they represent to pay dues. This means that the unions' real payout comes from the states that permit forced-dues collection.[22]

But JFK let the camel's proverbial nose under the proverbial tent. Quite quickly after that, the camel came all the way into the tent and brought a bunch of his friends with him. More specifically, this Executive Order triggered a wave of copycat legislation in the states. These new laws authorizing collective bargaining over state and local government workers started in Wisconsin in 1959 but proliferated once Kennedy's Executive Order was issued. Labor commentator Daniel DiSalvo notes, "In 1959, only three states had collective-bargaining laws for state and local employees; by 1980, 33 states had these laws."[23] Now, forty-three states permit collective bargaining over state or local government employees.[24] And twenty-seven states permit forced-dues provisions in union contracts, and twenty-two states actively force unionized state and local workers to pay union dues as a condition of employment.[25] These forced-dues states include heavily populated California, New York, Illinois, Pennsylvania, Ohio, and Michigan.

But how did things go so terribly wrong in most of the states? To tell this story, you will have to go back a few years and meet a little, bespectacled, unpleasant man named Jerry Wurf.

Angel of Death

Jerry Wurf had been afflicted with polio from the age of four, making even walking a struggle, but Wurf never shied away from a brawl. He got his start in union agitation organizing cafeteria workers in New York City in the mid-1940s. To get inside the cafeterias to organize the workers there, Wurf got himself hired as a cashier. Then he played rough. If a cafeteria owner resisted the union's demands, Wurf suggested that busboys "drop a tray laden with dirty dishes at the end of a serving line."[26] The Yiddish-speaking cafeteria owners quickly gave Wurf the nickname of *mal'ach hamaves*, which means the "angel of death."[27]

In 1947, the *mal'ach hamaves* went to work for the labor union American Federation of State, County and Municipal Employees (AFSCME) to help them in their early efforts to organize government workers.[28] Their first goal was to get New York City to grant unions collective bargaining power over city workers.

There's an old joke about a donkey trainer known far and wide for training donkeys in a gentle way, a "donkey whisperer." One day, a man who had a recalcitrant donkey brought him to the donkey whisperer for training. The donkey trainer immediately pulled out a two-by-four and whacked the donkey right between the eyes. The man was taken aback. "Why would you do that?" he asked. "You're supposed to be the donkey whisperer!" he cried. "Well," said the donkey whisperer, "before you whisper, you need to get their attention."

Wurf knew how to get the attention of the government: by smacking them between the eyes with political muscle. In return for giving the union the power to organize government workers, Wurf pledged direct political support to politicians—not just money, but turn-out-the-vote support in the streets. He offered Democrat Robert F. Wagner Jr. (the son of Senator Wagner, who sponsored the Wagner Act) support in his run for New York City mayor in 1954. In return, Wagner agreed to support giving unions collective bargaining power over city workers. AFSCME then went out into the streets and delivered the votes needed to elect Wagner mayor. Thus began the great synergistic alliance between politicians needing election support from unions and unions needing political support from politicians.[29]

Burn, Baby, Burn

Wurf's innovative arrangement with Mayor Wagner in New York City led to a groundswell in unionization of state and local government workers across the country—from 341,000 in 1961 to 5 million under union collective bargaining control a brief fifteen years later.[30] Wurf's true agenda was to extend the New York City model across the country. In that effort, he was backed in full by the radical progressives who thought that a socialist America was just around the corner. Of course, it would take until 2008 for the real socialist America to come into being with the election of Barack Obama...but we'll get to that.

Not all politicians were as accommodating to Wurf as Wagner. And to get less accommodating politicians on board, Wurf would have to break out a figurative two-by-four: the classic union threat of violence and coercion. Violence has always bubbled under the surface of the union movement. Labor unions had always relied on the implicit threat that if things didn't go their way, they'd bring out the lead pipes. In many cases, this meant inciting violence and then allowing it to spin out of control.

In other words: burn, baby, burn.

Let's look at what happened when Wurf got involved in 1968 in the union-hostile territory of Memphis, located in right-to-work Tennessee. Wurf came to woo the new Memphis mayor, hoping to secure monopoly bargaining and automatic dues check-off privileges for the local AFSCME sanitation workers union.

Memphis Blues

Working conditions for Memphis sanitation men were degrading and dismal at the time. By then, the famous Dempster Dumpster technology—that's that sound that wakes you up at 5 a.m., when wheeled waste containers are mechanically tipped into a garbage truck—had already been available for three decades. But not in Memphis. There, sanitation men still had to pick up and carry metal garbage cans and dump them into heavy leather tubs. Then, they had to sling the tubs over their shoulders and carry them through people's yards. Many of the tubs leaked, "and during the course of the day the caustic flow from the garbage caused huge welts on the men's shoulders, arms, and torsos."[31]

There were still more indignities: white crew chiefs typically addressed black sanitation collectors as "boy," and black men were not promoted to the job of supervisor.[32] Also, the sanitation men were paid to cover a certain number of city blocks per day, no matter how long it took—with no overtime. And in 1968, their average weekly pay was a bit over $70 a week.[33] In a sense, the situation in Memphis was one of those situations where workers were actually being exploited and mistreated, and where organizing the workers could perhaps produce improvements in pay and working conditions as it had in the earlier part of the twentieth century for garment workers and others. But this is not the lesson of this particular story.

By adopting existing wheeled waste container technology, the city of Memphis could have dramatically reduced the number of man-hours needed for sanitation services. Why hadn't the city of Memphis implemented such changes? The government didn't want to change the existing system, which worked fine for the supervisors, at least. Wurf himself noted, "One of the real problems in public service is that the people who make management decisions may not be as concerned with efficiency and profit and loss as management in private industry would be."[34]

In any case, the sanitation workers called a strike in February 1968. Wurf got involved, both to make sure that the strike succeeded and to get the city to recognize the AFSCME local as the sanitation workers' exclusive bargaining representative.[35] It might not have been the perfect moment to strike, because it violated a few important principles that Wurf had developed for a successful strike. First, Wurf said that you are "stupid if you have a garbage strike in January or February. It doesn't stink as much as if you have it in the middle of the summer." He also noted that Memphis mayor Henry Loeb was new in office, and "you don't go after a politician the moment he gets into office. You haven't had time to get people mad at him and you have to develop this."[36] Wurf didn't call the strike, and "would have advised anyone against it," but once the workers were out on strike, he was not going to send them back to work without getting concessions from the city.[37]

When faced with striking sanitation workers, Mayor Loeb agreed to institute overtime pay and uniform retirement benefits, and to fight racial discrimination. But he refused to recognize AFSCME as the sanitation workers' exclusive bargaining representative and claimed that Tennessee law gave him no authority to hand union officials special privileges. He also refused to allow "dues checkoff"—which would have required the city to collect union dues on behalf of the union. Dues checkoff was critical to the union, but not very important to the workers themselves.[38] Because AFSCME wouldn't be recognized and they wouldn't get dues checkoff, Wurf kept the workers out on strike. As the strike dragged on for weeks, both the sanitation workers and the city of Memphis faced real hardships.

MLK in Memphis

Then the sanitation workers and AFSCME received a ray of hope from the Rev. Dr. Martin Luther King Jr. Dr. King knew about the labor unions' long history of sanctioning racial discrimination in employment, which union officials had not yet fully repudiated.[39] But he supported the rights of working men and women as part of his civil rights mission.[40] He therefore agreed to speak at a pro-strike rally of fifteen thousand people in downtown Memphis, and then to come back and lead a march through the city's streets.

The procession, however, quickly turned violent—marchers and police clashed; youths broke away and began looting local stores.[41] Having declared for many years he would never lead a violent march, Dr. King returned to his motel under his advisors' recommendations and then went home to Atlanta.[42] But Dr. King soon announced he would return to Memphis for another march on April 5.

And on that well-publicized return to Memphis, escaped convict James Earl Ray shot King to death. Ray had been planning to murder King in Atlanta, but he soon learned through the newspapers of King's Memphis visit. Dr. King's stalker arrived in Memphis on April 3, and was able to learn from the thoughtlessly informative local papers not just the motel, but also the very room number where his target was staying.

Always philosophical about the possibility of his being assassinated, Dr. King refused to maintain any security detail. On the night of April 3, King addressed a large crowd and gave his famous and prophetic speech. He said, "I just want to do God's will. And He's allowed me to go up the mountain. And I've looked over, and I've seen the Promised Land. I may not get there with you, but I want you to know tonight that we, as a people, will get to the Promised Land."[43] The next day, early in the evening, Dr. King was standing on his motel balcony. A single fatal shot by Ray brought down the great civil rights leader. Although the assassination was not connected with the sanitation workers' strike, Wurf would make sure that AFSCME would be forever linked with Dr. King's martyrdom when the history of the labor movement was written.

Never Waste a Good Crisis

Tragic as the assassination was for our nation, it was somewhat less tragic for Wurf and AFSCME, who quickly used the crisis to their advantage. Wurf might have agreed with President Obama's first chief of staff, Rahm Emanuel, who made the famous statement, "You never want a serious crisis to go to waste." Emanuel explained further that what he meant by that is that a crisis gives you "an opportunity to do things you think you could not do before."[44] Dr. King's assassination gave Wurf the opportunity to end the strike on terms favorable to AFSCME.

On the very evening of the murder, Wurf called William Welsh, then an assistant to Vice President Hubert Humphrey and later to become AFSCME's political director.[45] Unless the White House quickly intervened to settle the strike in favor of the sanitation workers, Wurf warned, violence would be the rule of the day. "I don't know what buttons to press," Wurf said, "but, g——, Memphis is going to burn."[46]

The day after the King assassination, the White House dispatched Undersecretary of Labor James Reynolds to Memphis to prevent the violence that Wurf had predicted by bringing the strike to an end. The strike was quickly settled with the city, and indeed, riots did not occur in Memphis.[47] Sanitation workers continued to lug tubs with forty to fifty-five gallons of trash through people's backyards for low pay, but were now represented exclusively by the AFSCME local union complete with dues checkoff. AFSCME then quickly proceeded to go after other city employees in Memphis.[48]

Fortunately for Jerry Wurf and his cohorts, very few of the millions of Americans who sympathized with the plight of Memphis sanitation men during their strike in 1968 paid any attention to how it actually turned out for them. In the minds of many Americans, the Memphis sanitation strike led by AFSCME and Wurf was linked forever to the tragic death of Martin Luther King Jr.

The association between King's assassination and the Memphis strike thus "identified AFSCME, in the public mind, as a union linked to the surging civil rights movement." Wurf suddenly became a "unionist of national stature."[49] The AFSCME website today still proclaims proudly, "During the 60s, AFSCME's struggles were linked with those of the civil rights movement."[50] But it took another thirteen years, until late 1981, for the city of Memphis and the AFSCME Local union to eliminate the back-breaking tubs with the introduction of curbside collection and wheeled garbage bins.[51]

Nonetheless, the AFSCME victory over the city of Memphis and other union victories greased the skids for even greater union takeovers of our government workers.[52] Cascades of government workers in cities and states across America were going over the union falls—and worker freedom was going over those same falls in a barrel.

Memphis Blues Again

This was not the end of the story of union coercion in Memphis. Within a few short years, both the firefighters and police workers were unionized. Soon after, they struck. The story of these strikes shows us the true danger of unionizing critical public safety workers. Once organized, they can and will strike—even if striking is illegal. And when public safety workers go on strike, citizens are truly left unprotected.[53]

In July 1978, the local affiliate of the International Association of Fire Fighters ordered more than 1,400 firefighters to go out on strike. This union wasn't aiming for decent pay or better working conditions with this strike. Not even close: this strike was over "shift differential"—the fact that firefighters received less additional pay for working less desirable shifts than other city employees received.[54]

Faced with striking firefighters, the new mayor, J. Wyeth Chandler, cobbled together a force of 150 substitute firefighters made up of supervisors, National Guard troops, the few firefighters who did not go on strike, and National Parks Service firefighters. Many members of this skeleton crew were not even familiar with the streets in the city of Memphis.

From the beginning, the strike was marked by widespread violence, vandalism, and other misconduct. Within twenty-four hours of the strike, tire slashing, headlight smashing, engine tampering, and destruction of medical equipment put most of the fire department's ambulances out of operation.[55] Using vandalism, union strikers took away the tools that the substitute firefighters would need to keep the population safe. What better way to pressure a city than put its population in real danger of being without essential safety services?

On the first weekend of the strike, three times as many fires were reported as normal—stretching the skeleton crew very thin. At the sites of some of the blazes, union militants physically blocked their substitutes from getting to the fires. And so Memphis burned. In just two days, fires caused an estimated $3 million in damage to the city.[56] The Memphis police director reported that union agents were responsible for setting 90 to 95 percent of the fires. That's actual arson on the part of the firefighters union. The police director exclaimed, "Last night was one of the most unreal scenes I've ever seen. It was like a World War II newsreel."

After three days, the city's firefighters returned to work, complying with a court injunction against the strike. But Memphians barely had time to catch their breath before the next illegal public-safety strike. Less than one week later, police went out on strike. What were they aiming for? They wanted an arbitration clause added to their contract so that future disputes between the police and the government employers would be sent to a neutral arbiter.

Once again, violence and intimidation were the order of the day. Officers who returned to work heard from anonymous phone callers threatening to "make your families pay," to "take it out on your wife and kids," and to "teach you a lesson."[57] Union members trashed twenty-five police vehicles and three fire trucks and blew up a tear-gas bomb in the county administrative building, all in pursuit of that all-important arbitration clause.

While this strike raged, the firefighters rejected the tentative contract that they negotiated the previous month and went out on a second illegal strike. Now, Memphis had police and firefighters *both* out on strike at the same time, creating a public service emergency. To add to the crisis, Memphis sanitation and teachers union bosses launched sympathy strikes in support of the police and fire unions. Within eight days, Memphis was brought to its knees. The mayor was forced to cut a deal with these various government employee unions—and that deal included a provision giving all the illegal strikers amnesty, except for those who had actually been caught committing felonies.[58] That, naturally, was a small number, since the police were striking—so who would arrest the felons?

More Unions, More Strikes

Rather than avoiding strife, unionizing our essential public safety workers actually puts our government in the position of being unable to protect our public safety in the case of strike. Breakdown in government services is possible only when government workers are unionized. Strikes of public safety workers actually create emergency situations, causing citizens to panic.[59] And citizens' fears make public safety worker strikes both short and enormously effective.

And with greater unionization

Breakdown in government services is possible only when government workers are unionized. Strikes of public safety workers actually create emergency situations, causing citizens to panic. And citizens' fears make public safety worker strikes both short and enormously effective.

of government public safety workers, strikes increased dramatically. In New York City, where unions were king, the unions were no kinder to their subjects—illegal strikes and violence were the order of the day. On July 1, 1975, sanitation workers staged a wildcat (illegal) strike, letting garbage pile up in the city—in the heat of the summer, just as Jerry Wurf had advised for a successful garbage strike. During the strike, police officers marched on City Hall, blocking access ramps to the Brooklyn Bridge and carrying signs that read, "Cops Out, Crime In" and "Burn City Burn."[60] Even the liberal *New York Times* editors admitted, "Last week's illegal sanitation strike...was the end product of three decades in which one New York mayor after another systematically fostered the growth of centralized union power."[61] Instead of bringing cooperation and labor peace, growing union power resulted in greater strike activity.

In Pomona, California, in 1975, police officers went on strike and then proceeded to vandalize cop cars and stop volunteers from assuming police duties. "I am ashamed of this kind of activity on the part of policemen," said a police captain there. "The citizens feel the officers have abandoned them, and they have."[62] That same year, policemen went on strike in San Francisco. When the mayor threatened to fire them, the officers firebombed his home.[63] Firefighters in Dayton, Ohio, let fires burn out of control during their strike in 1977.[64] The same thing happened in St. Louis that year.[65]

From the late 1960s to the early 1980s, sanitation, public safety, and public hospital strikes hit not just Memphis, New York, Chicago, and San Francisco, but also Kansas City, St. Louis, Huntsville, and many other American cities, large and small.[66] Time and again, homes and businesses were destroyed and lives were jeopardized as a consequence of government employee union strikes, most of them illegal. As Al Shanker, the legendary head of the American Federation of Teachers, explained, "One of the greatest reasons for the effectiveness of the public employee's strike is the fact that it is illegal."[67] He was making the point that illegal strikes inflict harm on cities and frighten residents, which make these strikes even more successful than legal strikes. And calling an illegal strike rarely hurts the union or its members—after illegal strikes, unions have almost always been able to negotiate for amnesty for the illegal strikers as part of the strike settlement agreement.

Americans who live in towns and cities that have given power over their public safety workers to the government employee unions can never again truly rely on those workers to protect their safety. Union objectives come first, even when life and property are at stake. Once the union toughs like Jerry Wurf got their feet wedged in the government door, they had no qualms about breaking into the house, stealing the silverware, and then setting the structure ablaze.

More Strikes, More Violence

Strikes by public safety workers charged with protecting our citizens are very different from strikes by factory workers. In the private sector, strikes by workers put economic pressure on the owners of a business. The owners will seek to end the strike before it becomes too costly for the business or drives too many of the business's customers to its competitors.

In contrast, strikes by public sector workers are not economic, but rather undermine the whole role of government—to protect its citizens. As labor policy analysts Armand Thieblot and Thomas Haggard noted, "When strikes involve employees charged with protection of public safety they are inherently violent." They continue, "Denial of protection is itself a form of violence."[68] The point is that the job of the fireman or policeman is to protect citizens, and failing to do this job is itself a form of extortion.[69]

Beyond merely not performing their duties, strikes of union workers have often used outright violence as a tactic. According to the National Institute for Labor Relations Research (NILRR), union members have committed more than ten thousand incidents of union-related violence that were actually reported by the media since 1975, usually in the context of a strike.[70] These violent incidents include vandalism, assault, battery, and even murder. The actual number of incidents may be ten times greater, or even a hundred times greater than these reported incidents; the media tends to ignore such violence. As the director of the NILRR project, Stanley Greer, concluded, the past quarter century has witnessed "an enormous amount of union-related violence... which can hardly be dismissed as spontaneous or uncoordinated."

Of these media-reported violent incidents, no legal action at all was taken in almost four out of five of these cases. And a paltry 3 percent of these violent incidents resulted in convictions, even though there are usually plenty of witnesses in cases like these. One reason is that the law actually *discourages* prosecution of union officials and members for violence committed, particularly during strikes.

Legal Violence

You remember the story at the beginning of the chapter in which the union officials and members allegedly committed vandalism, threatened workers, and stabbed a company official to get them to sign agreements with the union? That case is still pending in federal court because the union claims that even if all the allegations of wrongdoing and violence are true, the union bosses and members are protected from prosecution under federal law.[71] In discussing the case, Mark Mix, president of the National Right to Work Committee, explains: "Time and again, federal prosecutors have amassed extensive evidence that Big Labor bosses have orchestrated, authorized and/or ratified violence, vandalism, and threats." He continues, "Nevertheless, because of the pro-union violence loophole... extortion prosecutions of the implicated union officials ultimately fail—or never even get off the ground."[72]

How could that possibly be true? Because the Supreme Court has essentially legitimized union violence in the furtherance of union objectives. In 1973, the Supreme Court ruled in *U.S. v. Enmons* that if union officials or members commit violence, they can't be prosecuted under federal extortion laws as long as they were doing the violence in pursuit of a "legitimate" union aim, like striking for higher wages.[73] The Supreme Court case involved several striking electrical workers who allegedly fired high-powered rifles at three utility company transformers, drained oil from a transformer, and blew up a substation. The court decided that their acts were not "wrongful" use of violence because they were in furtherance of legitimate union goals—these goals being improving the outcome of the strike.

Essentially, this decision means that union bosses and members aren't treated like everyone else when it comes to intimidation and violence; only "little people" are prosecuted for violence. Former Attorney General Edwin Meese III said the federal law as interpreted by the Supreme Court "in effect, permits union officials alone among corporate or associational officers in the United States to use violence and threats of violence to life and property to achieve their goals."[74] It's just another way that unions and union officials get special treatment under the law that is not available for regular Americans. If you burn down your office building on behalf of your boss so he will get insurance money, both you and your boss will be prosecuted. If you burn down an office building on behalf of your union during a strike, no one will likely be prosecuted.

> *Former Attorney General Edwin Meese III said the federal law as interpreted by the Supreme Court "in effect, permits union officials alone among corporate or associational officers in the United States to use violence and threats of violence to life and property to achieve their goals."*

Although some violent crimes committed by union members during strikes can be prosecuted under state law, the *Enmons* decision itself encourages states and localities to drop prosecutions. The unions love this "end justifies the means" logic—after all, stronger federal prosecution of union crime might have a "chilling" effect on union violence during strikes which might make unions less effective in achieving their goals. And we certainly wouldn't want that.

How many times has this law actually prevented union officials and members from facing prosecution? No one knows. We *do* know that at least 203 Americans have been murdered and at least 5,869 Americans have been injured in union-related violence since 1975. These are just the cases that are reported on and classified as union violence by the press, which is not always able and willing to cover these incidents.

Many states have similar laws providing exceptions to their extortion laws for union officials and members. Why? Because these state laws follow model legal codes that include this exception, which are written by pro-union law professors and leaders of the American Bar Association.[75]

To close this loophole in federal law, Congressman Paul Broun (R-GA) reintroduced the Freedom from Union Violence Act in 2012, which Congressman Joe Wilson (R-SC) and others introduced in earlier sessions of Congress. How many Democrats have ever cosponsored a Freedom from Union Violence bill? You guessed it: absolutely zero.[76] If Democrats won't oppose union violence, they won't oppose unions on anything—especially not union coercion and intimidation.

Thuggery

Unions also use extreme intimidation tactics to force their opponents to back down. Service Employees International Unions (SEIU) have allegedly used brutal intimidation tactics in several campaigns to unionize corporate workplaces. While these examples involve SEIU's private sector organization efforts, they show the extreme intimidation tactics that are allegedly in the union's playbook and that unions could apply in government contexts as well.

One of the most egregious alleged cases of union pressure tactics involved SEIU's campaign against the multinational food services company Sodexo, whose workers SEIU was seeking to unionize. If the employer permits it to do so, a union can be certified as the representative of workers in a business by simply collecting cards ("card check") from workers without conducting a secret-ballot election. SEIU demanded that Sodexo let it unionize the company's workers using card check, but the company refused. So, the union allegedly retaliated by launching a negative public relations campaign against Sodexo claiming food safety and other violations against the company.[77]

Sodexo fought back in court with a lawsuit against SEIU under the Racketeering Influenced and Corrupt Organizations Act (RICO). Sodexo issued a press release explaining that the company "filed the lawsuit seeking to halt SEIU's extortionate threats and barrage of unlawful tactics."[78] In this press release, Sodexo alleges that the union engaged in "blackmail, vandalism, trespass, harassment, and lobbying law violations designed to steer business away from Sodexo USA and harm the company." In the suit itself, Sodexo accuses SEIU of numerous acts of threatening behavior, intimidation, and property destruction, some so extreme as to be comical. For example, in its legal complaint, Sodexo accused the SEIU of using "false pretenses to infiltrate a prestigious medical conference catered by Sodexo and, once inside, throwing plastic roaches onto the food being served at the conference."[79] Sodexo also alleges in its complaint that the SEIU attempted to "instill fear and disgust in hospital patients and their loved ones by passing out 'patient surveys' asking—without a shred of factual justification–whether patients had encountered 'bugs, rat droppings, mold or flies' in the food they were served by Sodexo employees."[80] Pretty nasty allegations indeed.

Faced with a RICO lawsuit, SEIU ended its public campaign against Sodexo. The case settled out of court, but not before the lawsuit exposed an SEIU manual entitled "Pressuring the Employer" which showed SEIU's own coercive tactics, honed in disputes with private companies. This corporate campaign playbook "describes in detail its preferred tactics for harassing, intimidating, smearing and psychologically and financially punishing employers that are unwilling to yield to its extortionate demands," alleged Sodexo in its complaint in the case.[81]

The manual begins, "It's not enough to be right. You need might as well."[82] In an expose in the *Washington Times*, labor law analyst Vincent Vernuccio reported that the SEIU manual suggests local unions use community groups to "damage an employer's public image and ties with community leaders and organizations." He notes that the manual also suggests unions attack company leaders personally in order to get decision makers to take the union's side in a dispute or to allow the union to organize workers in a company under more favorable conditions.[83]

SEIU allegedly put intimidation tactics into practice in another matter by driving fourteen busloads of protestors to the residential neighborhood of the deputy general counsel of Bank of America, and protesting on his lawn with bullhorns. The SEIU protestors were said to have scared the daylights out of neighbors and the counsel's teenage son, who was home alone.[84] *Fortune*'s Washington Bureau chief Nina Easton, who happened to live next door and witnessed the five-hundred-person protest on the quiet suburban street, concluded, "Intimidation was the whole point of this exercise."[85]

The SEIU manual also explains that union representatives can use a legal form of blackmail against managers to get them to change their positions on union issues. The SEIU manual clarifies, "It may be a violation of blackmail and extortion laws to threaten management officials with release of 'dirt' about them if they don't settle a contract." But, as the manual points out, "there is no law against union members who are angry at their employer deciding to uncover and publicize factual information about individual managers." In other words, extreme pressure tactics and personal revelations are union-prescribed techniques for getting opponents to give in to union demands.

Conclusion

With the unions now representing more government workers than private workers, unions generally use political persuasion to get what they want. Simply buying cooperation from politicians is much easier for the unions than using strikes, violence, and intimidation—and far better from a public relations perspective.

But don't think for a second that union coercion and violence is a thing of the past. Just because unions may now represent far more white collar workers than blue collar workers, far more postal workers and teachers than burly steel workers and truckers, doesn't mean that violence and coercion aren't still front and center in the unions' playbook.

Today's Shadowbosses may dine at the White House and be more refined and polished than union bosses of old (in many cases, at least). But they still use strikes, and threats of strikes, by our nation's public safety workers to put communities at risk and win concessions from them. They still use extreme pressure and blackmail-like tactics to get politicians and corporate leaders to decide their way. Also, outright union violence is still with us and is about three times more prevalent in union-controlled states than in less union-controlled, right-to-work states.[86] Funny how this type of violence doesn't bother liberals who are usually so focused on "tolerance" and "peace."

Union advocate Robert Reich, who was President Bill Clinton's secretary of labor, admits, "To maintain themselves, unions have got to have some ability to strap their members to the mast. The only way unions can exercise countervailing power is to hold their members' feet to the fire."[87] In other words, a union supporter explains that sometimes unions need to exercise coercion over their own members to achieve union objectives.

In nearly every chapter of this book, we will see how unions will use coercion and violence in order to achieve their objectives. But next, let's see how government employee unions use dues money to buy the government that is supposed to represent us all.

Chapter 2 Summary Points

- Even early labor leaders and Democrat politicians including FDR recognized the danger of collective bargaining for government worker unions.
- Whenever unionization increases, the economy suffers, as happened in the 1930s when the Wagner Act was first implemented.
- JFK's Executive Order No. 10,988 opened the door to our union-dominated federal government and encouraged states and localities to unionize their workforce as well.
- Only 341,000 state and local government employees were under union collective bargaining control in 1961, but this number increased to 5 million over the next fifteen years.
- Violence and intimidation has been a constant in union activity from the earliest days until today. Over ten thousand incidents of union-related violence have been actually reported in the media since 1975.
- At least 203 Americans have been reportedly killed in union-incited violence, and almost 6,000 injured, but union violence is probably significantly underreported.
- Union violence is rarely prosecuted. The law actually condones union violence in cases of strikes.

IMPORTANT MILESTONES IN LABOR UNION LAWS

Popular Name	Law	Date	Brief Description	Coverage
RLA	Railway Labor Act	1926	• Governs labor relations in the railway and airline industries (since 1936). • Denies right-to-work protections to all railway and airline workers even if they work in right-to-work states (which is why airlines can be forced-dues operations all over the United States). • Arose out of a period of intense strike activity and provides extensive dispute resolution procedures designed to prevent strikes and the resulting disruptions to interstate commerce.	All Railway and Airline Employees
Wagner Act/ NLRA	National Labor Relations Act	1935	• Signed by President Roosevelt into law as part of New Deal legislation with the purposes of encouraging collective bargaining and unionization of private sector workers. • Prohibited unfair labor practices by employers, set forth mechanism for certification of unions and created National Labor Relationship Board for enforcement of the Act. • Does not apply to railway or airline workers, agricultural employees, domestic employees, supervisors, federal, state, or local government workers, or independent contractors. • Is considered by many to have bonded labor unions and Democrats together.	Private Sector Employees with Exceptions

Continued

Popular Name	Law	Date	Brief Description	Coverage
The Hatch Act	An Act to Prevent Pernicious Political Activities	1939	• Designed to prevent civil servants (including post office workers—but not including Presidential appointees) from engaging in partisan political activity and to remove political patronage from government jobs. • Originally prohibited partisan activities such as endorsing candidates and taking an active part in political campaigns, but were relaxed under Clinton in 1993. • Still prohibits political activity while at work, running for partisan office, soliciting political contributions, and certain other restrictions. • Also applies to state and local government employees in agencies paid for with federal funds and DC employees.	Federal Employees (and Certain State and Local Employees)
Taft-Hartley Act	Labor-Management Relations Act	1947	• A federal law regulating labor unions amending the Wagner Act (passed by Congress over President Truman's veto). • Passed in reaction to frequent strikes by labor unions which interfered with interstate commerce. • Prohibited unfair labor practices by labor unions (the Wagner Act had only prohibited unfair labor practices by employers). • Allowed states to pass right-to-work laws (codified in Section 14(b) of the Wagner Act); 23 states now have right-to-work laws on their books.	Private Sector Employees with Exceptions
Little Wagner Act	(NYC) Executive Order 49	1958	• Signed into law by New York City Mayor Robert Wagner Jr., son of Senator Robert Wagner who sponsored the federal Wagner Act.	Local Government Employees (NYC)

Popular Name	Law	Date	Brief Description	Coverage
			• Gave the unions collective bargaining rights over New York City workers, and a "forced dues" provision that made supporting the union a condition of employment was added in 1977. • Similar collective bargaining grants were subsequently adopted in other American cities.	
Landrum-Griffin Act	Labor-Management Reporting and Disclosure Act	1959	• Act was designed to curb labor union abuses, corruption, and racketeering violations in the 1950s. • Instituted secret elections for union officers, financial disclosure and worker protections. • Barred members of the Communist Party and felons from holding union office. • Required annual financial disclosure by labor unions to the Department of Labor. • Provides safeguards for protecting union funds and assets. • Extended to cover federal employee unions and their members by the Civil Service Reform Act, but unions representing solely state, county, and municipal employees are not covered. • Administered by the Office of Labor Management Standards (OLMS).	Private Sector Unions, Federal Employee Unions, and Their Respective Members
Wisconsin Collective Bargaining Law		1959	• In 1959, Governor Nelson of Wisconsin signed the first state law to permit collective bargaining over state employees. • Many other states added similar laws in the 1960s and 1970s. • Currently 34 states plus DC permit unions to engage in collective bargaining over state and/or local government workers, and at least 22 states require employees under collective bargaining agreements to pay dues or fees to unions as a condition of employment (forced-dues).	State and Local Employees (Wisconsin, then other states)

Continued

Popular Name	Law	Date	Brief Description	Coverage
Executive Order 10,988		1962	• Issued by President Kennedy. • Extended collective bargaining to federal workers for the first time, although federal workers already had the right to join a union. • Granted right-to-work protections to federal government workers protecting these workers' right to decide whether or not to support a labor union. • Inspired an extension of union collective bargaining power at the state level to state and local employees which led to huge growth in government employee union membership by the 1970s.	Federal Employees
Civil Service Reform Act		1978	• Signed into law under the Carter Administration, this law reformed the civil service of the federal government. • Title VII of the act governs labor relations between federal workers and the federal government and formed the Federal Labor Relations Authority (FLRA) which is charged with overseeing federal employees' so-called collective bargaining "rights." • Title VII also codified right-to-work protections for federal workers, limits union collective bargaining to codified working conditions, and prohibits federal workers from striking.	Federal Employees

CHAPTER 3

Follow the Money

IN the movie *All the President's Men*, Bob Woodward (Robert Redford) meets informant Deep Throat to get the story about the Watergate break-in. "All we've got are pieces," he tells Deep Throat. "We can't seem to figure out what the puzzle is supposed to look like." Deep Throat tells him, "Follow the money." And, of course, the money leads right to the top.

The same holds true for unions and the Democrat Party. Watch as billions of dollars in union dues and fees forcibly collected from America's workers flow into union coffers. Then, see the unions as they carefully separate that money into a series of buckets, reporting each amount on disclosure forms required by the government. Finally, watch with amazement as union officials pour almost all those different buckets, which they carefully filled and reported, right into the pockets of their favorite politicians and leftist groups—rewarding their friends and punishing their enemies.

But of course, that is just where the story begins. The next step is when the unions pull the strings *attached* to the money. They ensure that the union-friendly legislators pass laws that benefit the unions. These laws are then signed by executive branch officials who were also elected with union money. Once passed, the laws increase the number of workers forced to pay union dues, thus protecting the dues income that unions rely on. On and on, the river of money flows in a never-ending cycle of greed and corruption.

Why Unions Spend So Much on Politics

Unions (at the national, state, and local levels combined) collect an estimated $14 billion in dues alone every year, and more than half of this income comes from government workers.[1] That's more revenues than 65 percent of the Fortune 500 companies, giving unions huge money to spend on politics—almost all of which goes to Democrats.

Unions (at the national, state, and local levels combined) collect an estimated $14 billion in dues alone every year, and more than half of this income comes from government workers. That's more revenues than 65 percent of the Fortune 500 companies, giving unions huge money to spend on politics—almost all of which goes to Democrats.

Many Americans think that labor unions spend money on liberal causes and Democrat candidates because union officials are themselves socialists and leftists. There's some truth to that—there are plenty of old socialists in the union leadership who love to support the liberal agenda. But the *real* reason that they spend so much money on Democrats isn't ideological—it's good business. Buying politicians allows unions to keep their dues-based business surviving and thriving.

Influencing our political system is a big part of the unions' business model. Buying the cooperation of our government is far more critical for unions than for almost any other special interest group. Oil companies, Wall Street banks, or any of the other businesses that many people love to hate—none of them rely on government favors and grants of power as much as government employee unions do to keep growing and thriving.

Unlike private sector unions, government employee unions draw all their business directly from the government. The government actually gives government employee unions the power to unionize government employees—and, even more important, allows unions to collect dues forcibly in many states. As a result government employee unions spend far more of their dues income on politics than private sector unions do.[2] Government employee unions have to spend money on politics to be sure that politicians will support their forced-dues collection business.

But why do unions spend almost exclusively on Democrats? Legendary Democrat political strategist Pat Caddell frequently refers to our two political parties in America as the "corrupt" party and the "stupid" party. You can probably guess which party is which and also which party is more likely to enter into a quid pro quo arrangement with the unions. And, of course, the labor union movement's agenda of unfree labor markets, regulation of businesses, wealth redistribution, and bigger government fits well into the Democrat Party agenda of promoting a greater role for government in all aspects of our lives. Big government makes it easier to grab big dollars for your big union.

And so the government employee unions dump cash on the Democrat Party. According to the National Institute for Labor Relations Research, labor unions spent well over $1.2 billion during the 2010 election cycle, almost all going for the Democrats.[3] All the biggest government employee unions spend huge dollars on politics—especially, the American Federation of State, County and Municipal Employees (AFSCME); Service Employees International Union (SEIU); the AFL-CIO labor federation; and the two teachers unions, the National Education Association (NEA) and the American Federation of Teachers (AFT).

AFSCME was crowned as the biggest political spender in the 2010 election cycle, investing over $91 million in political campaigns.[4] "We're spending big. And we're damn happy it's big. And our members are damn happy it's big—it's their money," said AFSCME president Gerald McEntee.[5] Not that their members have much choice in the matter.

Voters are concerned that unions are using cash to influence our political process. A recent poll shows 68 percent of registered voters are concerned that government employee unions have too much influence over the politicians that pass laws and negotiate with them.[6] But even union members are largely powerless to stop the flow of cash from their unions to politicians and back to the unions again in political favors.

Where the Cash Comes From

Unions keep their dues collection data as vague as possible, but the vast majority of their cash comes from a special set of states—the forced-dues states. These are the states in which unions can force every worker they represent to pay dues or fees.[7] There, the money that government employee unions spend on politics is ripped out of the wallets of America's workers by government-sanctioned force.

As you'll recall, once the government gives a union collective bargaining over a group of workers, only the twenty-three right-to-work states expressly prohibit unions from forcing all workers to pay dues or fees. In most of the other states, the unions can and usually do get a forced-dues provision in their union contract with government, allowing them to extract dues from their members.

In forced-dues states, even workers who choose not to join unions have to pay fees to the union. These forced fees are named by unions, in Orwellian fashion, fair share fees—and these rates are generally set near the same rate as union dues to encourage all workers to actually join the union. In these states, the state basically gives the union a cut of workers' income—and this cost gets passed on to the taxpayer, since the government employees paying the dues still want the same take-home pay.

Even more incredible, many states and localities agree to collect union dues directly from their employees on behalf of the unions. *Dues checkoff* means the government deducts dues directly from the workers' paychecks, like tax withholding or Social Security, and delivers the dues to the union. From the union's perspective, why send reminder slips to workers to pay their union dues when you can get the government to withhold union dues directly from their paychecks? Imagine if your cable bill were deducted from your paycheck automatically each month, like withholding. Would you ever cut back on the premium channels? Of course not. Dues checkoff makes forced dues a bit easier for workers to swallow by hiding the costs of their dues in paycheck deductions. It also saves unions the cost and trouble of collecting union dues, and curiously,

From the union's perspective, why send reminder slips to workers to pay their union dues when you can get the government to withhold union dues directly from their paychecks?

makes that the government's obligation instead.

These forced-dues and dues checkoff provisions are *the* reasons that government employee unions are able to survive, thrive, and spend so much on politics. And these are the contract provisions that the unions will go to the mat for, again and again. As Robert Chanin, general counsel for the National Education Association, admitted, "It is well-recognized that if you take away the mechanism of payroll deduction, you won't collect a penny from these people."[8] By "these people," he meant the NEA members. The fight for forced dues and dues checkoff is literally a battle for survival for the government employee unions.

Some members of Congress are working to prevent forced dues, at least in the private sector. Republican senators Jim DeMint of South Carolina and Rand Paul of Kentucky have proposed a national right-to-work law, which would give most private sector workers in America the right to choose whether or not they want to financially support a union.[9] "Workers should have the right to provide for their families without having to pay for political activity they strongly disagree with," explains DeMint.[10] Senator Paul calls the national right-to-work law "an historic opportunity to break the cycle of tax-and-spend, political corruption and out of control budgets caused by Big Labor's compulsory union power."[11] This law is a step in the right direction but doesn't solve the problem of government employee unions influencing our political system. State and local government workers in forced-dues states would not be freed from paying union dues even if the law were enacted.

As scholar Lowell Ponte writes, forced-dues laws are essentially a giant "money-laundering operation" on behalf of the Democrats. "This union money is the mother's milk of the Democratic Party. If these millions in union campaign contributions vanished tomorrow, most Democratic officeholders would be bankrupt overnight, and the Democratic Party would immediately shrink to permanent minority status," says Ponte.[12] And what a beautiful world it would be then.

Where the Cash Goes

So what do the government union bosses do with all this forced-dues income?

"Well obviously," you might say, "they spend it on collective bargaining expenses and the cost of representing all those workers. After all, what are unions for?" You'd be partially correct—when the union bosses are divvying up the dues money into different spending buckets, there *is* a bucket for representational expenses. But that is certainly not where most of the dues income is going, as we will see in this chapter.

The unions have made sure that their activities and spending are fairly difficult to examine. Union financial reporting is largely limited to some basic financial information disclosed to the U.S. Department of Labor, making it difficult to pin down union spending and financial activities. Unlike public companies, unions don't issue audited financial statements or annual reports that would give more detailed information about their finances, subsidiaries, and spending. Because of their special status under federal law as labor organizations, unions are able to maintain a lack of financial transparency that is unusual in our world today.[13]

This lack of transparency, incomplete financial reporting requirements, reductions in union disclosures by the Obama Administration, and some creative accounting in union financial disclosures make it very difficult for outsiders to dissect and analyze union finances. President George W. Bush's secretary of labor, Elaine Chao, explains that before she overhauled union disclosure, "one union could get away with reporting a $62 million expenditure as nothing more than 'contributions, gifts, and grants to local affiliates'—with no further explanation." But the Obama Administration "wants to return to this nontransparent standard of financial disclosure."[14] Transparency does not seem to be a priority for the Obama Administration when it comes to union finances.

Other complexities complicate union finances. For example, unions are structured as an interrelated group of national, state, and local unions that are treated as separate organizations for legal and tax purposes. Some local unions are not required to disclose their finances publically. This makes it difficult to determine the total spending of any union. For example, to determine the spending of the largest teachers union, the National Education Association, you would need to aggregate the financial disclosure of the NEA and every state- and local-level NEA subsidiary teachers union—if in fact all this information were publically available.

For all these reasons, it is almost impossible to get the full picture of union financial activities. But we will make some important observations about how unions spend their dues income from the financial information that is available for the largest government employee unions.

Before unions start dividing up the money by activity, they take overhead off the top. Union staffing, salaries, and benefits for union fat cats, building rental, and the like, seem to take about 10 to 20 percent of union dues.[15] Of course, since unions are heavily engaged in political activity, a big portion of overhead actually relates to political activity even though it is disclosed as "overhead."

Each of the fifty-six unions that are part of the AFL-CIO federation, including the American Federation of State, County and Municipal Employees (AFSCME), pay about 10 percent of their dues income up front to AFL-CIO. Members of Change to Win, like the SEIU and the Teamsters, pay a similar charge to their federation. Of course, the AFL-CIO and Change to Win use these dues to pay for political activities of their own, so we should consider most of these amounts political spending, too.

Once overhead and transfers to their federation are paid for, the unions put that still-huge pile of money into three buckets: one for political spending, one for union charitable giving, and one for representational activities.

Bucket #1: The Political Bucket

The first bucket into which unions dump their cash is the political bucket, which is used to pay for the unions' vast political organizing activities. The actual amount of union political spending cannot be accurately parsed from the limited union financial disclosure, as we mentioned before, but political spending is huge. Reported political spending is about 20 to 30 percent for government employee unions,[16] but this certainly understates the true amount of union political spending.

Remember, unions have an interest in reporting as little political spending as possible because "labor organizations" can lose their special tax-free status, or can be required to pay taxes on certain types of political spending, if they show too much political activity. An example of how unions may treat spending as nonpolitical when it has some political aspect to it is seen in the National Education Association's $80,000 payment in 2011 to Rock the Vote, an organization that works to engage young people in the political process and register them to vote, which the NEA identifies as an "advocacy organization." While the organization is officially nonpartisan, increasing the youth vote benefits Democrats—young people tend to vote Democrat and voted 2 to 1 for Obama over McCain in the last Presidential election. For financial disclosure purposes, though, the NEA treated this spending as completely nonpolitical; instead, they treated this spending as "union administration" for the purpose of "member/staff Education."[17]

Of the money that unions disclose that they spend on political activity, much of the cash is so-called soft money spending. This includes a wide range of political organizing, including phone bank support, voter registration drives, mail and advertising, and turn-out-the-vote efforts. Soft money spending does not involve direct campaign contributions to candidates, which is called hard money support.

The New York Times recently noted that labor unions realize that "their ground troops, not money, is labor's signal contribution."[18] What the Times means is that the unions spend far more on soft money political organizing activities that favor their candidates and the Democrat Party than on hard money campaign contributions through their political action committees (PACs). But who needs campaign contributions if the union will provide all the support—people, phone banks, mailings, and advertising—that campaign contributions would buy in the first place?

Unions also provide huge numbers of political "volunteers" for rallies, turn-out-the-vote efforts, and phone banks. But "volunteering" has a different meaning for unions than it does for most people. Republicans have a lot of independent grassroots volunteers—real people who give their time freely because of their love of country and of party. Democrats have some grassroots volunteers, too—but their real grassroots organizing work is performed by union members who can be paid to volunteer.

The Federal Election Commission (FEC) does not allow volunteers for federal candidates, including Presidential candidates, to be paid by third parties for volunteering, and state laws vary on the point. But the unions get around these rules by compensating volunteers to do general political organizing work and get-out-the-vote efforts for the benefit of specific candidates. Although unions try to keep the fact that they pay their political volunteers a secret, unions offer expense reimbursement and stipends to members who act as political volunteers.

The going rate seems to be $25 for two hours on phone banks for get-out-the-vote messaging, and $50 for a three-hour solidarity walk, plus meals and T-shirts are also provided.[19] Tea Party volunteers certainly don't get those benefits—but then again, they don't have a union representing them. Yet!

Another form of union political spending is "independent expenditures" or "outside spending," which can be made by unions directly or through political organizations known as super PACs. Unions make independent expenditures directly, or through a super PAC, on advertising, mailings, or other media in favor (or against) specific candidates, but which are not coordinated with any candidate's political campaign. After the Supreme Court ruled in *Citizens United v. Federal Election Commission* in 2010, which allowed unions and corporations to make unlimited expenditures on political advertising and other political activities, unions ratcheted up their game. The decision allows unions to send their political troops out to canvass all households, union and nonunion, to increase support for their candidates and get their supporters to the polls. The *New York Times* notes that this change is "expected to increase labor's political clout significantly in this year's elections."[20]

Labor unions can spend union dues on political advertising and other political activity directly or contribute to super PACs to do the spending for them. Most unions do both. Labor union super PACs accounted for 25 percent of all super PAC spending in the 2010 election cycle.[21] Many unions have their own super PACs and also contribute to other liberal super PACs like those funded by George Soros, the Hungarian-born magnate and huge donor to leftist causes.[22] Andy Stern's super PAC, founded in 2007 to help out President Obama and his buddies, was appropriately called Working for Us—the idea seems to be that the super PAC will elect politicians who will work for the unions and their agenda.[23]

But wait, there's more in the political bucket! Dig deeper and you'll find union cash flowing to the Democratic National Committee, the Democratic Governors Association, and various state Democrat parties. The unions also hire outside lobbyists directly and pay for them out of the dues in this bucket. Finally, many states allow unions to make donations to state and local candidates from their dues income (subject to certain limitations), which would also come from this bucket.

When there's a particularly hot-button union issue, unions also impose "special assessments" from their members, which gives the unions even more cash. Of course, they don't really ask. They just require these extra assessments, which can be several hundred dollars in extra dues, on top of regular dues. A recent lawsuit involving an assessment by an SEIU local showed that these assessments can be pricey—workers had to pay an assessment equal to one-quarter their entire annual dues—on top of the dues that they paid already.[24]

Union members are mostly kept in the dark about union political spending. While unions are required by law to make reports to union members on how their dues are being used, many unions simply don't comply. And even if union members *did* know, they couldn't do much about it.[25] Rank-and-file union members don't get a say in whether a special assessment is levied on them or generally whether their dues are raised. And most union members have very limited rights to prevent their union from spending their dues on politics.[26] About 60 percent of union members object to union political spending, but only union workers in a few states that have passed paycheck protection laws are consulted before their unions spend their dues income on politics.[27] And in those forced-dues states in which most union members reside, it is not as if they can leave the union or stop paying union dues if they are dissatisfied.

Bucket #2: "Charitable" Giving

Into the smaller second bucket, the unions put money for gifts, contributions, and donations to other organizations. And this bucket, too, is largely political. Union donations go to support left-leaning think tanks, political movements, and other organizations; the goal is to build alliances with like-minded political groups—the vast left-wing conspiracy, sometimes called the Shadow Democrat Party.

To see how this works, let's look at America's largest union, the National Education Association (NEA), which represents teachers. As part of its huge political spending, the NEA's national headquarters alone made over $88 million in direct grants and donations to various organizations, almost all to left-leaning organizations and political organizing projects.[28]

The teachers unions are able to draw attention away from their huge political influence because Americans generally like and trust teachers. "Because they represent people working with children, National Education Association and American Federation of Teachers benefit from residual good will in a way that the Teamsters and United Auto Workers do not," one commentator noted.[29]

A typical NEA grant would be the $250,000 that the NEA gave to Arizona State University, which, like the NEA, is highly critical of charter schools.[30] And just to ensure that NEA's agenda makes its way in the media, NEA has given $100,000 to Media Matters, the George Soros–funded liberal "charitable organization" dedicated to targeting mythical right-wing media bias; $110,000 to the Center for American Progress, another Soros-funded radical-left think tank; and other grants to many more leftist organizations.

Occupy Wall Street (OWS) is among teachers unions' favorite causes. The New York City teachers union provided logistical support for the protestors; the union president said, "Occupy Wall Street isn't a place—it's an idea, a movement that has brought national and international focus to the danger to our economy that we face because of growing income inequality."[31] Is income inequality an issue of direct importance to teachers? Of course not. But for future battles affecting the union more directly, the teachers union needs to be part of the grand leftist alliance that OWS represents.

While the teachers unions are almost 100 percent liberal in their public positions and support for other organizations, a solid 50 percent of NEA's members consider themselves "more conservative than liberal," according to NEA's own polling.[32] But that doesn't stop NEA from continuing to pick its members' pockets to support a hard-left agenda.

So what rights do union members have to control *donations* by their unions to liberal causes? Practically speaking, none. Union members aren't given rights to vote against or opt out of political spending, although nonmembers paying agency fees do have the right to opt out of political spending. Until that changes, unions will continue to use philanthropy and resolutions to build a very strong coalition of leftist organizations that will support unions getting more power over our workers and our nation.

Bucket #3: Worker Representation

Almost forgot about it, didn't you?

That's because representing their workers isn't as much of a core focus for government employee unions as political activity is. In this bucket, unions put funds for the actual cost of representing workers, negotiating contracts for them, handling grievances and, of course, organizing new groups of workers.[33] You thought these causes were the central focus of the unions. So did union members. But representing workers is not really a big part of the unions' business plan.

Because members and the public consider these to be core union activities, unions have an incentive to show as much possible spending on representational activities as possible. NEA shows about 13 percent of its national headquarters' spending on representational activities, whereas the top ten unions show an average of 30 percent of spending in this bucket at their national headquarters level.[34] The difference may be that other unions like SEIU may spend considerably more than the NEA on organizing new workers, which also goes into this bucket for financial reporting purposes but is really about business generation and improving the bottom line. It's likely that unions actually spend far less than 20 percent on real worker representation, especially at the state and national level, since negotiation and grievances are mostly handled at the local union level.

How do we know that this bucket actually holds so little in practice? When members have sued to find out where their dues are going, unions have been able to show only that they spend about 20 percent of their dues income on these core union functions.[35] An analysis of teachers union dues in Washington State found that 20 percent or less of dues income were used for "legitimate, chargeable union functions, such as collective bargaining, maintenance of the contract and grievances."[36] So politics is the name of the game for the government employee unions. Negotiation over worker contracts, in many cases is largely window dressing.[37]

Direct Contributions

Unions don't generally make direct contributions to federal candidates, or most state and local candidates, out of their general revenues.[38] If unions reported actual political contributions from union dues, they'd face negative tax consequences. Instead, unions set up special political action committees (PACs) for the purpose of making campaign contributions to candidates. Union PACs cannot be funded from union dues, but are funded instead from contributions collected from the union's members. (In contrast, super PACs can be funded with union dues, but cannot make campaign contributions to candidates and are used mostly for purchasing advertising and sending mailings in favor or against candidates.)

Member contributions to the union PACs are supposed to be voluntary and in addition to their union dues. In practice, however, unions frequently seem to extract these contributions from members without their consent. One recent FEC audit of a union showed that 93 percent of the time, the union was deducting PAC money from members without their written approval; in another case, the union was doing it 67 percent of the time.[39] The moral of this story: don't ever give your union the right to deduct amounts from your paycheck if you have the choice—of course, dues checkoff is mandatory for most union members.

Direct donations to candidates through PACs are a part of unions' political support for pro-union candidates, but the amounts aren't particularly large. Unions are estimated to spend ten times as much on soft money political activities as on hard money campaign contributions to candidates, but this suits the candidates receiving the support just fine.[40]

Reward Your Friends, Punish Your Enemies

The government employee unions have a very simple action plan: reward your friends; slice and dice your enemies Benihana-style. Most Americans think that members of Congress and political leaders live in fear of the opinion of their constituents. But as we will see, Democrats live in fear of the people that really impact their reelection campaigns—the union

"An honest politician," President Abraham Lincoln's secretary of war, Simon Cameron, supposedly said, "is one who, when he is bought, will stay bought." If the unions buy someone who doesn't stay bought, they work to replace him with someone who takes orders better.

Shadowbosses. And fear them they should, for hell hath no fury like a union official scorned.

"An honest politician," President Abraham Lincoln's secretary of war, Simon Cameron, supposedly said, "is one who, when he is bought, will stay bought." If the unions buy someone who doesn't stay bought, they work to replace him with someone who takes orders better. Of course, unions constantly try to replace Republicans with Democrats since, as a general rule, Democrats have less ideological objection to taking union orders. But they also replace Democrat defectors with more loyal Democrats. And if they don't support you, they are going to work against you—usually very effectively.

AFL-CIO president Richard Trumka now spouts that unions are going to be even more vigilant about holding politicians accountable: "For too long, we have been left after Election Day holding a canceled check waving it about—'Remember us? Remember us? Remember us?'—asking someone to pay a little attention to us. Well, I don't know about you, but I've had a snootful of that [expletive deleted]."[41] He added, "Unlike in the past, instead of saying 'OK, we've elected you, now do what's right by us,' we are going to keep our machinery in place." The point he is making is that the unions will stay focused on politics all the time—not just at election time—in order to get better service from their politicians. Trumka asserted, "We are going to make sure that our interests are considered at the front of the parade."[42]

AFL-CIO president Richard Trumka now spouts that unions are going to be even more vigilant about holding politicians accountable: "For too long, we have been left after Election Day holding a canceled check waving it about—'Remember us? Remember us? Remember us?'—asking someone to pay a little attention to us. Well, I don't know about you, but I've had a snootful of that [expletive deleted]."

Other unions echo this sentiment that they are keeping careful track of who is naughty and who is nice. Andy Stern, former head of the SEIU, told the *Wall Street Journal* in 2008 that he had set aside a $10 million fund just to get errant politicians unelected, and he said, "We would like to make sure people appreciate that we take them at their word and when they don't live up to their word there should be consequences."[43] Similarly, one California SEIU official exclaimed,

"We helped getchu into office, and we gotta good memory. Come November, if you don't back our program, we'll getchu out of office."[44] And this is no empty threat—of the top ten congressional candidates whom labor spent money to defeat in 2008, all lost their races.[45]

Secretary of Labor Hilda Solis knows all about how the unions enforce party discipline. That is exactly how she first got elected to the U.S. Congress. In 2000, she went to Congress as the labor unions' choice in California against an incumbent Democrat, Matthew Martinez, who had defied the unions to support the North American Free Trade Agreement (NAFTA).[46] Solis was seen as more controllable. As one of her colleagues in the California Statehouse said about Solis and unions, "She'll carry their water, no matter what."[47] And so, the unions helped her replace Martinez.

By contrast, when Democrats strayed from the beaten path on Obamacare in 2010, unions threatened to crunch them underfoot like fallen leaves in autumn. When Mike McMahon, Democrat House member from New York, was thinking of voting against Obamacare, a representative of the SEIU came to him and told him that the union would withdraw its support for his reelection.[48] Representative McMahon didn't heed the union warning; he voted against Obamacare. And McMahon was defeated in his bid for reelection.[49]

Labor Lapdogs

The unions use their political support to influence our government. Don't believe us? Ask Jon Corzine, former governor of New Jersey, who attended a Trenton rally of public workers and couldn't restrain himself: "We will fight for a fair contract," he shouted. It must have made the union bosses proud—except that his job as governor was to negotiate on behalf of the state, not to negotiate on behalf of the unions.[50] Even politicians are sometimes honest when they are speaking to their political allies and think no one else is paying close attention.

Unions spend money electing candidates for President, Congress, governor, state legislature, mayor, school board, and many other offices at the federal, state, and local levels. But let's take a close look at their spending on candidates for the U.S. House of Representatives. Overall, here is a look at the top ten federal U.S. House recipients of labor union

TOP 10 LABOR UNION SUPPORTED MEMBERS OF CONGRESS

Rank	Politician	Description	Union Contributions
1	Steny H. Hoyer (D-MD)	Minority Whip (2003–07, 2011–Present); Former House Majority Leader (2007–11)	$3,042,153
2	Richard A. Gephardt (D-MO)	Retired Congressman (1977–2005) now working as pro-business lobbyist; Former House Minority Leader (1995–2003)	$2,611,162
3	Neil Abercrombie (D-HI)	Governor of Hawaii (2011–Present); Retired Congressman (1986–87; 1991-2010)	$2,510,585
4	David E. Bonior (D-MI)	Current Labor Law Professor; Retired Congressman (1977–2003); Former Democrat Whip (1991–2002); Leader of Democrat opposition to NAFTA	$2,313,741
5	Tim Holden (D-PA)	Lost AFL-CIO endorsement when voted "no" on health-care bill	$2,275,654
6	David R. Obey (D-WI)	Retired Congressman (1969–2011) currently working for Gephardt's lobbying firm; Chairman of Appropriations Committee (1994–95; 2007–11)	$2,250,550
7	Nancy Pelosi (D-CA)	House Minority Leader (2011–Present); Former Speaker of the House (2007–11)	$2,240,800
8	Martin Frost (D-TX)	Retired Congressman (1979–2005); Former President of progressive Super PAC America Votes (2007–08); Former Democrat Caucus Chair (1999–2003)	$2,220,509
9	Frank Pallone Jr. (D-NJ)	Congressman (1993–Present); Anti-NAFTA and other free trade initiatives	$2,210,720
10	Sander Levin (D-MI)	Ranking Democrat on House Ways and Means Committee (2011–Present); Former Chair of Ways and Means (2010–11)	$2,200,543

The numbers on this page are based on contributions from PACs and individuals giving $200 or more. All donations took place during the 1989–2010 election cycle as released by the Federal Election Commission.

Courtesy: Center for Responsive Politics

cash from 1989 to 2010. Remember, these amounts represent only hard money campaign contributions, not their soft money political support, which would be much greater and for which no specific public information is available.

Notice anything? First, there are no Republicans. But by now, this probably doesn't surprise you.

Second, many of these members of Congress hold or held leadership positions in Congress or served on important committees. As minority whip, Representative Steny Hoyer can wrangle far more votes for pro-labor legislation than an ordinary member can deliver. In fact, Hoyer, Nancy Pelosi, and Richard Gephardt all have held multiple positions in the Democrat leadership of Congress.

Dick Gephardt was such a friend of labor as Speaker of the House that he clocks in at number 2, even though he hasn't served in Congress since 2005. But since leaving Congress, he is no longer bound by the golden handcuffs of Big Labor. Shadowbossed no longer, Gephardt now advises Boeing on labor conflicts and is a consultant to both the pro-business Chamber of Commerce and the most hated investment bank in America—Goldman Sachs.[51] Not only that, he recently brought number 6 labor lapdog David Obey into his lobbying firm. We can't wait to see what corporate interests House Minority Leader Nancy Pelosi, number 7 on our list, champions when she leaves the House!

Neil Abercrombie, now governor of Hawaii and number 3 on our list, is not only a friend of labor, he was a personal friend to President Obama's parents when he studied with them at the University of Hawaii and personally vouched for President Obama being born in the state of Hawaii.[52]

If you were expecting even higher contributions from unions, it is because these amounts are only the direct campaign contributions, made through labor union PACs—and that's only the tip of the political spending iceberg. The much greater contributions are the soft money political support—get-out-the-vote, mailings, advertising, phone banks, and super PAC political activity. Being a union-supported candidate is a great deal for these politicians; in return for carrying water for the union, you receive union support in the forms of money, organization, and troops of volunteers.

Union-Government Partnership

The union-government partnership works beautifully for both the unions and the politicians. Labor experts Daniel DiSalvo and Fred Siegel explain, "The result is a nefarious cycle: Politicians agree to generous government worker contracts; those workers then pay higher union dues a portion of which are funneled back into those same politicians' campaign war chests."[53] At its core, it is just that simple.

But if this sounds like an exaggerated conspiracy to you, consider this example of how the union-government partnership worked in practice in Washington State.

In Washington in 2002, the American Federation of State, County and Municipal Employees (AFSCME) invested significant dollars and used their political machine to support Democrat candidates for the legislature. In return, the Democrat-controlled legislature gave AFSCME what it was looking for—laws that gave unions the chance to win lucrative collective bargaining agreements over more workers.[54] Within three years of focusing their efforts in Washington State, AFSCME's membership in Washington had doubled, as did the fees the union collected there.

And the cycle continued. AFSCME supported the Democrat candidate for governor, Christine Gregoire, in 2004. After the election, it initially looked like she lost her race, but with $250,000 in cash contributions to the Washington Democrat Party, a recount was held. Gregoire was declared the winner by 129 votes—even though Republicans claimed to have found at least 489 felons who voted unlawfully in the election.[55] The Republicans challenged the election, but lost in court.[56]

Once Gregoire entered office, she "negotiated contracts with the unions that resulted in double-digit salary increases, some exceeding 25 percent, for thousands of state employees," explained DiSalvo and Siegel.[57] An advisor to Gregoire's 2004 opponent complained that the union's support of Democrat candidates created "a perfect machine to generate millions of dollars for her reelection" achieved at "taxpayer expense."[58]

In 2008, Gregoire was reelected. The Gregoire-union partnership was going great for both parties. But then the financial crisis hit, and Gregoire made the outrageous suggestion that state workers' pay raises be put on hold to address the ballooning state deficit. She was promptly sued by the unions for unfair labor practices and breach of contract. Perhaps not surprisingly, she did not seek a third term as governor.[59]

While the unions are hard on their opponents, they are great to their friends. We can see how politicians who support the unions' agenda are paid back for their loyalty by looking at congressional supporters of the card check legislation in 2007. Card check, a top union legislative priority, eliminates the requirement of a secret-ballot election for certifying a union and makes it easier for unions to organize new workers. Congressmen who voted in favor of card check in 2007 "collected 10 times more on average from union PACs during their careers ($862,065) than those who didn't ($86,538)."[60] And remember, those are only the hard dollar PAC contributions to candidates, not the much larger soft dollar support—the super PAC spending, advertising, political organizing support, and get-out-the-vote efforts that unions have bestowed on card check supporters. The unions haven't been able to collect enough votes to get the legislation enacted yet, but they are still working hard on it.

Purple People Eaters

The Big Daddy of the union-government partnership is the highly political SEIU, whose members wear purple T-shirts at rallies to identify themselves. The SEIU's former president Andy Stern "said, 'we believe in the power of persuasion, and if that doesn't work, we believe in the persuasion of power,'" according to political strategist Pat Caddell. The persuasion of power describes the SEIU's electioneering strategy, too. Caddell added, "Those guys are thugs, the SEIU."[61] He may call them thugs, but then they would be thugs with an awfully big checkbook.

SEIU is part of America Votes (AV), a coalition of labor unions and leftist organizations formed by a former SEIU official. America Votes was established as an umbrella organization to coordinate the get-out-the-vote effort among leftist organizations and labor unions and prevent duplication of effort. The organization claims to have built a "permanent advocacy and campaign infrastructure" for Progressive issues.[62] Other America Votes members included the Association of Community Organizers for Reform Now (ACORN), the AFL-CIO, AFSCME, the AFT, and the NEA. America Votes is just another organization that is part of the so-called Shadow Democrat Party, the coalition of labor unions, Hollywood, big donors, and leftist organizations that have been called the power behind the Democrat Party.[63]

The SEIU is just one union, but it conducts a huge amount of political activity. During the 2008 election season, the SEIU contacted approximately 4.5 million voters directly, especially in the top ten battleground states—many of which went for Obama by slim margins. According to the union, 88 percent of SEIU activities were person-to-person contact, comprising 40 percent of all voter contact in Indiana and 20 percent in Virginia, "exceeding even that of the campaigns and party committees."[64]

As the SEIU gloats, "From the top of the ticket on down, SEIU members helped win 82 percent of the critical races and ballot measures we targeted. Most importantly, Barack Obama won 17 of the 20 states that SEIU targeted."[65] The SEIU's impact in the Obama campaign perfectly illustrates how important union political support can be to candidates willing to fully embrace the unions' agenda.

Union Bad Boys

In alleged intimidation campaigns against companies (discussed in chapter 2) and even against other unions, the SEIU seems to be trying to stake out its claim to title of "bad boys" of the union movement. In April 2008, the SEIU allegedly came to bust up a labor union conference at which a rival union official was scheduled to speak and caught a lot of criticism even from labor movement leaders. John Sweeney, the President of the AFL-CIO, called the incident a "violent attack orchestrated by SEIU at the Labor Notes conference in Detroit," and chided that "No union should understand the corrosive effect of violence better than SEIU."[66] Hundreds of SEIU representatives came by the busload allegedly for the purpose of intimidating rank-and-file members of other unions at "progressive union gathering." These SEIU representatives allegedly stormed into the conference and precipitated a heated scuffle with conference goers, which resulted in at least one person going to the hospital.[67]

The reason for the fight? A rival union official that was battling the

SEIU to organize a group of hospital workers in Ohio was scheduled to speak at the conference. In other words, a fight over organizing workers and new union dues seems to have precipitated the SEIU's alleged violence and intimidation tactics. The rival official head called the SEIU "the new poster child for bad union behavior" and said that "compared with the corrupt Teamsters of old, the 'S.E.I.U. makes them look like choirboys,'" according to the *New York Times*.[68]

Michelle Malkin covered the story and wrote, "Team Obama and the Democrats—who together received more than $60 million in SEIU independent expenditure funds—remain mum about SEIU thuggery."[69] Malkin reminds us: "Obama, after all, promised the SEIU on the campaign trail: 'We look after each other!'" And they certainly do.

Unions are Anti-Gun

Union money doesn't just push forward pro-labor politicians—it advances liberal politicians that may take many views that are out of step with the views of the rest of America. Consider gun owners' rights.

While many union members all across our nation support gun owners' rights and the National Rifle Association—union members are even on the NRA's board—union money flows exclusively to anti–Second Amendment candidates and groups.[70] The contrast between union members' views on guns and union officials' views on guns is so extreme that the unions developed special advertising to persuade pro-gun union members to support the union's political candidates—specifically, Barack Obama. One union ad to union members read, "Barack Obama *won't* take away your gun; but John McCain *will* take away your union."[71]

Of course, it was a little hard to get some pro-gun union members into the Obama camp after Obama had proclaimed during his campaign in small Pennsylvania towns, "they get bitter, they cling to guns or religion or antipathy to people who aren't like them or anti-immigrant sentiment or anti-trade sentiment as a way to explain their frustrations."[72] Many pro-gun union members may have identified more with these small-town Pennsylvanians than with President Obama, which may explain why 39 percent of union households voted for John McCain while their unions endorsed Obama.[73]

Not surprisingly, Obama is fulfilling the dreams of the anti-gun crowd; he's advocated gun control and appointed numerous anti-gun federal judges. And he has more planned for a second term. He recently told an anti-gun activist, "I just want you to know that we are working on [gun control]. We have to go through a few processes, but under the radar."[74]

The AFL-CIO has staked out a series of anti-gun positions on legislation.[75] The teachers unions are also opposed to gun ownership; they explain their anti-gun positions in terms of curbing school violence. But the AFT, for example, is a member of the Coalition to Stop Gun Violence—a group that goes much further than fighting gun violence, instead focusing on wholesale banning of manufacture, importation, sale, transfer, ownership, and possession of handguns.

On the gun issue and many others, government employee unions don't care about the opinions of their members. Of the twenty congressional politicians most supported by labor union money in 2010, fourteen received a D or an F rating from the NRA, which the NRA reserves for politicians with spectacularly bad congressional voting records on Second Amendment issues. The unions are full-scale behind the anti-gun agenda, especially when the anti-gun politicians happen to be the Democrats that can best guarantee them their cash flow.

On the gun issue and many others, government employee unions don't care about the opinions of their members. Of the twenty congressional politicians most supported by labor union money in 2010, fourteen received a D or an F rating from the NRA, which the NRA reserves for politicians with spectacularly bad congressional voting records on Second Amendment issues.

It makes good political sense for government employee unions to support their leftist allies, but it's also clear that when unions spend to get their favored politicians elected, they undercut the beliefs of their own membership at the same time. And for the rest of us, even if you don't mind the growth of government and goodies that pro-union politicians deliver to government employee unions, you may mind how these same politicians vote on issues of importance to you personally.

Conclusion

The financial disclosure of government employee unions is intentionally difficult to penetrate and unenlightening. Even if union members knew where their dues money was going, they have almost no rights to ask that their dues not go for political spending. Unions can even force members to pay for additional spending through assessments beyond even their regular dues. Forced dues make this crony system of political spending on Democrat politicians and leftist causes possible, leaving the taxpayer unrepresented in the halls of power.

The game of monetary musical chairs continues on a daily basis. When the music stops, the only people left without chairs are the taxpayers, who have to foot the bill for the growth of government. The people sitting in the chairs are the people who really matter in the Democrat Party—the Shadowbosses, liberal organizations, the Democrat Party officials and the candidates themselves—all funded on the backs of American workers and taxpayers.

As we have seen, the chief goal of the Shadowbosses when it comes to national politics is keeping their political allies—almost always Democrats—in office. The unions have many friends, but they have never had a better ally in the White House than President Obama. As you'll see next, the unions paid up to get Obama into the White House, and President Obama paid them back many times over once he took the reins of power.

Chapter 3 Summary Points

- Despite limited annual financial disclosure to the Department of Labor, unions keep their finances largely hidden and impenetrable from outsiders and even from their own members.
- Unions (at the national, state, and local levels combined) collect an estimated $14 billion in dues alone every year, and more than half of this income comes from government workers. That's more revenues than 65 percent of the Fortune 500 companies, giving unions huge money to invest in politics.

- Labor unions spent well over $1.2 billion during the mid-term 2010 election cycle.
- Unions are a major part of the vast "Shadow Democrat Party," the political machine that has been called the power behind Democrat election success.
- Sixty-eight percent of registered voters are concerned that government employee unions have too much influence over the politicians that pass laws and negotiate with them.
- Unions also give "charity" dollars to leftist causes to create allies for their own agenda.
- When unions elect friendly liberal politicians to office, they get more pro-union votes but they also get more leftist votes on a variety of issues, like gun control, which conflict with the beliefs of many union members.
- Unions reward politicians who help them, and they punish politicians who oppose them.

CHAPTER 4

Union-Label President

THE Shadowbosses largely run our political system. They pull the strings. But in 2008, they had the chance of a union lifetime: the opportunity to place a full-blown union advocate in the White House. One of their very own. A man who'd worked in Big Labor, drank the Big Labor Kool-Aid, and battled for Big Labor.

His name was Barack Obama.

Barack Obama is the most union-connected president in the history of the country, a partner of and true believer in the labor movement. From card check to closed-door meetings in which health-care policy was run past former Service Employees International Union (SEIU) president Andy Stern and other Shadowbosses, union connections define Obama's presidency. He has stacked his staff and advisors with Chicago cronies—almost all of whom also have union connections. And the unions are betting that a second Obama term will bring them an even bigger payoff. After all, with a lame duck president who isn't worried about reelection, the sky's the limit.

The President doesn't mince words when it comes to his support of labor unions. And the unions support President Obama right back. The unions reportedly spent from $300 to $450 million to elect Obama in 2008, and it seems to have been well worth their investment.[1] For the unions, Obama's presidency is an opportunity for a partner in the White House and "change" that doesn't come around too often.

In 2007, Obama spoke to the SEIU. "I've got a history with this union," he said. "When I was a young organizer, I had just moved to Chicago. I started with working with SEIU Local 880, home health-care workers, to make sure that they were registered to vote." He continued, "I will judge my first term as president based on the fact of whether we have delivered the kind of health care that every American deserves and that our system can afford. And I'm not going to be able to do it on my own, so I hope that the SEIU will partner in that process."[2] The SEIU and every other government employee union have been more than happy to partner with the President in working toward a new "progressive" America that both the President and the unions believe in.

The SEIU is perhaps Obama's closest labor union connection—and no wonder, since, according to Andy Stern, the SEIU sent out one hundred thousand "volunteers" to help Obama during the campaign in 2008 and spent $60 million toward getting Obama elected.[3] Several SEIU state councils were among the first labor unions to endorse Senator Obama for President in January 2008, when both Hillary Clinton and John Edwards were still strong contenders.[4] And Stern has no complaints. "We get heard," he confirmed.[5] Stern celebrated Obama's first hundred days in office with a video message to SEIU members, during which he said, "SEIU is in the field, it's in the White House, it's in the administration!"[6]

Union Man on the Inside

Obama's relationships with the entire union movement go deep. As one who had worked inside the labor movement himself, Obama was able to make powerful pitches to the unions to work for his election. When Obama addressed the AFL-CIO, the federation of labor unions, in 2008, he promised his full support for the federation's agenda: "I know the AFL-CIO is tired of playing defense," he said. "We're ready to play some offense...We're ready to play offense for organized labor. It's

When Obama addressed the AFL-CIO, the federation of labor unions, in 2008, he promised his full support for the federation's agenda: "I know the AFL-CIO is tired of playing defense," he said. "We're ready to play some offense...We're ready to play offense for organized labor. It's time we had a President who didn't choke saying the word union."

time we had a President who didn't choke saying the word *union*."[7] President Obama certainly doesn't choke on the word *union*. In fact, his administration is more likely to choke those who choke on the word *union*.

The AFL-CIO federation bought the pitch—along with the presidents of all fifty-six unions in the federation. The AFL-CIO sent out 250,000 volunteers to help his campaign and pledged to spend $50 million toward his election. Obama had, after all, voted with the AFL-CIO agenda 98 percent of the time during his brief service in the Senate. The AFL-CIO said its top issues were health care, retirement, jobs, "economic equality," and card check.[8] Obama proceeded to work on all these issues for them.

When he's talking to his union friends, Obama is surely speaking the truth. He promised to give the unions exactly what they need to bolster the movement and increase their membership. That's exactly what he is delivering. With our President representing the unions' interests, who is representing you, the taxpayer?

The National Education Association (NEA) spent $50 million on Obama's election campaign in 2008.[9] When Obama spoke to the NEA in 2008, he emphasized that he would be able to deliver more dues revenue to the teachers union: "In the coming weeks, I'll be laying out the specific details of my plan to invest billions of new dollars into the teaching profession and recruit an army of well-trained, well-qualified teachers who are willing to stand at the front of any classroom and give every student the chance to succeed." Of course, more teachers may or may not be the fix that our failing education system needs. But we do know that by recruiting an army of teachers, Obama channels additional union dues right to the teachers unions. And that sounded good to the teachers unions in 2008, so they agreed to heavily support Obama's campaign.

Obama's Magic Formula for Socialism

Obama displayed his true vision for America most clearly when he addressed the American Federation of State, County and Municipal Employees (AFSCME) well before his election as President. In a speech to the AFSCME national convention, Obama first rewrote the history of AFSCME in glowing terms. He talked of the AFSCME sanitation strike of 1968, described it as an effort devoted to civil rights, a great victory for the workers (not true, as we've seen in our discussion of the sanitation workers strike in chapter 2).[10] Of course, he connected the strike with the assassination of Martin Luther King Jr., and he described the strike as culminating "in the union contract that the workers had sought for so long," although as we have seen in chapter 2, it is debatable whether or not the workers themselves won great concessions from the city in the strike.

After retelling the great mythical history of AFSCME—and ignoring its baggage—Obama continued, "This is the legacy you inherit today. It's a legacy of courage, a legacy of action, a legacy of achieving the greatest triumphs amidst the greatest odds."[11] Just the triumphant message that the AFSCME union bosses themselves wanted to convey to members at their convention.

But then Obama went on—and here we see where Obama's own philosophy and that of the government employee unions mesh perfectly:

> At the very moment that globalization is changing the rules of the game on the American worker—making it harder to compete with cheaper, highly skilled workers all over the world—the people running Washington are responding with a philosophy that says government has no role in solving these problems; that the services you all provide every day are better left to the whims of the private sector.

This is Obama's philosophy in a nutshell. Government can solve all your problems. And globalization is bad for the economy and bad for American workers, since American workers are inherently uncompetitive. Following from this, unions are needed to protect American workers, especially obsolete government workers from privatization of their services. This is Obama's essential ideology: wrap up unionism, bailouts, and bigger government in one well-articulated package, and bring European-style socialism to the United States as the end result.

Nanny state, cradle-to-grave care, and wealth redistribution, here we come!

Obama continued:

They're telling us we're better off if we dismantle government—if we divvy it up into individual tax breaks, hand 'em out, and encourage everyone to go buy your own health care, your own retirement security, your own child care, their own schools, your own private security force, your own roads, their own levees...It's called the Ownership Society in Washington. But in our past there has been another term for it—Social Darwinism—every man or woman for him- or herself.[12]

Obama encourages the union members in the audience to fear the free market, which he suggests will crush them. He uses this fear to push them to embrace the all-encompassing nanny state, complete with unions to represent them in making demands on their government employers. Obama was able to alarm these government employee union members and their bosses into fearing that Republicans would leave them to die at the hands of cruel market forces. And this is the same type of class warfare argument Obama continues to make today.

For this kind of protection against free market forces, AFSCME has pledged to spend $100 million reelecting Obama in 2012.[13] In Obama's first Presidential campaign in 2008, AFSCME joined up with the radical-left organization MoveOn.org to put up more than $500,000 for a commercial against John McCain. In the ad, a woman sits on a couch holding a baby. She talks about how she loves her baby. Then she looks into the camera and says, "So, John McCain, when you said you would stay in Iraq for a hundred years, were you counting on Alex? Because if you were; you can't have him." What a labor union had to do with the war in Iraq was anyone's guess.[14] But just like Obama's comments at the AFSCME convention, the ad promotes a visceral fear of Republican leadership—the idea that your survival is somehow at stake. And we don't have to guess at the true agenda of the unions in running ads like this: putting a true partner of the unions in the White House.

PARTYING AT THE WHITE HOUSE

Think that those cash expenditures by the government employee unions don't buy access? Think again. Since his election, President Obama's favorite White House guests have been his union buddies. Either he loves them for their sparkling conversation, or for their bags of cash. We'll guess it's the bags of cash.

This is a pattern going back to the Clinton Administration, when Bill and Hillary were said to have offered nights in the Lincoln Bedroom and dinner seats at major state dinners to raise campaign cash. Gerald McEntee, president of AFSCME, secured a seat for himself at a state dinner given by the Clintons in 1997 for the president of Chile. It may have helped that he spent millions in forced union dues on Democrat congressional candidates during the 1996 election cycle. McEntee, of course, denied the connection: "We've supported the Democratic Party and we've supported Republican candidates, and for anybody to think that we were invited tonight—when all of this is going on—because we gave a contribution would be absurd."[15] No connection at all.

Fast-forward a decade. The same union bosses are swarming the White House again. Same deal, different president—and much more access than ever before. Richard Trumka, head of the AFL-CIO, bragged that he visited the White House two or three times a week and talked with a member of the White House staff every single day—including weekends.[16] Trumka not only attended Obama's first state dinner but also sat in the First Lady's box for the President's September 2011 address to Congress.[17]

At Obama's first state dinner, honoring the Indian prime minister, not only was Richard Trumka welcomed but also the SEIU's then president, Andy Stern, and its then secretary-treasurer, Anna Burger (both since retired).[18] James Hoffa, Teamsters president, got his invitation to the state dinner in 2011 honoring German Chancellor Angela Merkel.[19] And

Randi Weingarten, of the American Federation of Teachers, got her turn in March 2012 at a state dinner for UK Prime Minister David Cameron.[20]

Although it's a close battle with Richard Trumka, Andy Stern may have won the award for "most frequent Shadow-boss visitor" to the White House during the early days of the Obama Administration. He visited the White House at least twenty-two times, meeting with the President personally at least six times—all in the first six months of President Obama's administration.[21]

Union Stimulus

Government employee union dollars have flowed into electing and working on reelecting President Obama, and taxpayer dollars are now flowing in the other direction from the Obama Administration to these same unions. The money cycle began with the first Obama cash giveaway: the misnamed, $787 billion American Recovery and Reinvestment Act signed into law by President Obama in February 2009, also known as the first round of "stimulus" spending.

A bunch of stimulus spending just happened to flow to the very same unions that supported Obama's election the previous year. For example, the U.S. Department of Labor sent $7.4 million in "green jobs training grants" to SEIU Local 32BJ and to a partnership between SEIU's health-care unions and major employers.

What exactly are these grants for—other than paying back the SEIU for its support? The goal of the grant was the creation of 5,200 jobs, but it is not really clear how this spending was supposed to lead directly to new jobs. The first $2.8 million was dedicated to a New York City program, "One Year, One Thousand Supers," that trains superintendents and other workers in New York City buildings to become "energy efficient building operators."[22] The president of an SEIU building services local union said, "With nearly 80 percent of New York's greenhouse gas emissions produced by buildings it's imperative for owners, workers, environmental groups and the federal government to jointly tackle this environmental challenge."[23] Can you read the coded language here? Jobs will be created by training people to comply with regulations, and then they can help work with the government to create more regulations, which will require more training and so on. The cycle of government jobs goes on and on! And the only green anybody sees is the cash that flows into union pockets.

As if that grant weren't useless enough, this program is just one tiny part of $500 million in stimulus funding to fund "workforce development projects" that promote green jobs.[24] One of these projects is paid for with another $4.6 million grant to SEIU to create "a new career ladder for 3,000 entry-level environmental service workers." An SEIU press release notes that SEIU locals "will serve as its lead partner to train and place workers in the health care field, and workers in environmental services (often called housekeepers) will learn methods for tracking and reducing the use of energy, water and waste."[25] Since when have housekeepers been known as "workers in environmental services"[26] anyway? And is this training anything more than how to sort trash into the various types of recycling bins?

Participants also receive "training in non-polluting cleaning technologies" and even get to "prepare academically for entry into more advanced and certified green occupations that are currently in development by their employers." "Currently in development" seems to mean that there aren't many actual "green jobs" of this type available yet, but that the government is working real hard to create some in the future—regardless of what the market requires.

The stimulus goodies went on and on for government employee unions, especially in the area of these phantom green jobs. When you can spend real green to create fake green jobs "currently in development," why stop there? In February 2010, another SEIU local won another $1.2 million in funding for yet more green jobs training. While green jobs remain hard to find, apparently running training centers for potential green job holders is a very lucrative side business for the unions.

Green jobs funding, said Secretary of Labor Hilda Solis, is "an investment that will help American workers succeed while doing good."

What was all this "good" that they'd be doing? They'll complete a curriculum "focusing on recycling, waste reduction, reducing water use, energy efficiency, and worker health and safety." How many "recycling and waste reduction" specialists do businesses need, anyway? To create actual jobs for all the people trained in green job technologies, the government would need to mandate that each workplace have its own "green czar" to oversee recycling, waste reduction, and the like.[27] These are exactly the types of regulations we should expect during a second term of the Obama Administration.

It's not even clear exactly what "green jobs" really are. As former real green jobs czar Van Jones admitted, "We still don't have a unified definition [for green jobs], and that's not unusual in a democracy. It takes a while for all the states and the federal government to come to some agreement. But the Department of Labor is working on it very diligently."[28] Word to the wise: when you need an entire department to define a term, and they haven't done it after a period of years, the term isn't real—like green jobs themselves, the term is "currently in development." And, by the way, Jones eventually resigned when he was accused of signing a petition questioning whether the George W. Bush Administration had used the September 11, 2001, terrorist attacks as a pretext for entering into the Iraq and Afghanistan military campaigns and possibly blaming the United States for these terrorist attacks.[29]

Another stimulus program gave the AFL-CIO Working for America Institute just under $1 million. The Working for America Institute is dedicated to creating "relationships in which workers obtain higher skills and better pay, employers become more successful and communities become better places in which to live and work." We all want that, don't we? What does the Institute *actually do* for a million dollars in stimulus? It will "provide technical assistance and support to labor leaders."[30] In other words, it's a big slush fund for the AFL-CIO. Another AFL-CIO related union that received extensive stimulus funds was the Communications Workers of America. This union received nearly $4 million to "provide training to individuals in the automotive and auto-related communities across Ohio which have been impacted by recent automotive related restructurings."[31] This sounds great until you realize that it was unions like those affiliated with the AFL-CIO that bankrupted the automobile companies in the first place.

Project Labor Agreements: Only Union Members Need Apply

The stimulus package and phantom green jobs programs were just the beginning of a strong Obama-union alliance during Obama's first term. Obama gave the unions another enormous payback when he recommended that major government projects use unionized labor.

The stimulus package and phantom green jobs programs were just the beginning of a strong Obama-union alliance during Obama's first term. Obama gave the unions another enormous payback when he recommended that major government projects use unionized labor.

As the *Wall Street Journal* noted, "There's almost a direct correlation these days between the Obama Administration's complaints about 'special interests' and its own fealty to such interests. Consider its latest decree that federal contractors must be union shops."[32] The *Journal* was referencing Executive Order No. 13,502, which President Obama issued during his first weeks as President. The Order encourages federal agencies to enter into Project Labor Agreements, or PLAs, with labor unions on projects of more than $25 million. As the *Journal* noted, "Only 15% of the nation's construction workers are unionized, so from now on the other 85% will have to forgo federal work for having exercised their right to not join a union." In contrast, the Bush Administration had preserved open competition for work on federal construction projects by expressly prohibiting PLAs.[33]

By favoring unionized workers, PLAs restrict competition and drive up the costs of construction projects about 10 to 20 percent—great for unions, but terrible for taxpayers.[34] And even though one of the major arguments in favor of PLAs is that they prevent work stoppages and strikes, studies have shown that PLAs don't prevent these costly events.[35] Even though their contracts forbid them to engage in work stoppages and strikes, some workers engaged under PLAs still do use these practices as a bargaining tool in negotiations for new contracts. In fact, construction on several of the new World Trade Center buildings and other New York City building projects has been delayed by unionized construction workers engaged under a PLA using work stoppages to bargain for new agreements.[36] President Obama, however, recently confirmed his support for PLAs for federal projects and we can expect him to mandate greater use of PLAs by the federal government during a second term.[37]

Washington Monument Syndrome

Paying back the teachers unions for their support is always a pretty easy political move, because we Americans love our teachers. Another reason that it's easy to channel money to education and the teachers unions is what journalist Steven Greenhut of the Pacific Research Institute calls the Washington Monument Syndrome.[38] This is a trick politicians and unions use to get the public concerned about budget cuts. When faced with cuts, politicians and unions will always suggest that the government will have to ax the very public services that we all most appreciate—as in, "Budget cuts will force us to close the schoolchildren's favorite tourist destination in our nation's capital, the Washington Monument!" In this case, it's the teachers unions telling you that teachers in your local schools are on the budgetary chopping block.

Of the initial stimulus spending, a whopping $115 billion was earmarked for education spending like the "Edujobs" program. The program is called Edujobs to focus the public on the fact that teachers' jobs are saved by the program. How did that work? The federal government gave money to the states, supposedly so that states didn't have to lay off teachers. But money is fungible—all this money didn't necessarily go to preserve teachers' jobs. The states basically used this cash to plug holes in their budgets generally and to delay necessary spending cuts—not just to education but to other government services as well. Of course, the discussion is framed in terms of preventing your local teacher from losing her job. The teachers unions are able to put a face—your local teacher's face—on the budget cuts to get you personally interested. As a result, stimulus spending for education is much more popular with taxpayers than stimulus spending in general. It's the Washington Monument Syndrome at work.

From the teachers unions' perspective, this spending is essential to keeping dues income up. By retaining teachers in forced-dues states, teachers keep paying union dues. If states have to reduce the number of teachers and school workers thanks to the budget crunch, teachers unions get hit.

While the stimulus didn't create many education jobs, it does preserve existing government jobs—and in most cases, that means union jobs. The U.S. Department of Education claims that the stimulus created—or, more accurately, retained—367,524 education-related jobs during the 2009–10 school year, which if true would also have preserved at least $165 million in teachers union dues annually.[39] One recent Edujobs grant program explicitly states that the grant money can't generally be used to pay the salaries of outside contractors in schools. Do these jobs matter less to our kids' education? Probably not, but they matter less to the teachers unions because outside contractors aren't generally unionized.[40]

More recently, Obama has been promoting the American Jobs Act, which is really almost more of a campaign promise than an actual piece of legislation. One part of this Act supposedly will create jobs by spending $593 billion more on propping up state budgets. The proposed legislation was designed, according to the White House, to preserve additional teaching jobs, but it will also preserve almost $50 million in dues income for the national teachers unions.[41] As one commentator on the legislation writes, "It pays to have friends in high places."

Not only did stimulus spending protect dues income, but Obama sent the teachers unions some more goodies. The AFT Educational Foundation received just under $5 million in stimulus via the Investing in Innovation Fund, which gives grants to applicants—that is, other liberal organizations—with a supposed record of improving student achievement. According to the AFT, the goal was to create "evaluation systems" for the teachers. Because, really who could be better at designing and implementing evaluations of teachers than their unions, right?[42]

In his 2012 State of the Union address, Obama continued to fulfill his promises to the teachers unions—this time by asking states to require all students to stay in school through the age of eighteen.[43] While this proposal may or may not help our nation's kids, it also just happens to mean more jobs for teachers and more dues for teachers unions. There are an estimated 1.2 million kids who drop out instead of graduating with their class.[44] For each additional year that they are kept in school, 150,000 additional teachers and other school workers would be needed to teach them, resulting in more teachers union members and more dues income once again.[45]

The National Education Association thinks that raising the school leaving age is such a great idea, for the union at least, that it has issued a proposal advocating students be required to complete a high school degree or stay in school until twenty-one![46] The evidence is mixed on whether or not raising the age of compulsory schooling actually improves education outcomes.[47] But whether "at risk" kids would benefit or not, Obama's proposal would certainly do two things: raise educational costs further, and increase the number of teachers our nation requires to fulfill this mandate which benefits the teachers unions.

Card Check and Intimidation

The unions' first legislative priority for the Obama Administration was passing card check legislation. Unionizing a workplace currently requires two steps: first, 30 percent of employees must turn in cards asking for a union, and then a secret-ballot election must take place, in which the union wins at least 50 percent of the votes cast.[48] In Orwellian fashion, the bill that implements card check was named the Employee Free Choice Act. It would do away with secret-ballot election and allow a union to be certified if the union could get 50 percent of employees to turn in signed cards supporting the union. The unions like card check because the protection of the secret-ballot election would be gone. Instead, winning union elections using worker intimidation would become the name of the game.

Up until recently, the National Labor Relations Board (NLRB) recognized that intimidation could corrupt the unionization process. For decades, the NLRB's standard was that if an election was marred by behavior that prevented an employee from exercising free choice, the election was invalid. But on August 22, 2008, the NLRB oversaw an election for the Communications Workers of America. After the election, some of the employees claimed that threats of physical violence had been made against them by pro-union employees. One of the employees received an anonymous phone call threatening to "get even" with him if he "backstab[bed] us." Another group of employees heard pro-union employees aggressively threaten them with battery if they "cost us the election." The NLRB, though, ruled that this behavior wasn't egregious enough to moot the election.[49] It's hard to imagine what would be *egregious* enough to moot an election if that kind of intimidation won't do it.

Union members understand that the protections of the secret-ballot election protect workers against union thuggery. A Zogby poll showed that 71 percent of *union members* wanted to keep the secret-ballot law on the books, while just 13 percent wanted to change the law.[50] But that didn't stop the unions and Obama from pushing card check.

Once he was in the White House, Obama doubled down on card check. He told a closed-door meeting of over a hundred labor executives in 2009, "We will pass the Employee Free Choice Act."[51] Reportedly, Obama also told the unions that he didn't "buy the argument that providing workers with collective-bargaining rights somehow weakens the economy or worsens the business environment." This, of course, pleased union officials to no end. "Him putting it on the record in public makes me feel better," one official stated.[52]

Obama has not been able to deliver card check to the unions, and this has been a very sore point for his union supporters. In 2009, Obama couldn't get his filibuster-proof sixty votes in the Senate to pass the card check—despite having sixty Democrats in the Senate. What happened to the Democrats who didn't support card check in the Senate? Well, we'll never know, since the issue never came to a vote, thanks to Majority Leader Harry Reid, who apparently didn't want unions cracking down on Democrats that voted against it. Several senators did come out against card check, including Ben Nelson (D-NE), Arlen Specter (D-PA), Blanche Lincoln (D-AR), and Thomas Carper (D-DE). What happened to them? Nelson has already announced he will not run for reelection in 2012; Specter was defeated in a Democrat primary challenge in 2010; Lincoln lost her seat to a Republican in 2010. And Carper is up for reelection in 2012.

Obamacare and Unions Go Together

One of the great mysteries of modern politics was the high level of union support for Obamacare. As we've discussed, government employee unions generally negotiate for the world's best health insurance for their members—the famed, wildly expensive Cadillac plans. Some unions even directly profit from this health insurance by negotiating for contracts that force states to purchase health insurance for government workers from union-affiliated insurance companies.[53]

Kimberley Strassel explains in the *Wall Street Journal* that unions often negotiate with states for control of state employees' health insurance: "In Wisconsin, for instance, the teachers union doesn't just bargain for more health dollars. It also bargains to require that local school districts buy health insurance for their teachers through the union-affiliated health-insurance plan, called WEA Trust." This arrangement actually costs the state at least $68 million more than the state's health-care plan for its other government employees costs, with the excess going directly to the union.[54]

The Service Employees International Union (SEIU), the American Federation of State, County and Municipal Employees (AFSCME), and other government employee unions spent literally hundreds of millions of dollars promoting Obamacare. The SEIU has focused like a laser on pushing for universal health care, stating that the union "will not stop until every man, woman and child has quality, affordable care they can count on."[55] Why would government employee unions identify large-scale nationalization of our health-care system as a top priority when it is not a critical issue for their members?

It can't be just that the unions wanted to help make President Obama's vision of a national health-care system a reality. There seems to be a more direct reason why unions supported health-care reform. Don Loos, former Labor Department official in the Office of Labor-Management Standards, suggests, "It is clear that Big Labor is banking on the probability that all healthcare workers eventually become federal, state, and municipal healthcare employees" who could then be subject to forced unionization.[56] He explains that the SEIU sent a memo to the Obama transition team pointing out that there were 17.6 million health-care jobs currently, and the Bureau of Labor Statistics had projected that the nation would need 3.5 million more health-care workers over the following years. The SEIU memo proposes that stimulus spending be used for training of new health-care professionals with the involvement of unions like the SEIU, and promises the SEIU's involvement in reforming health care in 2009.[57] Loos explains that the SEIU and other unions were involved in health-care reform to pave the way for greater unionization of health-care workers. He notes, "ObamaCare is an SEIU and AFSCME membership 'net' designed to eventually capture 21 million forced-dues paying government workers as all healthcare workers eventually become federal, state, and municipal healthcare employees."[58]

By having the government take over health care, the SEIU plans to get a greater hold over our nation's health-care workers. With Obamacare, most health-care workers would receive government funding and be subject to greater government regulation. As a result, more health-care workers could potentially be treated as "government employees" and be unionized.

Looking to our neighbor to the north, Canada shows us that national health care yields more unionized health-care workers. Canada has national health care, and "as a result 60 percent of Canadian health care workers and a stunning 80 percent of nurses belong to unions—more than quadruple the levels in America," notes labor economist James Sherk.[59]

Unions support national health care in America because, quite simply, it is good business for them. Unionizing all the health-care workers involved in implementing Obamacare could generate as much as $19 billion per year in forced union dues, but even unionizing a portion of these workers would significantly improve the unions' bottom line.[60] Obamacare could allow unions to potentially earn more in additional dues income than the gross domestic product of whole countries, like Paraguay, Iceland, and Jamaica!

This was the unions' agenda all along. The SEIU made a grab for organizing all health-care workers as early as 2007 when it consolidated all its over 1 million health-care members into SEIU Health Care, and claimed that its union would "guarantee a voice at work" for all health-care workers nationwide—not just its members. Its 2008 brochure shares its plan: "SEIU's health care profile—and power—will only continue to grow. And after we elect a pro-worker president and stronger pro-worker majorities in Congress, we will take all our energy, ideas, organizing strength, grassroots lobbying and political muscle, and make it happen."[61] SEIU also publically admitted its goals for national health care, which included creating "demand for SEIU-provided services" and crafting a health care "crisis" to convince Americans that we needed Obamacare.[62] Once the other unions bought in to these goals themselves, Obamacare became nearly inevitable.

Unions Win with Obamacare

In Obamacare, the government employee unions got exactly what they were looking for: massive growth of the federal and state bureaucracies, creating millions of potential new union members. But they still had a problem. What about their own members, whose Cadillac health-care plans would now be taxed? That is what the meeting of the Shadowbosses at the beginning of this book was all about—the unions bringing their demands to the President as a condition for their support for Obamacare.

> *In Obamacare, the government employee unions got exactly what they were looking for: massive growth of the federal and state bureaucracies, creating millions of potential new union members. But they still had a problem. What about their own members, whose Cadillac health-care plans would now be taxed?*

Faced with Shadowboss resistance to Obamacare, Obama acceded to union demands. He delayed a tax on Cadillac plans until 2018, giving the unions more time to find a legislative solution to the problem.[63] Obama also granted "lucky golden ticket recipients" waivers from the most onerous provisions of Obamacare, according to columnist Michelle Malkin.[64] Over half of the Obamacare waiver beneficiaries were union members—way out of proportion, considering just 13 percent of American workers are represented by unions. But the unions weren't the only ones getting special treatment—nearly 20 percent of all waivers took place in the home district of House Minority Leader Nancy Pelosi.[65]

There were extra goodies for Obama's union pals in the Obamacare legislation. A quiet Obamacare program called the Early Retiree

Reinsurance Program grants $5 billion to employers to provide "gap" health insurance to cover employees who retire before their Medicare coverage begins. An *Investor's Business Daily* editorial explained, "The little-noticed ObamaCare program was supposed to encourage companies to continue offering this benefit until 2014—when ObamaCare fully kicks in and will solve everything—by reimbursing companies for a chunk of their retiree health costs."[66]

What happened? Well, the unions were at the front of the line to apply for that federal cash. Pretty soon, the government had to shut down applications to the program because unions were flooding them. In the end, "10 of the top 12 recipients are either unions or public employee groups."[67] *Investor's Business Daily* concluded that "this ObamaCare money is really being used mainly to pay off unions and governments that would have provided these benefits anyway." The UAW Retiree Medical Trust alone netted over $220 million from this program, and several other unions got their piece as well before the program was closed to new applicants. The fire hose of cash from government to unions is hooked up, and the fire hydrant has been left wide open.

National Security Unions

In addition to receiving specific paybacks in the stimulus and Obamacare legislation, government employee unions have given President Obama a far broader directive. It is to help the unions to increase their control over America's national security employees. Take, for example, the unionization of Homeland Security's Transportation Security Administration (TSA) undertaken by the Obama Administration.

The 1978 Civil Service Reform Act explicitly bars monopoly bargaining over CIA, FBI, National Security Agency (NSA), and Secret Service employees; subsequent Executive Orders have extended this prohibition to many national-security-related federal agencies. George W. Bush used his discretion under the 2003 Homeland Security Act to ban union monopoly bargaining over federal airport baggage screeners employed by the TSA. In February 2011, however, President Obama's TSA Administrator John Pistole gave the unions collective bargaining power over airport screeners. At the same time, Obama moved to end a successful program that had allowed airports to privatize airport screening using strict federal security standards with substantial training and oversight, thus requiring more government, unionized screeners.[68]

What was Pistole's justification for this extension of union power over our airport security? Pistole explained that giving unions collective bargaining power over TSA workers would "ensure that a union's role would help to reinforce consistency and accountability across security operations at all airports."[69] Perhaps he was thinking about the fact that unionizing TSA would immediately bring up to $18 million in dues into union coffers annually.[70]

The two unions vying to unionize TSA, American Federation of Government Employees (AFGE) and National Treasury Employees

UNIONIZE THE MILITARY? CHECK.

What about some of the most important national security employees of all—the U.S. military? Could Obama actually unionize them? The law seems pretty clear on the point. Active duty military are forbidden from joining military labor organizations by a federal statute passed in 1978.[71] The law actually states that it is the policy of the United States that unionizing our fighting force "would undermine the role, authority, and position of the commander, and would impair the morale and readiness of the armed forces." It would take an act of Congress to unionize them. So is our military the one large government organization that the unions haven't been able to penetrate? Not quite. More than one-third of our full-time military employees are civilian employees, many of them ex-servicemen hired back into service in similar jobs as civilians. And 60 percent of those civilian employees are unionized. Of the 700,000 civilians employed by the Department of Defense in 2010, 450,000 are unionized—and they are represented by 45 separate unions.[72] So while the 1.4 million active duty troops cannot be unionized under current law, the entire military (not including reservists) is already more than 20% unionized without most people realizing that it could be possible.

Union (NTEU), already represent around 63,000 Homeland Security employees, many of whom work in very sensitive and critical areas.[73] AFGE represents employees at Federal Emergency Management Agency (FEMA), National Protections and Programs Directorate (NPPD), U.S. Immigration and Customs Enforcement, U.S. Citizenship and Immigration Services, U.S. Customs and Border Protection (border patrol agents), and the Coast Guard.[74] And NTEU represents 24,000 other Customs and Border Protection employees.[75]

After a close election and a runoff at TSA in 2011, the American Federation of Government Employees (AFGE) edged out the National Treasury Employees Union (NTEU) to become the exclusive representative for 44,000 TSA employees.[76] This single election significantly increased the number of Homeland Security employees represented by unions, and also represents another step toward unionizing all types of federal workers, no matter how critical their job function is to our national security.

Union Fingers in Every Federal Workplace Pie

Government employee unions hold collective bargaining power over almost 1.2 million federal workers on many employment matters, but not over federal wages or benefits.[77] This limitation on collective bargaining over wages and benefits—believe it or not—was put in place by Jimmy Carter in 1978. "Even Carter Democrats understood the difference between being in electoral debt to the unions, and being outright owned by them," Kimberley Strassel wrote in the *Wall Street Journal*.[78]

So at least there are some government workplace issues that the unions just don't have a say in, right? Well not quite. Thanks to President Obama, the unions representing federal employees suddenly have a lot more say in all workplace issues. Early in his term, President Obama issued an Executive Order which requires federal offices and agencies to consult with unions representing federal workers in "all workplace matters to the fullest extent practicable" before reaching a decision. Government agencies are required to consult the unions even on workplace matters that unions cannot bargain over by law. The order used an intentionally confusing term for this—"pre-decisional involvement," which seems to mean that no decision about the federal workplace can be made anymore without consulting the Shadowbosses.[79]

By requiring pre-decisional conferencing on all workplace matters, President Obama has given the unions representing federal workers an unprecedented (and almost unbelievable) voice in federal workplace matters, including military workplaces. It is almost hard to imagine what he could do to further augment their authority over the federal workplace during a second term, but we're sure that the unions have some ideas.

Unions Win the Auto Industry

Throughout his administration, President Obama has handed over new swaths of the economy to government employee unions. But the most egregious example may be the auto bailouts, where the Obama Administration not only handed partial ownership of the U.S. auto industry to the unions, but also circumvented our bankruptcy laws to do so.

Under the bankruptcy rules, parties owed money by a bankrupt company are paid out of any company assets in a certain order—first, the secured creditors such as bondholders are paid; then unsecured creditors like company employees are paid. But when the Obama Administration spearheaded the Chrysler bankruptcy in 2009, the Administration sidestepped these priority rules to give a better deal to the United Auto Workers (UAW), a hybrid private worker/government worker union that represented Chrysler's auto workers.[80]

The Administration forced a sale of Chrysler's assets to a new Chrysler corporation instead of letting the bankruptcy proceed. Investors who held Chrysler bonds were forced to take only 29 cents for each dollar of bonds that they held.

Meanwhile, the UAW retirement health-care trust received a 55 percent stake in the new Chrysler corporation in exchange for labor contract concessions. "Among the cost-cutting measures that the UAW leaders have accepted are a suspension of cost-of-living adjustments and new limits on overtime pay," reported the *Wall Street Journal*. "Workers will only be paid for overtime after they have worked at least 40 hours in a week. Chrysler workers will also lose their Easter Monday holiday in 2010 and 2011, according to the union summary."[81] The unions won yet again, even though the unions themselves virtually bankrupted Chrysler.

Similarly, when the Obama Administration took over the bankruptcy process for General Motors, it shortchanged the bondholders in favor of the UAW, which also represented the General Motors auto workers. As Speaker Newt Gingrich pointed out, "According to one analysis, while the bondholders will be lucky if they recover 15 cents on the dollar, the UAW can expect to recover up to 60 to 70 cents on the dollar—four to five times what the bondholders will receive."[82] The UAW argued, "Most bondholders are investors who can spread any losses over a broad portfolio."[83] In other words, the UAW claimed that only the 1 percent got hurt, and they could take it.

But actually, it wasn't just the fat cats that got soaked in the auto/UAW bailout. Other victims of the government reorganization were also people like Vicki Denton's family, as the *Wall Street Journal* reported. Denton died in a car crash when her Dodge's air bag failed to deploy. Chrysler lost a lawsuit against her family and was judged to owe them $2.2 million. But the family's right to payment got trampled in the bankruptcy reorganization deal. "Now, two years removed from a $12.5 billion bailout, Chrysler Group LLC still hasn't paid the damages, and doesn't have to," reports the *Journal*. "The reason: The company's restructuring allowed it to wash away legal responsibility for car-accident victims who had won damages or had pending lawsuits before its bankruptcy filing. The same holds true for General Motors Co."[84]

When government employee unions win, there are very real losses to very real people. But those real people don't include the President or the Democrat Party. As Mitt Romney pointed out, "I think the union folks basically bought and paid for [Obama's] last campaign, so he's taking care of them and they're taking care of him." And Speaker Newt Gingrich was more specific: "Between 2000 and 2008, the United Auto Workers (UAW) union gave $23,675,562 to the Democratic Party and its candidates. In 2008 alone, the UAW gave $4,161,567 to the Democratic Party, including Barack Obama. In return, the UAW received 55 percent of Chrysler and 17.5 percent of GM, plus billions of dollars. But nobody's calling this a scandal. It's time we start."[85]

It sure is nice to have a partner in the White House, although some union bosses have complained that what the President has done for unions has not been enough.

Back in Obama's Corner

The unions expected a 100 percent commitment to their agenda from Obama, and while the President has delivered a lot of the union agenda, he has fallen short on the unions' highest legislative priority—card check—and in a few other areas. Union bosses have complained that President Obama sacrificed card check to get Obamacare passed, has supported trade agreements opposed by unions, and has not created enough new jobs, presumably meaning union jobs.

Richard Trumka, head of the AFL-CIO, has been one of President Obama's most vocal critics in the union movement. In 2011, Trumka, who has been called a "thug's thug," criticized Obama for lack of leadership.[86] "I think he doesn't become a leader anymore, and he's being a follower," Trumka complained.[87] He also claimed the President had been doing "little nibbly things around the edge that aren't going to make a difference and aren't going to solve the problem" with a suffering economy instead of offering "bold solutions and some risk taking." He even threatened to pull the labor movement's support for Obama and other politicians: "If leaders aren't blocking the wrecking ball and advancing working families' interests, then working people will not support them," Trumka warned.[88]

Despite his criticisms, Trumka himself had experienced good times under the first Obama Administration. In addition to state dinners and White House visits for Trumka, Obama actually picked him to sit on his jobs advisory council.[89] Trumka accompanies Obama on some of his jobs speeches—which is sort of like having Dracula accompany you on your blood drive.[90]

In March 2012, Trumka jumped back on the Obama bandwagon, and the AFL-CIO endorsed Obama for reelection. Bloomberg reported: "The backing by the group representing 12 million members, less than a year after Trumka said enthusiasm for Obama had waned, suggests unions are warming to a second term."[91] And this seems to be the case.

The AFL-CIO's political director has stated publically that the union movement would expect even more from President Obama in the near future. "There's no question that the Obama administration has done many things that have helped working people and that have been positive for the labor movement," he said. "But on the other hand, this is the Democratic Party; it was elected on a platform to do much, much, much, much more."[92] For more, the unions will have to wait for a second Obama Administration.

Coming Next

Despite their grumbles with not getting everything that they wanted from the Obama Administration, union bosses lined up to endorse President Obama for reelection and will probably spend even more money on his reelection in 2012 than they spent on his election in 2008. Unions are projected to spend over $400 million on Obama's reelection, but the figure could ultimately go much higher.[93]

Over the July 4 weekend in 2011, Obama secured an early endorsement for reelection from the National Education Association.[94] It also passed a resolution that forced a new $10 assessment on members for political activities.[95] As columnist Kyle Olson observed, "Some teachers objected, calling it the union's 'Obama tax.' . . . $35.4 million can buy a lot of votes."[96] Shortly after receiving this endorsement, Obama started to pay back the teachers unions by offering more Edujobs spending in his American Jobs Act. The smaller American Federation of Teachers endorsed Obama a bit later, in February 2012.

When the SEIU endorsed Obama for reelection in November 2011, Mary Kay Henry, who succeeded Andy Stern as SEIU president, explained: "As Americans we face [a] stark choice. Do we want leaders who side with rich corporations, the 1 percent who are prospering, or leaders who side with us, the 99 percent?"[97] (They don't just steal your tax dollars—they steal Occupy Wall Street slogans, too.)

SEIU union bosses were well treated during the first Obama Administration. Former president Andy Stern continues to sit on Obama's deficit panel—ironic, considering that Stern's union has helped drive America's deficits to record levels. One commentator likened Stern's appointment to "a serial arsonist" organizing Fire Prevention Week.[98] Former secretary-treasurer Anna Burger was also an Obama appointee to the Economic Recovery Board of Advisors, working alongside AFL-CIO president Richard Trumka. John Sullivan, SEIU's associate counsel, was given a seat on the Federal Election Commission. Craig Becker, associate general counsel of SEIU, was appointed by President Obama to a seat on the National Labor Relations Board in a controversial

SEIU union bosses were well treated during the first Obama Administration. Former president Andy Stern continues to sit on Obama's deficit panel—ironic, considering that Stern's union has helped drive America's deficits to record levels. One commentator likened Stern's appointment to "a serial arsonist" organizing Fire Prevention Week.

recess appointment over the objection of a bipartisan group of senators. Current and former SEIU union officials are now operating from inside our government—only to shuttle back to the labor movement when Obama finally leaves office, taking with them inside knowledge of how best to pressure government into advancing their agenda.

When the American Federation of State, County and Municipal Employees (AFSCME) endorsed Obama in December 2011, the union also pledged $100 million in support for his reelection. Why so much? As AFSCME president Gerald McEntee explained, "President Obama is the only choice for the 99 percent."[99] Are these guys on message, or what?

Conclusion

What will a second Obama Administration hold in store for the unions? Endless new goodies.

We can expect a second Obama Administration would move the unions' agenda and control over our government workers much, much further. The unions' greatest dream is that they might one day be able to repeal section 14(b) of the National Labor Relations Act, which permits states to pass right-to-work laws.[100] Repealing right-to-work laws nationwide through an act of Congress would give the unions twenty-three more states in which to collect forced dues—and could almost double their dues income overnight. It is hard to imagine, but no dream is impossible with a second term for President Obama (and a Democrat House and Senate).

Already, the Obama Administration is also looking at requiring federal agencies to negotiate an expanded list of issues with the government employee unions.[101] This expansion would require agencies to negotiate with unions over the "numbers, types, and grades of employees or positions assigned to any organizational subdivision, work project, or tour of duty," and "on the technology, methods, and means of performing work."[102] In other words, government employee unions would have a lot more say in staffing and how employees perform their work, which is normally the prerogative of the government employer. What unions know about these issues is anyone's guess.

Government employee unions continue to expand and increase their control over our nation. But the greatest threat to the people of the United States by far is the undermining of the education system, thanks almost entirely to the teachers union bosses, as we'll see next.

Chapter 4 Summary Points

- President Obama is the most union-connected President in the history of the United States, both a partner of the unions and a true believer in the union movement.
- The unions spent $300 to $450 million to elect Obama in 2008 and have pledged to spend over $400 million or more to reelect him in 2012.
- Unions supported Obamacare heavily because it gives them an opportunity to organize millions more health-care workers—and add billions of dollars in dues income.
- During Obama's first term, the stimulus package was an enormous giveaway for the unions, particularly in the area of green jobs and education.
- The Obama Administration has allowed unions to gain collective bargaining power over the Transportation Security Administration (TSA). Our other Homeland Security employees and civilian military employees are also increasingly unionized, leaving our nation exposed to strikes.

- Card check, a top union legislative priority, would eliminate workers' rights to a secret-ballot election over whether or not their workplace will be unionized, and would be pushed hard during a second Obama term.
- An even higher legislative priority for unions during a second Obama Administration may be the repeal of section 14(b) of the National Labor Relations Act, which would destroy state right-to-work protections and make all fifty states in America forced-dues states, generating billions more in dues income for the unions.

CHAPTER 5

Schoolhouse Shadowbosses

IMAGINE sitting in a large room packed with human beings. Imagine that all of them are crying, or praying, or grimacing—because at the front of the room, a man is reaching into a basket of Ping-Pong balls. Each person in the room has been assigned a number. And each of those Ping-Pong balls carries a corresponding number. If your number is drawn, you have a chance at living a better life than your parents had—maybe going to college or to a technical school, getting a good job, making enough money to support yourself. If not, you'll likely end up dropping out of school, may face limited job prospects, and perhaps end up dependent on the government.

You don't have to imagine it. Each year, thousands of children across America enter into such lotteries, trying to get into decent public schools. Their normal public schools are educational sinkholes—kids fail out or they pass to the next level through social promotion without having met the learning objectives of the previous grade.

"Either the kids are getting stupider every year, or something is wrong in the education system," master educator Geoffrey Canada tells the camera in Davis Guggenheim's 2010 documentary *Waiting for Superman*. Guggenheim—the same man who directed Al Gore's propaganda film *An Inconvenient Truth* and President Obama's thirty-minute tribute reel at the 2008 Democratic National Convention—is no conservative. But he recognized that America's education system is in serious trouble.

Guggenheim points out that although we have doubled the money that we spend on K–12 schools in recent years, there has been little or no improvement in student performance. In the film, a huge share of the blame falls on the teachers unions—a conclusion Guggenheim desperately did not want to come to. "In this case, I'm a Democrat, and I believe, I really believe in unions, I'm a member of a good union," he lamented. "So that was an uncomfortable truth for me to have to talk about, but I've tried to make a reasonable film." He notes that "somehow it's written that you can't criticize the unions. Otherwise, you hate teachers."

What's wrong with the teachers unions? Guggenheim explains that union contracts run to 200 pages and control so many aspects of how our schools are run: "School day ends at 3, principals can't visit the classroom, can't fire a teacher, can't reward another good teacher."[1] Teachers union control over schools stops innovation dead in its tracks and stifles creative solutions to our nation's educational crisis.

This isn't a partisan issue—Jonathan Alter, liberal columnist for *Newsweek*, puts it well in the film: "It's very, very important to hold two contradictory ideas in your head at the same time. Teachers are great, a national treasure. Teachers unions are, generally speaking, a menace and an impediment to reform."

Guggenheim documents the effects of teachers unions in the film and what a big part chance has in the outcomes of these children's lives. Most heartbreaking, he shows five students sitting, biting their nails at those lotteries, waiting for their names to be called. One young girl wants to be a veterinarian, but she's stuck in a dead-end school, and doesn't win the lottery to attend a charter school; another young boy also doesn't win the school lottery and has to stay in his failing school, while his brother has the opportunity to attend a successful charter school; a few others win spaces in better schools and perhaps also win the chance for a better life.

And what are the chances of kids in failing schools getting into better ones? Unfortunately, their chances are very slim. For example, one charter school in Harlem had 792 applications for forty spots, and its numbers are fairly typical. There are far too many kids who want to go to successful charter schools than spaces at those schools. Clearly, kids want to learn; parents want them to learn; teachers want to teach them. But the teachers unions are keeping most of them in rotten schools.

Worm in the Apple

The teachers unions have carefully framed the debate about spending on education as taxpayers not willing to pay their fair share for the education of our nation's children. But their attack on spending is just smoke and mirrors. Every year, Americans spend more and more cash on education—and the teachers unions always claim that to fix K–12 education, we just need to throw more money at the problem. More money at the problem, of course, generally translates into more union dues for the teachers unions.

The United States spends almost $10,000 a year per elementary schoolchild.[2] We spend 68 percent more per schoolchild than Germany, 33 percent more than Japan, 84 percent more than Korea, and 14 percent more than the United Kingdom.[3] And yet, our children finished far behind these nations in math and science over the last decade.[4]

What do we get for enormous spending? An educational system that no one, certainly not teachers unions, wants to take credit for. Our rates of high school graduation have shown no improvement, and even declined slightly, over the last forty years.[5] There is basically no good news on the educational horizon whatsoever in terms of our spending producing measurable educational gains for our students. Except, as one commentator notes, "American students get terrible math scores compared to their international peers, but they think they're great in math—in fact, they have more confidence in their math skills than students from any other country."[6] But while confidence is great to have, it is no substitute for real student performance.

Many public school teachers are tremendous educators, motivated and caring people who want the best for our children. But behind the friendly principal at your school, the loving teachers that instruct your children, and the civic-minded school board that makes decisions about schooling in your district lurk their Shadowbosses—teachers unions and their bosses. The two national teachers unions are two of the largest unions of any type in our country. Not coincidentally, they are also among the largest financial contributors to Democrat Party politics. Their grubby fingerprints are all over America's dysfunctional education system, all over Congress, and all over the Obama Administration.

If the fifty individual states developed their own educational policies, you could expect a wide range of models for education in America—a thriving diversity of schooling ideas that would reveal startlingly different models for teacher pay, school schedules, and subject matter content. But in fact, public schools across America share almost uniform characteristics. And—surprise, surprise!—those characteristics typically benefit teachers unions.

With their immense dues income, teachers unions extend their political influence across all fifty states, even the right-to-work states. They are able to keep educational policies remarkably consistent across most school districts in America. Policies common to most school districts include: paying teachers based on seniority and educational attainment rather than merit and performance; seniority-based layoff policies known as "last in, first out"; and tenure policies that make it very difficult to fire bad or underperforming teachers. All of these policies are beneficial to teachers unions, but none are in the interests of our children. Worst of all, teachers unions keep many of our kids in failing school systems and give them very few real chances for success.

If the fifty individual states developed their own educational policies, you could expect a wide range of models for education in America—a thriving diversity of schooling ideas that would reveal startlingly different models for teacher pay, school schedules, and subject matter content. But in fact, public schools across America share almost uniform characteristics. And—surprise, surprise!—those characteristics typically benefit teachers unions.

Teachers Unions' Dues Machine

The story of teachers unions is a story about power and money. The money comes from teachers in the form of union dues payable to the National Education Association (NEA) and the American Federation of Teachers (AFT), and their state and local affiliates. The NEA, headed by Dennis Van Roekel, is the single largest and most powerful labor union in America. Its rival and sometimes partner is the much smaller AFT, headed by lawyer-turned-educator Randi Weingarten.

A veteran of many teachers union battles, Weingarten took over as head of AFT after eleven years at the helm of New York City's teachers union, the United Federation of Teachers (UFT). The NEA and the AFT generally act in concert to control our educational policy through their political activity and propaganda. Local and state teachers unions are generally affiliated with either the NEA or the AFT, or in some cases both unions.

> The teachers unions—the NEA, AFT, and their state and local affiliates—collect an estimated $2 billion in dues and fees from educators every year. Just how extensive is the teachers union control over our nation's teachers? Two-thirds of America's three million K–12 public school teachers are now under union monopoly bargaining control, and an estimated three-quarters of teachers are members of a teachers union.

The teachers unions—the NEA, AFT, and their state and local affiliates—collect an estimated $2 billion in dues and fees from educators every year.[7] Just how extensive is the teachers union control over our nation's teachers? Two-thirds of America's three million K–12 public school teachers are now under union monopoly bargaining control, and an estimated three-quarters of teachers are members of a teachers union.[8]

How many current teachers actually voted in an election to have a union in their district? Not even 10 percent of current teachers have.[9] States granted unions the power to unionize teachers in the school or district in the late 1950s and held elections in the school districts. If more than 50 percent of the teachers voting in the election chose the union, then the teachers union was certified as the teachers' exclusive bargaining representative. From that day forward, the teachers union represented *every* teacher in the district—even those teachers that voted no or didn't vote at all. And all future generations of teachers in that district are also bound by this *fifty-year-old* union vote. No recertification of the teachers union has likely ever been required since then. The teachers union in their school was there before most current teachers at the school were born and will likely remain there well after they die. And this works exactly the same for all other government employee unions. The Communist Party in the former Soviet Union would have been pleased with this type of arrangement.

Grading the States

Take a look at the map in which we gave each state a letter grade based on how much control the state gives teachers unions over the state's teachers (which correlated strongly to how much control the state gives unions over all its government workers).[10]

The F-grade states give teachers unions extensive powers over their teachers. In these twenty-two states plus the District of Columbia, state law grants the teachers unions collective bargaining power over teachers. This means that the teachers unions will represent teachers in all their contract negotiations and all other dealings with their employer. But the big advantage for the unions in the F-grade states, versus the other states, is that teachers are forced to pay dues to the union or be fired (and here you thought this was a free country).

In these forced-dues, F-grade states, teachers don't have to actually join the union. But if they don't join, they still have to pay agency fees about equal to union dues.[11] So, in these forced-dues states, teachers usually join the union to get the benefits of union membership (some liability and other insurance, camaraderie) since the cost is almost the same. Although these F-grade states employ less than half of our nation's teachers, teachers unions collect over three-quarters of all their dues and fees from these states.[12]

The twelve C-grade states give teachers unions collective bargaining over all or almost all teachers in the state but don't give them the power to collect forced dues from these teachers. In these states, the teachers union will be a big presence in teachers' working lives, and there will be a lot of pressure to join the union. But if a teacher declines joining the union, she doesn't have to pay dues.

The nine B-grade states allow individual school districts to decide whether or not to impose collective bargaining in their districts, but these states don't have state-level collective bargaining laws. In these states, unions do not collect forced dues even in the districts where they have collective bargaining power over teachers. The teachers unions' strategy in these states is to increase the number of districts under their control, because more teachers join the union where unions have collective bargaining power over them. If the union already represents you in contract negotiations and grievances against your employer,

GRADING THE STATES: WHICH STATES GRANT TEACHERS UNIONS THE MOST POWER OVER TEACHERS?

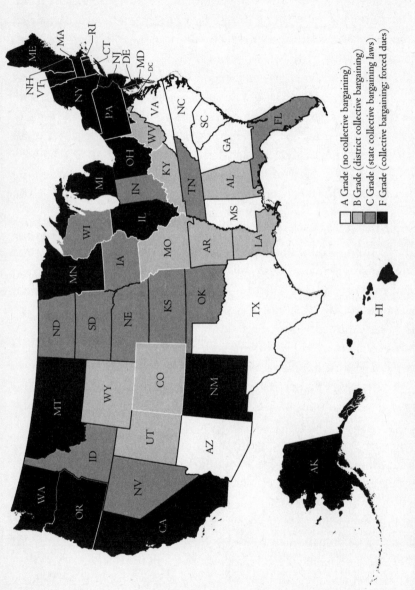

Legend:
- A Grade (no collective bargaining)
- B Grade (district collective bargaining)
- C Grade (state collective bargaining laws)
- F Grade (collective bargaining; forced dues)

Adapted from data provided in Terry M. Moe's Special Interest: Teachers Unions and America's Public Schools (Washington, D.C.: Brookings Institution Press, 2011), and updated for changes in the law.

Chart courtesy of Milton L. Chappell, the National Right To Work Legal Defense Foundation you already feel the power of the union in your workplace, and you are more likely to join the union than if no union represents you.

Finally, there are the seven A-grade states, where there is no collective bargaining or forced dues for teachers. As one would expect, far fewer teachers join teachers unions in the A-grade states than other states.[13] This suggests that if all states operated like the A states, the unions would collect less than one-sixth of the dues that they collect now, a huge financial blow for the teachers unions and their power.[14]

You might expect that all right-to-work states would be A-grade states that don't allow unions to have collective bargaining power over teachers. But this is not the case. Sixteen right-to-work states do have collective bargaining over at least some teachers. Right-to-work laws don't protect teachers and other workers from having collective bargaining imposed on them. But teachers in

> *Right-to-work laws don't protect teachers and other workers from having collective bargaining imposed on them. But teachers in these states are protected against having to pay dues and fees as a condition for getting or keeping their jobs.*

PERCENTAGE OF ALL TEACHERS UNION DUES COLLECTED IN "A" THROUGH "F" GRADE STATES

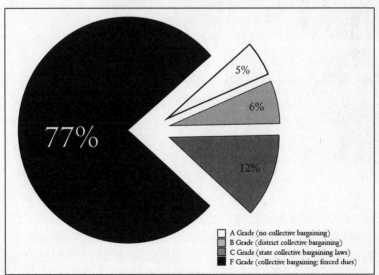

5%
6%
12%
77%

☐ A Grade (no collective bargaining)
☐ B Grade (district collective bargaining)
☐ C Grade (state collective bargaining laws)
■ F Grade (collective bargaining; forced dues)

Data from the Education Intelligence Agency and Terry Moe, Special Interest: Teachers Unions and America's Public Schools, *table 2-2* these states are protected against having to pay dues and fees as a condition for getting or keeping their jobs. And right-to-work laws hit unions where it hurts—in the pocketbook; only about 18 percent of total teachers union dues are collected in right-to-work states, although about 44 percent of teachers work in right-to-work states.[15]

Similarly, you might also expect that all non-right-to-work states would be F states. But this is also not the case. As you can see from the chart, five states do not have right-to-work laws but don't force their teachers to pay union dues either.

American Federation of Teachers president Randi Weingarten argues that states that have a lower proportion of unionized teachers, like the A-grade states, have lower academic achievement than states that have heavily unionized teachers, but this is really comparing apples to oranges.[16] Typically, the academic success of a state's students can be most easily gauged by how much their parents earn or by their parents' educational achievement, not by how unionized the state's teachers are.[17] Actually, there appears to be no demonstrable correlation between unionization and educational quality on a state-by-state basis.[18] In reality, teachers unions harm our K–12 educational system in all 50 states by exerting control over educational policy and practices nation-wide.

Why Teachers Join Unions

In forced-dues states, most teachers find it a pretty easy decision to join the union. After all, teachers have to pay union dues anyway, so they may as well join the union and get whatever benefits of membership are offered. In the states in which teachers are not forced to pay dues to a union to get or keep their job, the unions have to entice, cajole, trick, and pressure teachers to join the union.

One of the ways teachers unions develop their membership in the least unionized states is to capture young, impressionable college students who are training to be teachers. A young teacher from an A-grade state told us that when she entered her mandatory student-teaching period, her teachers college strongly advised her to obtain professional liability insurance. This insurance would cover her in the case that she was sued by one of her pupils' families during her student-teaching period. During student-teaching orientation, teachers union representatives offered all student teachers a discounted union membership rate, which included this liability coverage, and many of them joined. The takeaway message was "Welcome to the teaching profession—meet your teachers union!" Once student teachers join the union, the teachers union simply works to keep them as members when they take full-time teaching jobs.

A veteran teacher who worked in a number of A-grade states says that teachers union representatives pressured her to join the union throughout her whole career. Again, the union reps presented liability insurance as a major reason why she should join the union. They told her that if a student sued her, the union would provide her with a lawyer and she would be protected by liability insurance—but only if she was a member of the teachers union. Otherwise, she would be on her own. The unions were so successful at planting this fear in her that she always felt exposed to liability and uneasy about not joining the union. Of course, the states could fix this issue by providing liability insurance coverage to all teachers, but it hasn't happened yet. Teachers can also purchase this insurance inexpensively from other sources, but teachers unions have been very effective at presenting themselves as the sole source for professional liability insurance.[19]

Teachers unions are also effective at using sorority-style recruiting to sell the union as a social club for teachers. One teacher in an A-grade state recalls that union representatives were present with lots of fun giveaway items at the events that she was required to attend as a first-year teacher: "Here's a mug, and come join this fun club where you will meet new friends and share your experiences—the local teachers union!"

In states that impose collective bargaining on teachers, teachers unions have much more control over schools and are much more intrusive in their recruiting. A young teacher who has worked in several B-grade right-to-work states recalls that in Arkansas and Alabama, she was under intense pressure to join the teachers union. As a new teacher in Arkansas, union representatives were present at the orientation meetings for new teachers. She was directed to meet her school representative, who explained all the benefits she would receive as a union member and signed her up for membership and for her dues to be automatically deducted from her paycheck. When this teacher realized a few months later how much dues she was paying each month for union membership, and considered how little she benefited from the union, she decided to quit. But to do this, she had to visit the same in-school union representative and explain to her why she was quitting the union before her name could be taken off the union rolls. She recalls that this was a very intimidating process for her.

When this same young teacher moved to a school in Alabama a few years later, she was firm in her decision not to join the union. Shortly after she arrived at her new school, she was teaching a lesson to her kindergarten class when two other teachers barged into her classroom. Was there a fire or an emergency that demanded her immediate attention? No, these teachers were representatives of the teachers union. They proceeded to bully this young teacher in front of her class, urging her to join the union and help them achieve "100 percent participation" in the school. This teacher, experienced in the ways of union representatives by now, bravely refused. But although her experience of union intimidation may be typical, she's the exception in staying out of the union—when pressured, teachers tend to join unions.

Unified Dues

In many right-to-work states—especially the A-grade states that forbid collective bargaining over teachers—most teachers will tell you that unions don't affect their classroom experience at all. But is it really true that the teachers unions have little power over education in these states?

Of course not. Teachers unions have woven a web that spreads over the entire United States, covering every state and nearly every locality. The teachers unions' "support at the local level plays a major role in political campaigns."[20] Stanford professor Terry Moe notes, "While the stereotype is that the teachers unions are 'weak' in the states without collective bargaining, this is usually far from true. In any absolute sense, the unions tend to be quite powerful—just not as powerful as their counterparts in collective bargaining states."[21] But how have the unions built their state and local operations in states that have little dues income? They do it with an innovative funding technique called "unified dues."

Here's how it works. In the late 1950s and early 1960s, the teachers union bosses realized that they had a problem. Teachers were joining their local unions in droves, but not many teachers were joining their state and national teachers unions. After all, most education was local—so why pay to join the state and federal teachers unions?

The bosses found a solution: they forced local affiliates to charge unified dues. Now when teachers joined the local union, they automatically joined their state and national unions as well. Voila! Unified dues send tons of cash upstream to the state and national unions, giving these upper-level unions more funds for political activity and infrastructure building. The unified-dues system is now common to all government employee unions.

Here's an example of how unified dues works in practice. For example, a full-time teacher in Westport, Connecticut, pays $852 in dues for the 2011–12 school year, of which $178.00 is sent to NEA national headquarters, $484.50 is sent to the state-level NEA-affiliate union, and $190.00 is sent to the local NEA-affiliate union.[22] The national union then redistributes a portion of its funds to build infrastructure and fight important union battles all across the nation. The national teachers unions send representatives and resources to "underrepresented" right-to-work states where there are fewer union members, less dues income, and more limited teachers union infrastructure. Teachers union representatives invade right-to-work states like kudzu, colonizing new territory and taking it over: organizing workers, influencing educational policy, and supporting pro-union candidates there.

One observer explained, "In some states, the teachers unions [have] become the functional equivalent of a political party, assuming many of the roles—candidate recruitment, fund-raising, phone banks, polling, get-out-the-vote efforts—that were once handled by traditional party organizers." [23] And, of course, the teachers unions overwhelmingly support Democrats. When you look at the teachers unions, former Secretary of Education William J. Bennett said, "you're looking at the absolute heart and center of the Democratic Party."[24] E. J. McMahon of the Manhattan Institute adds, "NEA and American Federation of Teachers have been powerful forces in the Democratic Party for decades."[25]

Teachers Unions Dominate Politics

If you are surprised by the connection between teachers unions and politics, don't be. Teachers unions, like all government employee unions, survive only by putting their loyal friends in our government.

If you are surprised by the connection between teachers unions and politics, don't be. Teachers unions, like all government employee unions, survive only by putting their loyal friends in our government. The degree to which teachers unions influence state politics is so extreme that in many states "the legislatures, no less than the educational bureaucracies, function as wholly owned subsidiary of the teachers union," according to one education commentator.[26]

Nationally, teachers unions have political operatives in every congressional district in the United States. These political operatives have a dual job—assisting in day-to-day union work and managing teachers union political activity in the congressional district. These operatives are the backbone of the Democrat Party machine. They manage turnout-the-vote efforts in local school board elections and Presidential elections alike.

In all fifty states, teachers unions elect their own bosses—the district school boards and other educational decision makers who can give unions power over teachers and educational policy. In his book on teachers unions, Terry Moe points out that under this corrupt system, "democracy is turned on its head."[27] Even in states with few union members, "the teachers unions can use their political power to help choose the very people who will be running their districts and making all the authoritative decisions about money, personnel and policy," explains Moe.[28] Because few local taxpayers pay close attention to school board elections, for example, teachers unions elect their candidates almost every time. Eighty-four percent of school board candidates that the unions endorse in heavily Republican-controlled districts actually win their elections![29] And let's be serious—who among us bothers to investigate school board candidates and votes in local school board elections?

State-level teachers unions present themselves as educational policy think tanks and the defenders and reformers of the public schools. These sham policy institutes provide legislators and decision makers with research, support, and guidance on educational issues from the "teachers' perspective." Well, maybe not actually the teachers, but at least the teachers unions! Many government officials rely on these

THE NEA'S POLITICAL ARMY

The NEA stations about 1,800 UniServ directors, who are paid political organizers, in every congressional district in America.

What does this political army do for the teachers unions? UniServ's official function is to help local unions negotiate contracts and manage grievances. But UniServ directors are also there to make the federal, state, and local unions work together like one huge, well-oiled political machine. They organize local political action programs, including turn-out-the-vote efforts and other electioneering activities. They lobby for legislation and interview local candidates for mayor or school board.[30] A former teachers union boss explains that UniServ's "political role is at least as important as their bargaining role."[31] The NEA's own policy manager confirmed that UniServ is the political arm of the NEA when he told attendees at an NEA conference in 2003, "Politics move our policy. We work through UniServ."[32] UniServ directors are the backbone of the NEA's powerful political organization in all fifty states.

Like much political spending by unions, the NEA's spending on UniServ directors is considered nonpolitical spending by IRS rules. Even the NEA's spokesperson agrees that a reasonable person might consider UniServ spending to be for "political activity in the general sense of the term."[33] Try that sort of creative accounting yourself with the IRS, and you'll find yourself in jail. Try it as a union boss, and you'll find yourself with a comfortable seat at the State of the Union Address.

teachers union policy institutes for "objective" advice on educational issues. The teachers unions even set up front groups "to give the impression of public support of NEA policies," reports Phyllis Schlafly.[34] Often these faux-independent educational associations are funded by teachers union funds and staffed by current or former teachers union officials, but present themselves as nonpartisan, pro-education groups.[35] Generally, no strong pro-parent and pro-taxpayer organizations exist at the state or local level to counter these front groups, or if they do exist, they certainly don't have the funding and organizational power of the teachers unions or their front groups.

Even in the right-to-work states, state teachers unions are hard at work pushing their agenda and lobbying their legislatures. In Texas—one of the A-grade states—the Texas affiliate of NEA known as the TSTA explains on its website that "our lobbyists work with legislators before, during and after the biennial legislative session. They keep members informed of developments and alert them when action is needed, and they equip members with the skills and knowledge to elect pro-education candidates to national, state, and local office." And if the state teachers union does all that in right-to-work Texas, just imagine what teachers unions do in heavily unionized states like New York and California.

Keeping the Bad Apples

There's an old joke about doctors. What do you call a doctor who graduated in the bottom of his class in medical school? Answer: Doctor. The point of the joke is obvious—just because your doctor has his M.D. doesn't mean he's competent.

The same is true of teachers. Most teachers are good, but there are a few bad apples in every barrel. And unfortunately, teachers unions make it extremely difficult for school districts to separate the good apples from the bad, and to turn out the bad apples. Poorly performing teachers generally remain in the classroom for their entire careers, wasting the time, talent, and effort of countless American children.

Teacher quality is a leading driver of student achievement, concluded consulting firm McKinsey & Company in a report on why some nations have more successful K–12 education systems than others.[36] The report noted that "students placed with high-performing teachers will progress three times as fast as those placed with low-performing teachers." The report also explained that students placed with low-performing teachers for several years in a row tragically face an "educational loss which is largely irreversible."

Most teachers are good, but there are a few bad apples in every barrel. And unfortunately, teachers unions make it extremely difficult for school districts to separate the good apples from the bad, and to turn out the bad apples. Poorly performing teachers generally remain in the classroom for their entire careers, wasting the time, talent, and effort of countless American children.

Good teachers can even improve students' future earnings. As the Hoover Institute's Eric Hanushek concluded, excellent teachers can significantly increase students' lifetime earnings, whereas low-performing teachers can decrease their earnings.[37] Firing the bottom 5 to 10 percent of teachers based on their classroom performance and replacing them with average ones would improve student achievement significantly.[38] In fact, the world's best K–12 education systems intentionally weed out the lowest-performing teachers based on their classroom performance.[39] But in the United States, teachers unions stand in the way and prevent this from happening.

Teachers unions represent all teachers and protect the job security of good and bad teachers alike. As one school principal said of Randi Weingarten while she was head of New York City's powerful teachers union, "Randi Weingarten would defend a dead body in the classroom. That's her job."[40] And she sure does it well, now as the head of the American Federation of Teachers (AFT).

Teachers unions make sure that teachers who have taught for a few years are given tenure, making it almost impossible to fire them. Even in the case of serious wrongdoing, separating teachers from their government paycheck and benefits requires a lengthy, union-ordained legal process that can take years and can cost the school district hundreds of thousands of dollars. And it is virtually impossible to fire teachers who are merely incompetent—they are usually just left in the classroom, boring your children half to death.

When teachers are laid off, the last teachers hired are the first to be fired. This "last in, first out" firing policy doesn't take teacher merit and classroom performance into account, just seniority. This means that a young teacher who wins teacher of the year will be fired before all teachers hired before her, even the bad ones. It sounds fair to teachers unions at least.

What Teachers Unions Negotiate For

When teachers unions negotiate teachers' contracts, they demand single salary schedules and limits on class sizes, as well as tenure and "last in, first out" layoff policies, as we have seen. Even in those districts in which unions don't have collective bargaining power over teachers, teachers unions still promote these same inefficient policies using their political influence.[41]

The single salary schedule requires school districts to pay teachers based on their level of education and their years at the desk. They aren't paid more for good performance or because their teaching area is in high demand. Physical education teachers are paid on the same scale as physics teachers. As a result, the single salary schedule generally drives teachers who have more in-demand skills right out of the teaching profession, and it creates shortages of specialists in math, science, and other subjects. As a scientist, would you rather work at Lockheed Martin and be paid based on your skills and performance, or work as a teacher and be paid based on seniority and on the same scale as teachers with less marketable skills?

But, you say, at least the single salary schedule pays teachers with more education more salary. Don't we want to encourage teachers to get graduate degrees to improve their teaching? Well, there's a problem with that idea: teachers get the bump in pay regardless of whether their graduate degree relates to anything that they actually teach in the classroom. If your degree is in modern dance but you are a math teacher, why should the extra degree entitle you to a raise? Plus, research shows that having a master's degree or additional professional development credits does *not* make teachers more effective in the classroom.[42]

Teachers unions also have been unrelenting in their demands for smaller class sizes. A recent report shows that the ratio of student-to-educational staff (both teachers and assistants) nationally has dropped from 18-to-1 in 1960 to less than 8-to-1 currently.[43] Sounds great, right? Except that our children are just as poorly educated as they were before, even though the drop in class size has more than doubled the "labor intensity" of public schooling.[44] Out of the 112 studies researching the impact of class size on student performance, 103 studies concluded that smaller class size did not improve student performance at all.[45] So reducing class size doesn't appear to benefit students much at all, and existing teachers would certainly prefer education dollars be spent to increase their own salaries or on other priorities. But making class size smaller has driven up teachers union membership substantially because of increased teacher hiring.[46] So the main beneficiary of smaller class sizes seems, once again, to be the teachers unions, who have more teachers to unionize and collect dues income from.

Putting America in a Rubber Room

The union rules against firing tenured teachers are so extreme that many school systems have to warehouse hundreds of teachers who can't be trusted in the classroom but have to be put on paid leave for years until they can be fired. Seriously. "Rubber rooms"—offices that suspended teachers report to each day pending disciplinary and termination hearings—would seem to be the stuff of urban legend. Only they were real.

Required to report there every day during regular school hours, except for school holidays and vacations, suspended teachers found ways to pass the time. Some practiced yoga, some painted, some got into fights with other teachers to quell the boredom.

In New York City, these holding pens for errant teachers cost New York City taxpayers an estimated $30 million to $65 million annually for the seven hundred or so teachers assigned there at any one time. Some teachers were on leave for sexual harassment, corporal punishment, or insubordination; some were even suspended for sexual misconduct in the classroom.[47]

Bad publicity about rubber rooms led Mayor Michael Bloomberg to officially abolish them in New York City in 2010.[48] But union contracts still require school districts to give teachers years of expensive and extensive due process before they can be fired, about two to five years in New York City. The city is still putting errant teachers on paid leave for years, and the city is now sending them back to the classroom, giving them administrative duties, or sending them home instead of penning them in rubber rooms.[49]

Of course, teachers aren't the only ones we put in the rubber rooms. By leaving bad teachers in the classroom, we're essentially relegating our children to thousands of rubber rooms across the country in our public schools. As we have seen, America's public schools could be greatly improved by simply taking our worst-performing teachers out of our classrooms. With this change, American students could jump ahead of most countries in the world in mathematics,[50] instead of falling below students in almost all Asian and Western European countries as they do now.[51] But teachers unions are consistent in their position that this must never happen, and so far they are winning on this point and many other points.

Teachers Unions Win—And Kids Lose

In 2008, Michelle Rhee, then chancellor of the Washington, D.C., public schools, looked at D.C.'s schools and saw that they were a full-scale nuclear disaster area.[52] She recognized that many teachers performed so poorly that they didn't deserve to keep their jobs. So she offered D.C. area teachers unions a deal: teachers could choose one of two new compensation options, the green tier or the red tier. Under the green tier, teacher compensation would jump dramatically, increasing almost 100 percent, with much of the pay increases financed by private sources. But in return, the teachers would have to give up their tenure for a year, and at the end of the year, they would need the recommendation of their principal to continue teaching or face dismissal. Under the red tier, teacher compensation would jump a little less, and teachers would have to waive seniority rights that would help them keep their jobs in the case of layoffs ahead of more junior teachers. "Tenure is the holy grail of teacher unions," Rhee told the New York Times. But it has "no educational value for kids; it only benefits adults. If we can put veteran teachers who have tenure in a position where they don't have it, that would help us to radically increase our teacher quality. And maybe other districts would try it, too," she said.[53]

That's right where AFT president Randi Weingarten stopped her. Weingarten, who is militant in proclaiming that what's best for the unions *must* be best for kids, says that seniority is "the best mechanism we have. You have cronyism and corruption and discrimination issues…We don't want to see people getting laid off based on how much they cost."[54] But, of course, cronyism is the name of the game for the teachers unions—and teachers *should* be laid off if they are not producing enough value for their cost.

Weingarten, whom Newsweek called "well dressed and well educated" and who herself makes $425,000 a year as a union official, criticized Rhee as someone who "does not view teaching as a career…She sees it as temporary, something a lot of newbies will work very hard at for a couple of years, and then if they leave, they leave, as opposed to professionals who get more seasoned."[55] And faced the possibility of real tenure reform, Weingarten and the Washington Teachers Union president took the green-tier/red-tier proposal right off the table and didn't put the proposal to a vote of their members. The ultimate agreement between Rhee and the unions left teacher tenure basically intact, while "weakening seniority and job security" somewhat and providing much more modest teacher raises than Rhee's original green tier would have provided.[56]

Reform does not come easy in school systems controlled by the teachers unions. In addition to resisting changes to teacher tenure, the teachers unions fight pretty much any form of school choice, including voucher programs and charter schools which would implicitly allow parents to judge the quality of their teachers and schools. The teachers unions oppose these programs essentially because they allow students to escape from unionized public schools, reducing the number of unionized teachers needed and the amount of teachers union dues generated.[57]

Teachers unions often seem to want to take all choice away from parents over their children's education. In fact, it sometimes seems that teachers unions officials think they're *our* parents, and we children don't know what's good for us. When Louisiana's Republican governor Bobby

Jindal talked about the possibility of vouchers which would allow parents greater choice over where to send their kids to school (and would partially subsidize private and parochial school tuition), a Louisiana teachers union official dismissed the idea. The union official said, "If I'm a parent in poverty I have no clue because I'm trying to struggle and live day to day." The implication seemed to be that poor parents can't make meaningful decisions about their kids. Jindal responded, "To me that is incredibly offensive and exactly what is wrong with the top down approach." And as one mother of three children stated, "Nobody knows my child better than me. I can't imagine not having a choice."[58]

Teachers unions are well aware that making the fight over the future of our children allows them to claim the high road, but this is a public relations and bargaining tactic. A Michigan teachers union bargaining manual makes this point perfectly clear. The manual instructs its members to phrase their demands in terms of the children, stating, "In terms of a bargaining message, the public responds most positively when we talk about children, quality in the classroom and the future."[59] The manual suggests that the right type of slogan might be, "It's not about dollars and cents; it's about our children."[60] If only it *were* actually about our children!

Indoctrination

It's not just that bad educational policy drives out the most worthy teachers who can be paid more elsewhere. It's not even that math and science teachers make the same kind of money as teachers of ceramic arts. Or that young "teachers of the year" get fired before tenured rule breakers sitting in rubber rooms. It's that teachers unions are exercising considerable influence over what our students are taught.[61]

If the unions are focused on their own growth, we'd expect their curriculum choices to teach the benefits of bigger government and more education spending. And we'd expect the unions to stick their noses in every liberal issue across the spectrum. And lo and behold, that's exactly what happens.

The famed economist Ludwig Von Mises pointed out that in Germany, the university system was controlled by the government, and as a result university professors taught appreciation for big government. In America, we should not be surprised that our Shadowbosses are actually training a new generation of activists dedicated to the union cause right in our nation's public schools. Now, in addition to having your kids bug you to recycle, reduce your carbon footprint, fight global warming, and buy a hybrid car, you can expect that Junior will regale you with bits of union history and will try to convince you that joining together in solidarity with other workers is the noblest expression of a free people.

The teachers unions realize that the best way to build young unionists is to start early—in kindergarten, if possible. The unions have actually pushed a children's book called *Click Clack Moo: Cows That Type*. The book tells the story of a bunch of cows who go on strike. Unlike in real life, they aren't just shipped off to the stockyards for slaughter. The cows use collective action to win the day. And lest you think that the teachers union officials were just drawn to the colorful illustrations and amusing story: "One lesson plan...calls for students to read the book and learn four new vocabulary words: *union, strike, laborer* and *negotiate*," noticed one commentator.[62]

In another case, teachers at a teachers union conference were encouraged to have their kindergarteners put on a puppet show called *Trouble in the Hen House*, a union propaganda play put out by the California Federation of Teachers, a union affiliated with the AFT.[63] The story is about barnyard animals that fight unfair working conditions and is designed to teach the kids "about the strength and value of organizing unions." In the play, Daisy the cow hammers the point home to the chickens about the importance of organizing themselves into a union: "We're a group of working cows. We're strong because we all stick together and help each other. We decide what we need and we pick leaders to go talk to Farmer Brown, but he knows we stand behind our leaders. Now he gives us better hay, and we're not always so tired from having to give him so much milk." The teachers union materials explain that "*Students can make puppets and learn about the potential for power in collective action*" and that the play could be perfect for celebrating Cesar Chavez Day.[64] Other materials suggested for small children by the California Federation of Teachers include *Along the Shore*, a coloring book focusing on longshoremen, and "simply but effectively showing the importance of unions in workers' lives"; and *Autoworks*, a comic book history of the United Auto Workers.[65]

Partisan teaching is a huge action item for the teachers unions. A teachers guide for teaching globalism explains, "Partisan teaching... *invites* diversity of opinion but does not lose sight of the aim of the curriculum: to alert students to global injustice, to seek explanations, and to encourage activism."[66] Meanwhile, the NEA has opposed David Horowitz's Academic Bill of Rights, which would ensure that people of differing political views be allowed to teach on campuses.[67] Political diversity is not a type of diversity permitted by teachers unions in our schools.

Most of all, teachers unions want teachers to teach support for the union movement. In a model for all our states, Wisconsin governor Jim Doyle, the Democrat who served before current Republican governor Scott Walker, signed a bill requiring "labor history and collective bargaining" be taught in Wisconsin public schools. According to the Wisconsin Labor History Society, that bill's sponsors were interested in "returning balance to our school curricula by providing more teaching of labor in the schools."[68] Similarly, a California teachers union has a Labor in the Schools Committee dedicated to "educating K–12 students about the role and contributions of unions and the labor movement to American society."[69]

Late Socialist and leftist historian Howard Zinn was a huge proponent of just this sort of indoctrination of schoolchildren. "If teacher unions want to be strong and well-supported," he wrote, "it's essential that they not only be teacher-unionists but teachers of unionism. We need to create a generation of students who support teachers and the movement of teachers for their rights."[70] What a great self-serving idea—and the teachers unions have taken it to heart. As a labor organizer in Chicago says, "Some teachers don't want to talk to their students about unions; they see it as somehow unethical and misusing their position. That's ridiculous. Teachers need to help sow the seeds of the future of unionism."[71]

The NEA is heavily promoting activism in the early grades. In October 2011, teachers from an elementary school in Wisconsin received a $5,000 grant from the NEA to help them "develop a course of study with a team of colleagues to help first or second grade students understand the role of power in their lives, including how they can use technology and podcasts to create activist messages around issues important to the students."[72] Sounds like teaching school kids to be activists. But what happens when they want to strike for chocolate milk in the lunchroom and more recess? This school later returned the grant, but as progressivism takes a greater hold on our society, we can expect many schools to buy into new, well-funded teachers unions' initiatives to build young activists and praise the activist's mantra of "standing up to power."

Of course all that education about the labor movement and political indoctrination leaves little time for old-fashioned reading, writing, and arithmetic. Phyllis Schlafly explains: "Elementary and secondary school education used to be organized around subjects such as reading, math, history, geography, language, and science. While smatterings of those subjects are still taught, the focus has been shifted from academic subject matter to teaching attitudes, beliefs, values, themes, behaviors, and job skills. This is indoctrination, not education."[73] And it's a misuse of our students' valuable time and energy.

Protesting: A Lesson Plan

If you had any doubt about whether or not teachers unions consider students as tools in their hands, look no further than the recent protests over Governor Scott Walker's decision to rein in collective bargaining over teachers in Wisconsin. The teachers unions didn't just call rallies for the teachers; they encouraged teachers to bring their students with them. "High school students in Wisconsin have staged walk-outs in support of their teachers over the last two days, much to the delight of liberal sites such as *The Nation* and the blog of the AFL-CIO," reported *TheBlaze*.[74] Another report described a similar protest at another school, "Yesterday, more than half the student body of Madison East High School walked out with the support and assistance of their teachers."[75] The AFL-CIO cheered the move to give students their first taste of government employee union power. "The students have been so energized," celebrated one union leader.[76] Did the students enjoy the activism, or was it just a great excuse to miss school?

Teacher and student protests prompted Sarah Palin to write a note to the protestors: "I greatly admire good teachers and will always speak up in defense of the teaching profession," she wrote. "But Wisconsin teacher unions do themselves no favor by closing down classrooms and abandoning children's needs in protest against the sort of belt-tightening that people everywhere are going through."[77]

But, you say, that was just in Wisconsin, where battles over collective bargaining have reached a fever pitch. How could we possibly suggest that mobilizing students in favor of labor union causes is a common occurrence?

Maybe because it happens all the time. In Los Angeles, teachers protested in May 2011 against cuts in education funding in California. And the Associated Press reported, "Students were seen leaving Panorama City High School [during school hours] and lining the streets with signs to protest the cuts to education. The teachers are holding signs saying 'Keep Schools Open' and 'Education Can't Wait.'"[78] Well, apparently, *education can wait* while the teachers are protesting and bringing their students along with them. It has also happened recently in Texas, Florida, Pennsylvania, and other states.

Of course, when kids are not on school time, they have the right to go to protests. But protesting shouldn't be a school-sanctioned activity unless schools are training young unionists, which is exactly what teachers unions are working to do.

Rise of Online Education

Right now, only a few trends in education have the potential to curb the enormous influence of teachers unions over our educational system. Perhaps the most promising of these trends is online education.

Fortunately for Americans, and unfortunately for teachers unions, technology is changing everything. The rapid spread and obvious appeal of high-quality online schooling is so dramatic that even the well-organized teachers unions will not be able to hold it back—although, if we are not careful, they may be able to co-opt it and make it their own.

Imagine a customized program of online education which allows every schoolchild to develop his or her strengths and work on his weaknesses—even in the evenings, weekends, and over school breaks.

We are not talking about iPad apps here, but about high-quality online education programs increasingly available for K–12 students. Your child could attend live classes in school for a few hours a day, followed by several additional hours of customized online education in a study hall at school or at home. If your school doesn't offer a subject that your child is interested in, he could sign up for a virtual class in that subject with a live teacher interacting with him and a group of other students across the state or nation via Skype. He could drill in areas in which he is weak, and use programs designed for his particular learning styles. And if you and your child want to, he could continue his customized learning program over the summer so he doesn't slip back over the long school break.

Many states are now offering virtual public school programs that are provided by private companies for a fraction of the cost of public education. Florida Virtual School Full Time is now available free to every Florida resident as a substitute for public schooling; already 122,000 have enrolled at least on a part-time basis. Florida's online program employs 1,200 accredited, nonunion teachers, and it is available seven days a week, from 8 a.m. to 8 p.m.[79] Like most virtual schooling options, Florida Virtual School Full Time is much cheaper for the state to operate than a regular school—at least 30 percent cheaper per student. Many other states use national online companies like K–12, also staffed with nonunion teachers, to provide online schooling in their districts, again saving money for the state.

Online education threatens teachers unions because the world of online schooling is "flat." Content can be developed anywhere, offered freely or cheaply on the web. Live teacher support services via the Internet can be staffed by nonunion teachers, or even outsourced to teachers abroad, for that matter. The virtual world of online education has no bounds, no districts to keep children captive and subject to teachers union supervision. This makes online education very difficult to control, even by the crafty teachers unions.

Innovative educational platforms like the online Khan Academy challenge the teachers unions' control over K–12 education by promising to provide "a free world class education to anyone anywhere"— without public schools. It is a revolutionary idea, and one that millions of Americans are starting to embrace, at least as a supplement to school-based education.

Teachers unions may be able to dismiss a private Internet company like the Khan Academy, but as America's esteemed universities and top education companies join the revolution, there will be no stopping online education from toppling "school" as we know it. Johns Hopkins offers high-quality self-paced courses as enhancement or in substitution for school classes.[80] MIT now offers extensive online courses for free, and will even be offering certificates to people who complete its programs and take certain testing for a small fee.[81] Stanford and other top universities are already dipping their toes into this open access model.[82]

The biggest challenge for teachers unions is that online education, for the first time, puts education back in the hands of parents. Online education predicates itself on the notion that parents are in charge and able to choose a program for their own children. Brick and mortar schools, on the other hand, operate under the idea that parents hand their children over to a caretaker-teacher who is given full control to raise a child for the seven to eight hours that they are in school each day.

Online education has the potential to benefit many students. Students and parents win because they have another educational option; taxpayers win because they get more for their educational dollars with online education. Teachers win because online education gives them more employment opportunities. The only group that doesn't win is teachers unions, who lose control over K–12 education.

The biggest challenge for teachers unions is that online education, for the first time, puts education back in the hands of parents. Online education predicates itself on the notion that parents are in charge and able to choose a program for their own children. Brick and mortar schools, on the other hand, operate under the idea that parents hand their children over to a caretaker-teacher who is given full control to raise a child for the seven to eight hours that they are in school each day.

Taxpayers need to watch carefully how teachers unions respond to this latest challenge to their control of our education system. Generally, if there is a new platform or technology which will change the way things can be done, watch for unions to resist it. If you see them start to embrace it, you can bet that unions will try to take it over and become the gatekeepers once again.

Teachers unions are trying to get online education under union control—at least with respect to programs paid for with state education dollars. Teachers unions want to bog down state-supported online education with the same inefficiencies that plague public education—unionized teachers, restrictive work rules, and content restrictions.[83] If the teachers unions succeed, innovation in this field will slow, and the diversity of options available in online education will recede. Soon, the escape valve that online education is now providing may be stopped up by union gunk.

School? Who Needs School?

Another group of students that "escape" from the public schools are homeschoolers. Homeschooling is on a huge growth trajectory. While the number of private school students has declined slightly in recent years, the number of homeschoolers has increased a whopping 74 percent in a recent eight-year period and shows no sign of decreasing anytime soon.[84] Just over 2 million American school-aged children, about 3.8 percent of all school-aged children, were homeschooled in 2010.[85] In comparison, 5.5 million American students attend private or parochial school, representing 10 percent of all schoolchildren.[86]

One of the reasons that homeschooling is on the rise is that online education has made homeschooling much easier for parents. Twenty years ago, homeschooling parents had to locate books and materials to teach their children all the subjects they needed to learn. Today, homeschoolers can choose instead to sign up their children for a full online school program, such as K–12, which supplies all coursework, testing, and online tutors. And many states even provide comprehensive online school programs for free. Technology has lowered the barrier for families to homeschool and provided many more educational opportunities for homeschoolers—from remedial programs to AP and college courses.

Homeschooling brings educational costs down for our states and municipalities because parents generally pay the cost of the schooling, which is great for taxpayers. But its growth is a big problem for teachers unions. State-supported virtual homeschools take educational dollars away from teachers-union-controlled schools. And by taking large numbers of schoolchildren out of schools, homeschooling also reduces the number of unionized teachers and school workers needed in schools.

Imagine how pleased teachers unions would be if they could force those 2 million homeschooled children back into the public schools. The schools would have to hire 250,000 additional teachers and other school workers to keep the current union-mandated student–educational worker ratio of eight-to-one. Using current membership and dues rates, this represents a missed opportunity of over $100 million in potential dues income for the teachers unions annually![87] And as the number of homeschoolers grows every year, so does the amount of union dues forgone.

Watch for teachers unions to chip away at protections for homeschoolers across the country. Teachers unions will suggest that homeschoolers follow the state's subject matter standards and take assessments showing their mastery, all developed by teachers union educational specialists and proctored by union teachers. Teachers unions will try to require homeschooling parents to be certified by the state. And if they're successful, they may try the ultimate power grab: they'll try to force homeschooling parents into teachers unions.

This battle is on. Will technology and homeschoolers take down the teachers unions?

Conclusion

We have seen how teachers unions control education policy and classroom content across America. As Michelle Malkin rightly observes, "Instead of incentivizing fixes, politicians—dependent on teachers union campaign contributions and human shield photo-ops—incentivize more failure."[88] In the face of their huge organizational advantages, how can we possibly pull teachers unions' tentacles out of our system of education?

A critical first step toward reclaiming our K–12 schools is for taxpayers to pay attention to elections for the state superintendent of education and the local school board members. After all, many of these state and local government officials are elected with teachers union help while we are not paying attention, and they significantly determine educational policy in our states and school districts. We need to elect government officials that truly represent the interests of families, children, and actual teachers—not just teachers unions.

A second line of attack is to hit teachers unions where it really hurts—the dues income that they extract from teachers in forced-dues states. Teachers, like all workers, should have a choice over whether or not to pay union dues, a choice that they don't have currently in the F-grade states. Also, states with dues checkoff arrangements should stop collecting union dues for teachers unions—or any other unions, for that matter. Dues are payments to private organizations, so why should the state collect them on the unions' behalf? States also should require school districts to hold new elections to recertify the teachers union on a regular basis. This would give teachers an actual vote on whether or not they want to have a union represent them, instead of sticking them with a union that was elected many years before by their predecessors. Elections are not useful or fair unless they're regular.

Third, we should encourage our states to try innovative solutions in education that put our children's needs before those of the teachers unions. Even if we don't have kids in the local school system, we all have skin in the game as taxpayers and citizens.

Finally, we need to pay attention to what our children are being taught in their classrooms. Do we really agree with what is going on in the classroom and the lessons and values taught there? And if not, are we willing to stand up for what we believe in?

If we don't rein in the teachers unions soon, our nation and our children will continue paying a high price.

Chapter 5 Summary Points

- Two-thirds of America's public school teachers are under union collective bargaining control; three-quarters of teachers are union members.
- The two teachers unions collect over $2 billion in dues each year at the federal, state, and local levels.

- The United States spends almost $10,000 on school per elementary schoolchild. We spend 68 percent more per schoolchild than Germany, 33 percent more than Japan, 84 percent more than Korea, and 14 percent more than the United Kingdom, with far worse math and science scores than all these countries.
- About 77 percent of teachers union dues are collected in the twenty-two states plus the District of Columbia that force teachers to pay union dues, even though those states employ less than half of our nation's teachers.
- Teachers unions exercise considerable control over education and politics even in right-to-work states through paid political operatives that they maintain in every congressional district in the United States and the teachers unions' extensive national organization.
- Under contracts negotiated by teachers unions, it is nearly impossible to get rid of bad teachers. If we just got rid of 5 to 10 percent of the worst-performing teachers, our children's educational outcomes would improve dramatically.
- Teachers unions have demanded and received decreases in the student-to-staff ratio at schools from 18-to-1 in 1960 to 8-to-1 in 2009. Decreasing the student-staff ratios hasn't helped students much at all, but it does dramatically increase teachers union dues.
- Teachers unions encourage teachers to indoctrinate students with leftism and government worker unionism.
- We should expect teachers unions to try to take over state-sponsored online education and regulate homeschooling as a way to deal with these threats to their control of K–12 education.

CHAPTER 6

Shadowbosses Bankrupt Our States

A lion and a wild mule once decided to hunt together. During that hunt, the mule observed a group of gazelle from afar. "Lion," said the mule, "let's make an arrangement. I'll chase down those gazelle and drive them toward you—and as they reach you, you strike them down with your mighty claws. Then, we will share the spoils of our hunt together." The lion agreed.

The plan worked beautifully—as the mule drove the gazelle toward the lion, the lion killed them, one by one.

Then the lion curiously divided the meat into three piles. "Why three piles?" asked the bewildered mule.

"The first share is mine," said the lion, pointing to the first pile, "because after all, I am king of the jungle." The mule nodded. The lion pointed to the second pile and explained, "The second share is half of what is left, also mine because, after all, I killed the prey." The mule looked confused and then looked hopefully at the last pile. The lion concluded, "And the third share— well, let's just say that you'll give it to me also, and run off as fast as you can in case I get hungry again."

AS we've seen, the lion of American politics is the government employee unions. And just like the lion in Aesop's tale, government employee unions operate under the principle that might makes right. And we are the wild mules, hunting for food that the unions will take for themselves, losing our own hard-earned share of the spoils. How much longer can we keep hunting?

Tapping Out Our States

Overly generous pay contracts, featherbedding, and pension schemes have been negotiated by the government employee unions and achieved with union political activities and donations in support of union-friendly politicians. Remember when we said that the problem with government employee unions is that they don't have to worry about their employers going out of business? Well, they didn't. Until now.

A number of states actually are on the verge of insolvency, although no one really understands what that will mean for the states and for America. "The ultimate check on the growth of public sector unionism is municipal insolvency," writes scholar Eileen Norcross.[1] She's right. And we are approaching that ultimate check.

The *New York Times* reported "some states have deep structural problems, like insolvent pension funds, that are diverting money from essential public services like education and health care."[2] This illustrates a very important point—as states spend more money on salaries and benefits for current government workers and pension costs for retired workers, these states have less and less left in their budgets for essential services. But currently there is no way for states to get out from under crushing compensation and pension arrangements that were negotiated with the government employee unions. States are not permitted to declare bankruptcy and seek protection against their creditors, although cities are.[3]

While they can't declare bankruptcy, states can become insolvent. It happens when a state doesn't have enough cash to pay its bills, including its employees' salaries and pension costs. A number of states are approaching insolvency fast. If one state reaches this point, the federal government will probably step in to pay the bills and spread the cost over all the taxpayers in our nation. But does even the federal government have enough money, or ability to borrow, to prop up Illinois, California, and New York, the three states most likely to default over the next five years?[4]

Already the federal government is providing huge subsidies to the states to plug holes in their budgets. Basically, the federal government allocates cash to the states, which they then use to keep up their spending. Federal subsidies for state government spending are a great deal for the states, but a terrible deal for America's taxpayers. Over the last ten years, the federal government has subsidized more and more state government spending, covering 34.1 percent of all state spending in 2011, up from 25.7 percent ten years before.[5] And as the financial condition of many states worsens, we can expect more federal subsidies to fill the gap between state spending and revenues.

How does our federal government do this when it is already running a deficit? It simply borrows more. But there is a limit. Our nation may be able to bail out a few states, but eventually America's debt will be so large that our line of credit with China, the Arab oil states, and other nations will dry up. Our nation's debt compared with the size of our entire economy is getting into the extremely unhealthy range.[6] What happens if we continue in this direction? We become Greece.

Greece actually provides an example of precisely this disaster in the making. Recently, as Steve Forbes explains, the Greek government has cut expenses, but "not one civil servant from the bloated public sector was sacked. Thanks to fierce union resistance, privatizations have stalled...It's no surprise that the economy is still sputtering and that deficits remain gargantuan."[7]

Welcome to Greece.

As we'll see, more and more states are now trying to cut back on the unwise, overly generous promises that they made to the government employee unions in the flush years. Now in the lean years, the unions are still holding states hostage, while negotiating for more in salaries, pensions, and other benefits. How exactly will this story end?

Government Behemoth

The battle over whether to grow government or reform government spending is *really* a battle between the net tax receivers and the taxpayers. Net tax receivers always benefit by the growth of government—and so do government employee unions. Taxpayers, including members

Net tax receivers always benefit by the growth of government—and so do government employee unions. Taxpayers, including members of private sector unions, pretty much always lose.

of private sector unions, pretty much always lose. There's a well-known bumper sticker that states, "Work harder. Millions on welfare depend on you." But the problem is much bigger than just welfare recipients. The bumper sticker *should* more correctly say, "Work harder. Millions of net tax receivers depend on you."

Here's the sad fact: the pie that taxpayers make isn't growing as fast as the amount of pie redistributed by government employee unions. Just like the mule in the fable, we can keep on hunting, but we are not going to get much meat for dinner with the lion hanging around.

State and local governments already spend about half their total revenues on government employee pay and benefits, and this percentage is projected to rise in future years.[8] How much more of the budget can government employees possibly consume?

You might ask why legislators and government officials don't stop this nonsense. But you know by now that many legislators and government officials are supported by government employee unions, and they aren't about to bite the hand that feeds them.

One of the reasons our government gives away so much to the unions in negotiations is that the government negotiators are themselves government employees. Sure enough, these negotiators feel a natural kinship with other government employees. *I need a raise*, the government negotiator thinks. *And I'm a government employee. That guy's a government employee, too. He probably* also *needs a raise. Why shouldn't I just give it to him?* As one commentator put it, "The public sector employer is also a public sector employee," and they share similar goals about growing the size of government.[9] Plus, the elected officials like governors and mayors that have the final say in approving union contracts may themselves be supported by the union on the other side of the bargaining table in their own reelection efforts.

The situation for taxpayers is the same as that of the benevolent parents of a spendaholic teenager. Let's say little Suzie goes out and breaks the bank buying clothes and shoes, then comes home with a $1,000 credit card bill. She expects her parents to pay the bill. The credit card company has a hold on her parents, no matter how much she runs up. Suzie keeps on spending; her parents keep on paying.

That's the problem right now. Suzie is the unions, negotiating burdensome contracts with state and local governments; the credit card company is the state and local governments giving the unions what they ask for; and Suzie's parents are the taxpayers who are ultimately responsible for paying the bill. But eventually, Suzie is spending so much that her parents can't afford to keep paying her bills, yet they remain on the hook. They go into debt. Then, they go bankrupt.

That's precisely what happens when unions represent government employees. The unions run up such a massive tab for our government that the taxpayers can't possibly continue paying for it in the long run. And this is the principal reason that the economies of highly unionized states are faring much worse than states freer of union control.

Unions Kill Prosperity

Government employee unionism hurts states' economies. As Chris Edwards of the Cato Institute explains, "Unions reduce the ability of government managers to cut costs and increase efficiency in many ways. They protect poorly performing workers, they push for minimum staffing levels, they resist the introduction of new technologies that threaten their jobs, and they create a rule-laden and bureaucratic workplace."[10] And this hurts states with a highly unionized government workforce.

Lightly unionized states do much better than highly unionized states. As economist Arthur Laffer points out, "The economies in states with right-to-work laws grow significantly faster than those in forced-union states. They have higher employment growth, attract more residents, and have more rapid growth in state and local tax revenues than forced-union states."[11] Similarly, "decades of empirical research in economics shows that the *absence* of right-to-work laws hinders economic development," commentators point out.[12] That is, states with forced unionism and forced dues are failing in comparison with other states.

High rates of unionization kill private sector jobs. In New Jersey, for example, where two-thirds of all public sector employees are unionized, the state's private sector employment rate is down for the last decade.[13]

REAL PERSONAL INCOME GROWTH

In Most Populous States, 2000–2010

Right-to-Work States		Forced-Dues States	
Texas	26.0%	California	10.6%
Florida	21.2%	New York	12.8%
Georgia	13.7%	Illinois	5.1%
North Carolina	17.1%	Pennsylvania	10.2%
Virginia	24.7%	Ohio	1.1%
Arizona	29.0%	Michigan	−7.5%
Tennessee	15.3%	New Jersey	9.1%
Average	24.9%	Average	7.8%

Sources: Bureau of Economic Analysis, U.S. Commerce Department, Bureau of Labor Statistics, U.S. Labor Department

Courtesy: National Right to Work Committee

But the politicians kept spending as if there were robust growth in the state's economy.[14]

Now take a look at Texas. Texas is a right-to-work state with far less powerful government employee unions—less than one in five public employees is a union member.[15] Job growth in Texas was nearly double the national average in recent years.[16]

So, would you rather start a business in New Jersey or Texas? Unless you're Tony Soprano, the answer's clearly Texas.

The chart above illustrates this point exactly. Its message? The states experiencing the most personal income growth are right-to-work states. The largest right-to-work states experienced almost three times as much growth as the largest forced-unionism states. For vibrant private sector growth, head to the right-to-work states, which also are the states with low levels of government employee unionism.

Budget Busters

In 1980, Frank Sinatra covered the song "New York, New York." Today, we hear it every time the Yankees win a ball game. "Start spreadin' the news," Frankie Blue Eyes warbles. "I'm leaving today. I want to be a part of it: New York, New York!"

Unfortunately, in the '70s and early '80s, nobody really wanted to be a part of New York City. New York was a disaster zone. From 1965 to 1975, the city lost half of its million manufacturing jobs, rendering its increasingly bloated public sector payrolls unaffordable.[17] In 1966, the transit workers went on strike. In 1968, the sanitation workers went on strike, and huge piles of garbage bags were piled high in the streets. In the 1970s, in the state of New York, there were twenty teachers' strikes per year.[18]

Eventually, New York recovered. But overly generous union contracts and terrible pension obligations are driving the Big Apple down the road back to the mid-1970s. Unless Gotham's elected officials change course soon and begin aggressively reining in government employee compensation costs, the dark days of three and a half decades ago are bound to be returning soon.

It isn't just New York. It is the same in many states with a heavily unionized government workforce.

"But," you ask, "how can you be sure that it's the unions that create this problem?"

Well, let's take a look at two counties that border each other: Montgomery County in Maryland and Fairfax County in Virginia. Both are home to many federal contractors and federal employees. Both are dominated by Democrats.

One of these counties is not like the other, though.

In May 2010, the *Washington Post* declared, "Montgomery County has just completed a nightmarish budget year."[19] Montgomery County in Maryland was forced to jack up taxes because its deficit amounted to one-quarter of its budget. Meanwhile, Fairfax County in Virginia was "all sweetness and light by comparison." Fairfax erased its far-smaller deficit much more easily.

These counties not only border each other, but also have similar populations with similar demographics. So, what was the difference between Montgomery and Fairfax Counties? In Montgomery County, government employee unions wield great influence and hold collective bargaining power over teachers, police, firefighters, and other government employees.[20] In Montgomery County, the teachers unions in particular are so powerful that "politicians who received the teachers' endorsement in the most recent elections reached into their pockets and wrote checks to the union," instead of the other way around. And elected officials in Montgomery County can't make budgetary policy unless their union masters agree to it. Even the far-left *Washington Post* was forced to admit that Montgomery County's collapse was due to "irresponsible governance, unsustainable commitments and political spinelessness—particularly in the face of politically powerful public employee unions."

In Fairfax County, Virginia, in contrast, there is no collective bargaining for government employees. And that has made all the difference. As the *Post* confirms, "Fairfax, though facing tough choices and further cuts in an economy clouded by recession, has a brighter future."[21]

Union States vs. Free States

Not every place has to end up like Montgomery County, Maryland.

America is still a country that believes in letting states decide their own policies, at least on the issue of government employee unions. Unfortunately, the trends show that our future looks more like Montgomery County than Fairfax County.

In 2011, in eighteen states, more than half of public servants were covered by a union contract.[22] If you're in one of these heavily unionized states which we call "Union" states, you're in serious trouble: Alaska, California, Connecticut, Hawaii, Illinois, Maine, Massachusetts, Michigan, Minnesota, New Hampshire, New Jersey, New York, Oregon, Pennsylvania, Rhode Island, Vermont, Washington, and Wisconsin.

That same year, fewer than 30 percent of government employees were under a union contract in twenty-two states. If you're in one of the lightly unionized states, which we call "Free" states, you still have hope: Alabama, Arizona, Arkansas, Colorado, Georgia, Idaho, Kansas, Kentucky, Louisiana, Mississippi, Missouri, New Mexico, North Carolina, North Dakota, Oklahoma, South Carolina, South Dakota, Tennessee, Texas, Utah, Virginia, and Wyoming.

Ten states fell in the middle, with a public sector union density of between 30 and 50 percent. If you live in these states, which we call "Halfway" states, you can expect your state to do better than the Union states and worse than the Free states. These Halfway states are Delaware, Florida, Indiana, Iowa, Maryland, Montana, Nebraska, Nevada, Ohio, and West Virginia.[23]

In each of the Union states, public servants can be fired for refusing to pay dues or fees to an unwanted union—except Wisconsin, which has banned the practice recently for almost all government workers except public safety workers. And just one of the twenty-two Free states, New Mexico, authorizes such firings.[24]

So, what's the effect?

Quite simply, the Union states are worse off than the Free states, and the Halfway states fall in the middle.[25] On a 2010 list of the nine states "most likely to default" determined by the Business Insider,[26] all are Union or Halfway states. And the average unionization rate for government employees for the most-likely-to-default states was 20 *percent higher* than the average for all other states.[27] And it almost goes without saying, but let's say it anyway: *not one* of the twenty-two Free states was on the "most likely to default" list.[28]

Correlation doesn't always equal causation. But in this case, we think it does. The Union states have experienced slow private sector job growth, while government job growth has been brisk.[29] The Union states have higher amounts of state debt per person than less unionized states. Among states with more than 60 percent of the government workers unionized, the median debt per person was a whopping $6,380. This is *double* the level of debt per person of the middling-unionized states, and *triple* the level in less-unionized states.[30]

Okay, you say, that's still not proof. Doesn't the higher cost of living in the Union states account for the higher debt per person? California is expensive territory. So's New York. So it should cost more for government services there, right?

It certainly does cost more, but let's look at why it's more expensive to live in these states. One of the main drivers for the high cost of living in California or New York seems to be all the superfluous regulations on housing construction, energy generation, and land use, usually passed by pro-union politicians.[31] And the more regulated a state is, the more government employees it needs to ensure regulatory compliance, which drives up cost. And as we know by now, more government employees means more union members and more union dues. Cause or correlation?

Your Taxes Are Too High

For years, tax burdens in the United States have been substantially greater in the Union states than in the Free states. The average tax burden on individuals in New York is 12.1 percent, New Jersey is 12.2 percent, and California is 10.6 percent.[32] The average tax burden in the Free states is only an average of 8.8 percent.

Let's take the supposed leader of the Free states, Texas. While the average American paid 9.8 percent of their income in state and local taxes, the average Texan pays almost 20 percent less than that—7.9 percent. And Texas has also experienced brisk long-term growth, which has significantly increased its tax revenues. From 1990 to 2010, Texas state government revenues nearly tripled, even though Texans have a lower tax burden than other states.[33] But tax burdens are still too high everywhere, driven up largely by growth of government payrolls.

Spreading the Wealth

So you're paying high taxes nearly everywhere thanks to the increased numbers of government workers and their high salary and benefits. Most disturbing, your tax dollars are probably supporting someone who *makes more money than you do.* A recent analysis of government worker compensation confirms that state and local government employees are raking it in compared to their private sector counterparts.[34]

In America's Pacific region, where close to two-thirds of state and local government employees are unionized, government employees' hourly compensation is more than twice as high as private employees' hourly compensation. Even in lightly unionized regions, government employees' compensation is still 25 percent higher than private sector compensation.[35] Similarly, economist Larry Kudlow reports: "Nationwide, state and local government unions have a 45 percent total-compensation advantage over their private-sector counterparts...The politically arrogant unions are bankrupting America."[36]

So can't taxpayers in Union states just organize ourselves into "good government" groups, cut back excesses, and work to lower taxes in these states? It's not going to work, says Steven Malanga of the Manhattan Institute. "The next lesson we are likely to learn," he writes, "is that voter revolts against new taxes are no longer effective because of the might that these public-sector groups now wield."[37] Basically, the unions are so powerful in the heavily unionized states that taxpayers can't even organize effectively against the union machine there. It's like you're sitting in the ejector seat of a fiscal helicopter, and you're buckled in tight.

Featherbedding

"What have unions done to cripple the Union states financially?" you ask.

"How much time do you have?" we might reply. Government unions don't just negotiate for contracts that increase pay and benefits for the workers. They also negotiate for union work rules in employment contracts that allowing "featherbedding," which is requiring that more workers be hired than are really needed for the job, or paying workers for more time than is actually worked or is necessary. These are hidden costs that unions negotiate for in employment contracts for their government employee members.

For example, police in the northern New Jersey town of Englewood

UNION WORK RULES

Many officers in Englewood, New Jersey, and other jurisdictions rake in $25,000 or more annually in "extra-duty" pay at construction and utility-repair sites. Ever wonder why construction sites seem to have so many police standing around them? It is not because the police are lazy; it's because union work rules require it. New Jersey law mandates police presence at construction sites and during utility repair, even on quiet residential streets. That means a 6–11 percent price markup on every construction project, paid for by the taxpayer.[38] And this is great for the police, who can earn up to $65 an hour for these shifts. We love police officers, but they could be doing more good work walking the beat in high-crime areas rather than standing around on neighborhood blocks, watching road workers tar over speed bumps.

can earn roughly $3,000 extra a year in so-called "muster pay" by showing up for work just fifteen minutes prior to their shift and changing into their uniforms. Is it really necessary to pay them for this time? When was the last time you got paid extra for showing up a bit early to work to get ready for your day?

It isn't just the police that have featherbedding rules. An audit of the New Jersey Turnpike Authority found $30 million in featherbedding. Abusive practices included extensive non-merit bonus payments to employees and management, extra bonuses for workers who worked on their birthdays, and a practice of cashing out sick days every year to get around a $15,000 limit on sick-day cash out at retirement.[39] All this excessive pay was for tollbooth workers who have been kept on government payrolls under union contracts—even as automated tollbooths have made many of these jobs obsolete.

Pension Padding

Unions also negotiate terms that allow manipulation of overtime pay and pensions. For the rest of us, working overtime is a normal part of the job. And for small business owners, staying late is part and parcel of keeping their businesses alive. That used to be part of government service, too—government workers made an effort to go the extra mile just to do a good job. Now, however, overtime is a union-negotiated perk of being a government employee.

The government employee union representing New York City's Metropolitan Transit Authority (MTA) appears to be driving the bus over the city's taxpayers. In 2010, a *New York Times* reporter explained how union contracts jacked up taxpayers' cost of compensating an employee to *double* his base salary. For example, one recently retired MTA conductor allegedly made nearly a *quarter million dollars*, more than the authority's chief financial officer. The conductor's base salary was a bit less than $68,000, not extraordinary in a very high-cost city. All the other money came from overtime and money from unused sick days and vacation time he got upon retirement. All in all, nearly eight thousand MTA employees raked in more than $100,000 in salary in 2010.[40]

Thanks to the unions, staying late often means juicing your retirement income. This was the conclusion then New York attorney general

Andrew Cuomo came to in 2010 when he launched a probe into public-sector "union contracts that allow abuses to happen."[41] When a union-supported Democrat like Cuomo (now governor) gets up in arms about government union-boss skullduggery, you know there must be a worm in the Big Apple.

Cuomo gave an example of one police officer who had a $74,000 annual salary. He received another $125,277 in overtime pay. How did he log so much overtime? This officer, like many unionized public employees who monopolize overtime shifts in any given year, was nearing retirement. His taxpayer-funded lifetime pension benefits would be based on the average of his last three working years' income. So he purposefully arranged for extra overtime shifts so that he could bulk up that three-year average prior to stepping down. Such "pension-padding practices" cause a "one-two punch to the taxpayer," charged Cuomo.[42] Actually, they cause a one-two-three punch to the taxpayer. First, we have to pay the officer's inflated salary. Next, we have to pay his inflated overtime. Finally, we have to pay his inflated pension based on his inflated salary and inflated overtime.[43]

In nearly any business, large or small, a supervisor who allowed even one employee to get away with more than doubling his annual base salary by racking up overtime would get canned in short order. But let's remember—it's the government employee unions pulling the strings, electing their own bosses. And under current rules, neither the government nor the government workers would have an easy time firing the unions.

No wonder New York State is in serious trouble, as Herbert London, president emeritus of the Hudson Institute, reminds us: "There is no doubt New York State has extraordinary assets: an educated workforce, potable water, cheap hydro-electric power, magnificent scenery. But these assets have been surpassed by manipulative leadership, profligate spending, and the appeasement of municipal union demands."[44] Despite all its assets, New York State and other heavily unionized states are headed in the wrong direction.

And if New York is bad, the crony union city of Chicago is even worse. In Chicago, a 1991 law allowed union officials who once worked for the city to have their city pensions determined by their higher union salaries. The *Chicago Tribune* reported that this law allows union officials to "land public pensions that far exceeded their pay as city employees—even as they continued to earn lucrative salaries from their unions."[45] But union officials took this abuse one step further in a double-dipping pension scheme. Eight of Chicago's highest ranking union officials reportedly received pension credit *twice* for their union working years—once for determining their city pensions and once for determining their union pensions. "Some of those labor leaders were participating in up to three pension funds at the same time, accruing retirement benefits that reached as high as $500,000 a year."[46] One union official receives a "$158,000 municipal employees pension after being rehired at the Department of Streets and Sanitation for one day in 1994," working on union matters ever since. While officially retired from his city job, the union official continues to make $260,000 a year from his union job, from which he reportedly will receive an additional pension.[47]

These double-dipping pension schemes are considered abusive even by Chicago standards, but in a different pension-padding scandal, two union lobbyists there netted hefty city pensions perfectly legally with only a single day's work.[48] Legislation passed by the pro-union legislature allowed a brief window during which union officials could qualify for a teacher's pension by teaching in the school system for just one day. Two union officials who each substitute-taught school for a single day during the window are now legally entitled to a full teacher's pension—based on their union salaries and years of service to the union. Because their salaries are higher than the average teacher, their teacher's pensions are estimated to be double what a teacher would normally receive. The *Tribune* reported, "Over the course of their lifetimes, both men stand to receive more than a million dollars each from a state pension fund that has less than half of the assets it needs to cover promises made to tens of thousands of public school teachers."[49] Is it any wonder that the heavily unionized states are heading for an abyss?

Income for Life

And there is even more bad news. Government employees are extra burdensome for taxpayers because they retire earlier than other Americans. Early retirement is a union creation—and makes no fiscal sense.

Retiring government employees early places a huge burden on the next generation of taxpayers.

For example, in New York City, "firefighters and police officers may retire after 20 years of service at half pay—which means

Government employees are extra burdensome for taxpayers because they retire earlier than other Americans. Early retirement is a union creation—and makes no fiscal sense.

that, at a time when life expectancy is nearly 80 years, New York City is paying benefits to 10,000 retired cops who are less than 50 years old," notes labor analyst Daniel DiSalvo. That's twenty years of work for thirty years of retirement income.[50]

The unions *love* these early retirement schemes. Why? Because for every retiree, there's a new hire. Which means that both the retiree and the new hire have to pay dues to the union. It's two for the price of one for the government employee unions—and one for the price of two for the taxpayers. Of course, retirees pay less union dues than active members do, but they still do pay some dues and fees to the union. Plus, by substituting a new worker for an old worker, the union gets a longer payout—the new employee has his whole government career ahead of him during which he will pay the union dues. It is a great scheme for the union to guarantee its future income stream.

As virtually everyone recognizes at this point, pensions have destroyed full-fledged industries like the American auto industry. General Motors drove itself into bankruptcy because it had triple the number of retirees and widows as actual workers. GM provides one million people with health-care coverage, but has less than 100,000 people working for it. As Mark Steyn writes, "How do you make that math add up? Not by selling cars: Honda and Nissan were making a pretax operating profit per vehicle of around $1,600; Ford, Chrysler, and GM a loss of $500 to $1,500. That's to say, they lose money on every vehicle they sell."[51]

The U.S. car manufacturers are no longer car companies—they are pension companies. Our government will soon be a pension company itself as a greater and greater percentage of state and local revenue goes to pay for retirees instead of active government workers. And ultimately, being a pension company will even prove unsustainable for our government. The cost of paying for retired government workers with rich union-negotiated pensions ultimately will be too much for the taxpayers to bear.

Extreme Pensions in California

California has the notorious, budget-busting "3% at 50" scheme. At first, this deal allowed only California Highway Patrol officers to retire at 50 and a full pension based on 3 percent of their final year's pay times the number of years worked. For example, an officer hired at 20 years old and retiring after 30 years on the job gets a pension equal to 3 percent times 30 years, or 90 percent of his final year's pay, which is later indexed for inflation. Sweet deal for police officers, right? Then, the California Legislature authorized cities, counties, and school districts to negotiate the same deal for their employees.[52]

This is usually the way this works—once one group of government employees gets a benefit, government employee unions demand the same benefit for other groups of workers, even though being a policeman is more demanding and dangerous than being an office worker. And extending the greatest possible benefits to the greatest number of government employees drives up costs exponentially.

Largely as a result of the "3% at 50" system, California's pension costs increased *by an astonishing 2,000 percent* from 1999 to 2009. You read that statistic right—it's a two followed by *three* zeroes.

There is a basic immorality to this system. It is worth asking yourself how it became your job to pay for somebody else's generous retirement when you're having a hard enough time saving for your own.

The Vault Is Empty

And then the worst problem of all—unfunded pension liabilities. In addition to very high current pension contributions that strap state and local budgets, there is a much worse problem on the horizon. States and municipalities have promised their workers pension and retiree health-care benefits that there is almost no way that the government will be able to pay.

Of course, the lightly union-ized Free states don't necessar-ily have any better policies when it comes to underfunding their future pension and health-care obligations than the highly union-ized Union states. But the Union states will have greater future obligations because of bloated union-negotiated pensions and retiree benefits.

In addition to very high current pension contributions that strap state and local budgets, there is a much worse problem on the horizon. States and municipalities have promised their workers pension and retiree health-care benefits that there is almost no way that the government will be able to pay.

The contributions that governments have made each year to pay for these future pensions are simply not great enough to cover the future costs of these pensions. So, in future years, states will have to make astronomical payments out of their general treasuries to make up for these shortfalls.

Imagine that instead of saving what you need for retirement, you take half that money that you should put in your retirement account and try your hand at the slot machines. Your plan? Either you will win the jackpot, or your only son will make a whole lot of money and sup-port you in your old age. It is such a good plan that you realize you can cut back your contributions to your retirement account further, and spend even more on the slot machines. The only looming problem is that you haven't hit the jackpot yet, and you sense your son is having a hard time getting the lucrative job that you are counting on.

Just like you counting on a jackpot or your son's future earnings to make up for your retirement savings shortfall, the states are betting that a raging bull market will solve their shortfall problem. If the bull market fails to materialize, though, future taxpayers will have to make up the shortfall.

Most government employee pensions across the country are under-funded, meaning that in future years, taxpayers will have to make up the shortfall in order to pay out pensions to all those government workers who are counting on receiving them. Government officials have given in to union demands for greater pensions without anyone figuring out how to possibly pay for them. And anyway, future pension obligations don't impact the current budget too much, so why not? After all, these government officials will be retired anyway by the time the bill comes due. By then, it will be somebody else's problem.

There are two components of states' unfunded liabilities, both heavily affected by union-negotiated contracts. The first is the fixed pension amount that retirees have been promised, which we have discussed. The second is the future cost of retiree health care. When government workers retire early, the state provides full health-care coverage for them until Medicare kicks in (and even after that to some extent). With so many government workers retiring at fifty-five, fifty, or even earlier, these health-care costs are considerable. But nineteen states don't put aside any money at all to pay these health-care costs, they just use a "pay as you go" plan and pay the health-care costs for the current year. But in future years, health-care costs and pensions will crowd out other important items in the state or local budget, like public safety and education. But again, that's tomorrow's problem.

Unfunded state liabilities for health care and pensions amount to over $1.36 trillion, based on states' own actuarial calculations.[53] The only problem is that these gloomy calculations are *too optimistic*—because most states assume that they will earn an 8 percent annual return on their pension fund investments. Who can expect a return on their investments that high, especially without taking on risky investments? Not you and me, and not state pension funds, either. In reality, America's state pensions earned under 4 percent annually from 2000 to 2010, about half the rate the actuaries use for their calculations.[54] The U.S. Senate Finance Committee recently came out with a more realistic estimate of the unfunded state and local government pension obligations, finding that they may exceed $4 trillion.[55]

When the government assumes overly rosy investment conditions—an 8 percent annual return—and bases pension policy on those conditions—sooner or later, the government will come looking for your wallet. It's like buying your child a pony, assuming that your kid will go out and earn the $10,000 it takes a year to pay for food, medical care, and board for the pony. Your kid's going to come up short, and you're going to have to make up the difference. There's no such thing as a free pony—or a free pension.

Unfunded Liabilities in Union vs. Free States

What do unions have to do with all this? Well, heavily unionized states give their government workers amazing pensions. Unionized government workers have pension benefits that are on average 68 percent higher than nonunionized government workers.[56] So, the unfunded liability problem is much more problematic in the heavily unionized states, which have much larger obligations to their government employees in retirement than the Free states do.

In New Jersey, for example, as Governor Chris Christie stated, pensions and benefits are "the major driver of our spending increases at all levels of government—state, county, municipal, and school board." As Christie pointed out, the pension system isn't just unaffordable. It's a disaster area. He cited as an example a forty-nine-year-old retiree who had paid a grand total of $124,000 toward his retirement pension and health care, and was slated to receive $3.8 million in pension and health care—a 3,000 percent return on investment. Even Warren Buffett couldn't earn those returns. In fact, Buffett himself wrote in a letter to his shareholders of his concern over unfunded pension liabilities: "In a world where people are living longer and inflation is certain, those promises will be anything but easy to keep."[57]

Because government workers, like all Americans, are now living longer and retiring earlier, we're paying them forever. In California, a fifty-five-year-old male police officer or firefighter can expect to live until he is eighty-one, according to the California Public Employee Retirement System (CalPERS).[58] Allowing public-safety officers (and many other classes of government workers) to retire at age fifty rather than age sixty increases the cost of their pensions by nearly 50 percent. And even worse, spending on retirees starts to crowd out needed spending—like on *active-duty* firefighters and police.

Take a look at the magnitude of government worker union pension liabilities in the most heavily unionized states. To pay off the existing unfunded pension liability, Californians would have to pay $13,500 per person—which, of course, is never going to happen.[59] The per capita income of Californians amounts to about $29,000 per person. So Californians would have to spend nearly half their income to pay this off.[60]

Perhaps the worst news is that the fiscal instability of our states is already affecting our nation's credit rating. The unfunded pension liabilities at the federal, state, and local levels were one of the key factors when Standard & Poor's downgraded the United States' credit rating in August 2011.

Illinois's unfunded pension liability per person is over $17,230; New Jersey's is $16,838 per person; Connecticut's is $17,622; Rhode Island's is over $20,271 per person.[61]

By contrast, less unionized states have anywhere from one-half to one-third the pension liabilities per person—not good, but certainly better. The average per person unfunded pension liability for the Free states is $10,030.[62] In short—any amount of government employee unionization is bad. The more you have, the worse it is.

Perhaps the worst news is that the fiscal instability of our states is already affecting our nation's credit rating. The unfunded pension liabilities at the federal, state, and local levels were one of the key factors when Standard & Poor's downgraded the United States' credit rating in August 2011.[63] A recent Senate finance report explains the risk to the entire United States of unfunded pension liabilities: "The economy of California is nearly the size of Italy. Just as economic difficulties in Italy have stressed the European Union, fiscal problems in a large state such as California or Illinois could damage the fiscal health of the United States."[64] The problem created at the state and local levels affects all of us, wherever we live in the United States. We can't expect just the states with the worst unfunded pension liabilities to default without the rest of us being adversely affected as well.

The Great Migration

Government employee unions are unintentionally reshaping the demographic map of the United States. Burdensome government and high taxes in the heavily unionized states is causing residents to flee the states run by the Shadowbosses for the states run by the people.

It's happening in New Jersey, which is one of the nation's most unionized states. Overall, it's got the worst state tax burden in the country.[65] New Jersey has the top personal income tax rate, its corporate tax rates rank sixth nationally, and it has the highest property taxes. No wonder the wealthiest people in New Jersey work in waste management and evade taxes, or show their tans on *Jersey Shore*.

As of 2008, New Jersey was losing approximately fifty thousand of its citizens a year to the other states. And while its citizens were fleeing in droves, the state of New Jersey was still *increasing* its number of government employees.[66]

How then did then Democrat governor Jon Corzine respond to the dire news that his friends and neighbors were hightailing it for more hospitable climes? He accentuated the positive. Corzine drew attention to a Princeton University study that concluded that New Jersey was growing *more* prosperous relative to the rest of the nation, and that lower income people were leaving because it was just so darn affluent. (They didn't make the same argument with regard to, say, Mexico.) The study actually concluded, "While New Jersey has, for a long time, experienced net domestic out-migration, this is not a symptom of economic decline in the state... Out-migration from New Jersey is a byproduct of prosperity, not decline."[67] All this is good news for New Jersey according to the study: "We suspect that in a very high density state such as New Jersey, population growth is more costly and difficult to manage than out-migration."[68] So then, the population decline is a blessing in disguise? Corzine himself said, "I welcome the findings from the Princeton Study...which detail what we've surmised all along—that people are not fleeing the state at the accelerated rates that some pundits would have us believe...What this study shows is that migration is a byproduct of prosperity and not tax policy."[69]

While undoubtedly many lower income New Jersey residents are being squeezed out by the state's high housing prices and cost of living, other data seem to indicate that New Jersey is indeed suffering financially from hemorrhaging residents. U.S. Treasury Department data showed that from 2000 to 2008, over 1.4 million taxpayers and their dependents took off from the state. In the first year after leaving New Jersey, these households had an aggregate adjusted gross income (AGI) of more than $73,000 per individual or joint tax filer.[70] In other words, the vast unwashed weren't leaving New Jersey. The taxpayers were. Actual IRS data show that the average annual AGI for the taxpayers who moved *into* New Jersey was $1,800 *lower* than the average for those moving out. Over a nine-year period, then, New Jersey lost more than $13 billion in taxable income.

Kirsten and Keith Cuillard are the kind of family leaving New Jersey. They were paying a property tax bill of an outrageous $11,500. Then, they moved to North Carolina. "I would have loved to have stayed in New Jersey," Kirsten told the Asbury Park Press in 2009. "It's just that the cost of living was killing us." They bought a house twice the size of their New Jersey home, which cost nearly 30 percent less— and they'll pay 72 percent less in property tax annually.[71]

Just like in Jersey, Californians are leaving in droves, leaving for states that have no income tax, like Nevada and Texas. In fact, from July 1, 1990, through July 1, 2009, California lost a net total of roughly three and a half million residents as a consequence of out-migration to other states.[72] California's no longer a magnet state—it's a repelling state. Its residents are now heading for the borders.

For the past two decades, California has been embroiled in a grim competition with New York for status as the number one loser of residents (in absolute terms) to other states.[73] It's not just individuals leaving. Whole businesses are fleeing. California's increasing unattractiveness to middle- and working-class employees is a major factor in "encouraging their employers to move elsewhere."[74]

"In the relocation business, we're seeing higher percentages of employees willing to uproot themselves and their families," writes Joe Vranich of Fox & Hounds, a California business news website. In 2010 alone, Dr. Vranich was able to document 204 separate cases of companies either leaving California completely or building facilities in other states that normally would have been located in California. The vast majority of the cases he documented involve capital leaving California for the much less unionized states, the Free states of Texas, Arizona, Colorado, Utah, Virginia, North Carolina, and Georgia.[75]

And all this interstate migration has economic consequences on both the state losing population and the states gaining population.[76] Between 1999 and 2009, California lost almost $29 billion in taxable income because an estimated 1.2 million more people left the state than moved into the state over that period. North Carolina received an extra $16.6 billion in taxable income from the 505,000 more people moving into the state than leaving the state over that period.[77] Over time, America's demographic profile is shifting dramatically as Americans move to states with less union influence.

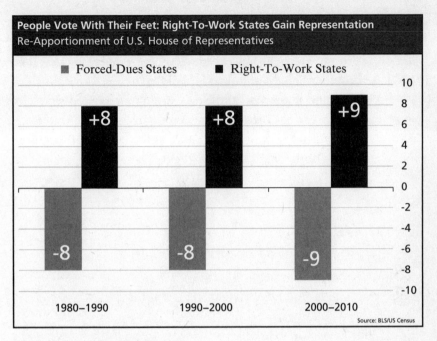

Courtesy: National Right to Work Committee.

This migration from Union states to Free states is having political as well as economic consequences. Right-to-work states gained a total of eight to nine representatives in the U.S. House of Representatives each of the last *three* times that representatives were reapportioned based on census data. Ultimately, as more representatives come from the Free states, government employee unions will have to look harder to find pro–labor union politicians to elect to Congress, because people in these new districts will likely oppose the union agenda.

Conclusion

Think back to the lion at the beginning of this chapter. Is there any doubt that the unions are "bleeding our country dry," as radio host Laura Ingraham puts it?[78] And as Michelle Caruso-Cabrera of CNBC writes, "The economy sat on the verge of abyss in 2008 and the massive decline in state tax revenues exposed just how much unions are costing America. It's time for Big Labor to adjust to the new world."[79]

But the government employee unions are refusing to adjust;

instead, they are doubling down. The unions are tapping out the taxpayers in the heavily unionized states. They're doing it with outrageous salaries, overtime, and pensions for government employees that they negotiate with their bought-and-paid-for politicians. They're killing private enterprise, and taxpayers are fleeing heavily unionized states for the greener and freer pastures of the less unionized states. America is becoming two distinct nations: the Union nation and the Free nation. And where we go from here is anyone's guess.

Chapter 6 Summary Points

- About half of all state and local government revenue is now spent on pay and benefits for state and local employees, and that is increasing.
- Many union contracts allow workers to hike their pay by performing largely useless work—like police officers in Englewood, New Jersey, being paid $3,000 a year extra for showing up to work fifteen minutes early to change into uniform, or being paid $25,000 or more in "extra-duty pay" to stand around construction sites.
- Union contracts also may allow government employees to increase their pensions considerably by working extra overtime in the last years before retirement.
- States with high rates of unionism have heavier state tax burdens and slower employment and income growth than less unionized states.
- The most likely states to default on their obligations have an average unionization rate 20 percent higher than the other states.
- Right-to-work states show far more growth in average real personal income (24.9 percent) than heavily unionized states (7.8 percent) from 2000 to 2010.
- Median state debt per person is nearly three times higher in heavily unionized states than in lightly unionized states.

- Government pensions are destroying state finances. California's per capita unfunded pension liability is over $13,500 per person, Connecticut's is $17,622, and Rhode Island's is $20,271. In contrast, less unionized states have an average unfunded pension liability per person of $10,030, still bad but much better.
- Unions are changing the demographic map of the United States as taxpayers flee highly unionized states and move to less unionized states. One consequence is that right-to-work states as a group gained eight to nine representatives, and heavily unionized states lost the same number of representatives, each of the last three times congressional representatives were reapportioned based on population.

CHAPTER 7

Corruption and Conspiracy

SOVIET dictator Joseph Stalin wasn't one to mince words. When asked once about democratic processes, he patiently explained: "I consider it completely unimportant who in the party will vote, or how; but what is *extraordinarily* important is this—who will count the votes, and how."

Government employee unions and their officials have taken this message to heart. Union officials sometimes cut their own members out of the union election process to stay in power. Worse, they extend those techniques to aggressive voter registration drives, which may include voter fraud, to win races for their political allies.

When it comes to government employee unions, as we've seen, their lifeblood is politics. To survive, the unions must put their allies in power, by any means necessary.

Culture of Intimidation

Remember *On the Waterfront* starring Marlon Brando, the Oscar-winning Hollywood study of union corruption and mob influence on the docks of New Jersey? It was pretty accurate. In 1956, a New York journalist was blinded with acid after writing a column about connections between New York unions and New York mob leader Johnny Dio. After he appeared on television wearing dark glasses, Congress was forced into action. Congress investigated, and found links between Dio, Teamsters head Jimmy Hoffa, and other criminal figures—but more on Hoffa and his associates later.

When Congress began investigating union corruption in the late 1950s, union bosses started talking about cleaning up the unions, too. George Meany, then head of the AFL-CIO, railed against union corruption at the 1957 union convention and said that the union bosses had been aware of corruption when the AFL and CIO merged together in 1955: "We thought we knew a few things about trade union corruption, but we didn't know the half of it, one-tenth of it, or one-hundredth part of it. We didn't know for instance that we had unions where a criminal record was almost a pre-requisite to holding office under the national union."[1] He went on, "We didn't know that there were trade union leaders who charged to the union treasury such items as speed boats, perfume, silk stockings, brassieres, color TV, refrigerators, and everything else under the sun." Previous union cleanup efforts had not worked because "you can't get much cooperation from a national union the officers of which are practicing the same sort of larceny on a national scale as is being practiced by their so-called local representatives on a local scale." Meany vowed to clean up the union movement.

Sadly, neither Meany nor Congress wiped out corruption in the unions. "Corruption remains deeply embedded in the way unions supposedly represent dues paying workers," observes Carl Horowitz of the National Institute for Labor Relations Research. "The sheer magnitude of corruption is staggering, both in the number of cases and the size of the take. American trade unionism is shot through with a culture of intimidation."[2]

> *"The sheer magnitude of corruption is staggering, both in the number of cases and the size of the take. American trade unionism is shot through with a culture of intimidation."*

We have seen this culture of intimidation in how unions deal with their rivals, how they treat corporations that don't cooperate with their unionization drives, and how they handle opponents to their strikes. In this chapter, we will learn about the culture of intimidation within the unions themselves—and we'll investigate how it affects our American democracy.

Become a Union Boss!

Would you like to become a union boss? It's a great job: large salary, terrific benefits, and visits to the White House. All you need to do is win the internal union election for leadership, right? Well, actually you can't. Many union bosses are handpicked by the previous bosses, use the union election process to keep themselves in office, and essentially rule for life like Communist leaders used to.

Gerald McEntee has been at the head of the American Federation of State, County and Municipal Employees (AFSCME) for over thirty years. John Sweeney headed the SEIU and then the AFL-CIO for a total of almost thirty years. But then there is Andy Stern. After less than fifteen years as president of the SEIU, he abruptly resigned in April 2010 for "personal reasons," which seemed highly unusual for a top union boss. A few months later, the press reported that he was under investigation by the FBI and Labor Department, although Stern himself denied it.[3] But don't feel too bad for Andy—despite these rumors, he kept his post on President Obama's National Committee on Fiscal Responsibility and Reform, known as the Deficit Commission, and was just appointed as the Ronald O. Perelman Senior Fellow at Columbia Business School.[4]

Sometimes it seems that only union bosses who are actual mobsters get thrown out of union leadership. Take a union boss of a local union in Chicago, for example. No one had challenged the local union president in a union election in quite some time. Then in 1998, union members allegedly discovered that their local union president was actually a "made member" of the Chicago mob. The U.S. District Court judge who adjudicated the matter pointed out that corruption should have been suspected because of "the alleged absence of contested elections during a twenty-five-year period." The alleged mafia boss/union boss was scheduled to begin talks with the city of Chicago to negotiate a new contract for the members of his union when his mob connections were revealed. As normally happens when mob influence is alleged, the local union was placed under "trusteeship" control of the national union in an attempt to clean up the local union.[5] Of course, this is like declaring martial law in order to restore democracy.

Then there is the most famous union boss of all time, Jimmy Hoffa of the International Brotherhood of Teamsters. When Hoffa was boss, the Teamsters represented mostly transportation workers like truck drivers, distribution plant workers, and loading bay workers. The Teamsters still represent these types of workers, but they also represent over two hundred thousand government employees including police officers, parole officers, public works employees, school bus drivers, and transit workers.

Hoffa served as Teamsters president from 1958 to 1971, serving his final four years as president from his prison cell in a federal penitentiary in Pennsylvania, where he was serving time for jury tampering. Hoffa was a thug through and through—his mob connections during his Teamsters career are extensive and well documented. Hoffa even channeled Teamsters pension funds into mafia projects like the construction of casinos on the Las Vegas strip.

Hoffa and his predecessors at the Teamsters were so corrupt that Congress passed the Landrum-Griffin Act of 1959 to stop them and other union bosses at certain notoriously corrupt unions. As James Mitchell, then secretary of labor, explained in advocating for the bill, "Teamster officials have crushed democracy within the union's ranks. They have rigged elections, hoodwinked and abused their own membership, and lied to them about the conduct of their affairs. They have advanced the cause of union dictatorship and have perverted or ignored their own constitution and bylaws."[6] Eventually, of course, Hoffa disappeared under mysterious circumstances.

While Hoffa disappeared, the Landrum-Griffin Act lived on. Under the Act, union members were supposedly guaranteed the right to vote for union leadership, freedom of speech, approval over dues amount, and access to collective bargaining agreements, although these rights have proved limited in practice.[7] The Act also required labor unions to file financial disclosure with the U.S. Department of Labor to explain their "financial condition and operations."[8]

When Congress passed the Landrum-Griffin Act, it was principally concerned with corruption at the very top of the leader hierarchy with the union bosses themselves. In recent years, however, much of the union corruption that has been detected has been at the level of local unions.[9]

Saga of the Teamsters

The Landrum-Griffin Act didn't stop the mob influence over the unions. In the 1970s and '80s, the federal government brought civil racketeering (RICO) charges against the International Longshoreman's Association and the Teamsters based on the mob connections of their union officials. Rudy Giuliani, then U.S. attorney in New York City, brought the 1988 RICO lawsuit against the Teamsters, alleging that union leaders let the mafia run certain local unions. In the same case, it was alleged that the mafia controlled the election process for union leadership and that the previous two Teamsters presidents had been selected by the mafia. One commentator noted, "The government's civil RICO complaint listed scores of murders and assaults of [Teamster] dissidents in order to document the Mafia's pervasive presence in union affairs."[10]

In settlement of the suit, the Teamsters agreed to court supervision over their union elections in order to purge the corrupt elements from the union. As part of the settlement, Teamsters had to hold rank-and-file secret-ballot elections of national union officials. Teamsters elections were designed to be much more democratic than most unions, which allow rank-and-file members to elect only delegates to a large representative assembly, which in turn elects the national bosses.

So everything would now be better, right?

Wrong.

This oversight of Teamsters elections would eventually make way for the election to Teamsters leadership of...James P. Hoffa Jr., Jimmy Hoffa's son. In 1997, Hoffa ran against incumbent Teamsters leader Ron Carey, who was considered a reformer. Hoffa's opponents claimed that if he won, Hoffa would reinstitute "the union's bad old days, when mafia chieftains used teamster officials as puppets and the union's treasury as their piggy bank."[11]

So Carey's backers created a "complex, interlocking fundraising scandal" to help keep Carey in power. The Teamsters even offered to give hundreds of thousands to the Democratic National Committee if the Committee found a friendly donor to give Carey's campaign a $100,000 check. The Democratic National Committee didn't get involved, but in the end the sides spent $3 million combined on the race for the union presidency. Carey won by 52 percent to Hoffa's 48 percent, only to see his victory overturned by the courts when this illegal funding scheme was uncovered.[12]

A court-appointed union monitor reviewed the election and found that Carey had funneled $700,000 of union funds to get himself reelected, a clear violation of union election rules. According to the union monitor, Carey had engaged in "significant electoral misconduct," and the monitor denied him the chance to run again. The monitor explained, "To allow a candidate to run under the rules which he broadly and intentionally violated would do direct injury to the credibility of those rules. Allowing Mr. Carey to run, under these circumstances, simply would not provide a clean slate and a level playing field in the rerun election."[13] So what was the final result? Hoffa Jr. took over the Teamsters.

According to the *New York Times*, the report also had one other interesting finding: "several other labor leaders, including Richard Trumka, the A.F.L.-C.I.O.'s [then] secretary-treasurer, and Gerald McEntee, president of the American Federation of State, County and Municipal Employees, had improperly raised money for Mr. Carey."[14] These leaders were not removed or charged, however. They remain at the heads of these unions to this day.

Fifteen years later, Hoffa remains in charge of the Teamsters. He vowed in 2011, "We got to keep an eye on the battle that we face: The war on workers...The one thing about working people is we like a good fight...President Obama, this is your army. We are ready to march. Let's take these son of bitches out and give America back to an America where we belong." It almost sounds like he is promising Teamsters thuggery for Obama. And Hoffa backs Obama to the hilt for a good reason. During the 2008 election cycle, Obama was said to have privately promised the Teamsters that he would terminate the strict oversight of the Teamsters by the Labor Department.[15] It hasn't happened yet, but maybe Obama is waiting for a second term.

And what happened to Ron Carey? After being expelled from the union for life, Carey was indicted for perjury, and then found not guilty. He was writing a book on union problems—including double-dipping by union officials—when he died of lung cancer in 2008. At least, unlike Hoffa Sr. his death appears to have been of natural causes.

Stealing Union Elections

"But," you say, "corruption exists within many organizations. What's different about unions?"

Union election fraud has a long history. In 1964, an electrical workers union held an election for president. Soon, those counting the votes realized that the incumbent candidate was going to lose. Stealing votes at the two election sites was going to be difficult because the challenger had witnesses at both sites. So the vote counters allegedly came up with an ingenious solution: they opened three new branches on the spur of the moment, and didn't let anybody in to watch them. Predictably, the incumbent president won. We know about this case because the scheme was uncovered, and when the U.S. Department of Labor examined the election closely, it found that that challenger had won by a large margin.[16]

Numerous cases have been uncovered of internal union elections being rigged. But are the cases we discover most instances of union election fraud, or just the tip of the iceberg?

In the late 1990s, New York City's largest union of city workers was shown to engage in particularly egregious examples of voter fraud as well as corruption and embezzlement. Union officials were charged with falsifying a 1996 vote ratifying the workers' five-year contract with the city. The officials stole the election by printing up thousands of blank ballots, marking each one with a yes vote and then mixing them in with the real ballots for counting.[17] An investigation resulted in the conviction of at least twenty union officials for voter fraud, embezzlement and other crimes, and with the presidents of two local unions being convicted of embezzling over a million dollars for personal use.[18]

From sea to shining sea, cases have been discovered of union elections being rigged and stolen, keeping the membership from having a say in the direction of the union itself. In St. Louis, the police officers union set aside its election results after a secretary's desk was allegedly found stuffed with blank ballots.[19] The election, in which a challenger won over the incumbent by fifteen votes, was invalidated, and a new election held. The scrutiny this time ensured a cleaner process; the challenger won again and was installed as president.[20]

Another case of alleged union election fraud occurred at a local union representing "academic student employees" at a public university in California. In a 2011 election, it looked like a group of reformers were about to win over the incumbent union officials. So the incumbent-friendly election committee reportedly simply cut short the vote count, disenfranchising half the voters. As the reform candidate for president lamented, "It's hard to understand why else the current union administration would abandon the vote count without having counted nearly half the ballots cast in the election."[21] Eventually, voting resumed, and the challenger won—but only after the members brought pressure to bear.

Union members who don't think they have been disenfranchised in union elections probably aren't watching closely enough.[22] Just visit the Department of Labor's website to see new examples of internal union election fraud reported. In November 2011, the Transport Workers Union of America allowed three board members to be elected who weren't even in good standing with the union; the same month, the National Emergency Medical Services Association was sued by the Department for failing to hold elections required by law; in October, the Department went after the International Union of Operating Engineers for rigging the election rules. The list goes on and on.

Some union officials may be willing to rig votes if necessary to get a contract approved or to stay in power. But they generally don't have to—union members don't vote in high numbers, and incumbents who control the union machine are better at getting their friends to vote than their challengers are. Participation rates in union elections are abysmal. For example, in 2007, only 22 percent of active union members voted in New York City's United Federation of Teachers (UFT) election.[23] But with 1,485 candidates running for 900 positions, whose name do you know on the ballot anyway? When Randi Weingarten was head of the UFT before moving up to become head of the American Federation of Teachers, she reportedly considered an election close when she received only 80 percent of the vote.[24]

Taking from the Union Cookie Jar

One of the most common types of union corruption that is actually uncovered is embezzlement. There are seemingly endless cases of union officials taking a little here and a little there, from the union cookie jar. Where extensive embezzlement is discovered, the national or international union usually takes over the local union, which is called trusteeship, in an attempt to rid the local union of corruption. Some have suggested that the parent unions sometimes expose corruption in local unions just to take over these unions and to put their own allies into leadership positions.

Former secretary of labor Elaine Chao reported that during the George W. Bush Administration, her Labor Department brought over 1,000 indictments for union-related fraud and achieved 929 convictions.[25] Many of the fraud cases discovered involve embezzlement, usually a union official taking $100,000 or less from the union cookie jar, often to feed his gambling habit.[26] In other cases, like a recent New York City case, the theft can be a whole lot more.

Melissa King administered employee benefits plans for the NYC "sandhog" union, the Laborers Union of North America. This local union represents subway diggers and others who work on underground construction projects. In 2010, King was charged with embezzling an almost unbelievable $42 million from the union.[27] Although King pleaded guilty, she claimed that the amount she embezzled was exaggerated. But she did manage to use embezzled funds to spend an estimated $5.5 million on keeping fine horses for her daughter, over $7 million on her American Express bill, and other millions on jewelry and a Park Avenue residence before her theft was discovered.[28] You know that there must be a lot of money available for the taking from unions if one person could embezzle tens of millions of dollars without detection for years.

Since 2001, the Labor Department's Office of Labor-Management Standards has prosecuted union bosses for over $100 million in embezzlement of union dues, but these federal cases represent only a fraction of all union embezzlement cases. The real take is probably much, much higher.

Union Hotel California

One reason unions aren't better run is that in general, union members can't leave one union for a better union. Remember the lyrics to the Eagles' hit "Hotel California"? You know—"You can check out any time you like / But you can never leave"? That's the unions. Once unions organize a workplace, the workers are essentially trapped inside the union. "Unionization is not like joining a club or trying out a new Internet service provider, where you can easily quit or stop paying if you aren't satisfied," reports the Center for Union Facts.[29] Union members are free to quit the union, but they can't stop the union from representing them, and if they live in one of the twenty-two forced-dues states, they can't stop paying fees to the union (which are the same or nearly the same as dues). If they try to stop paying the union, they will be fired.

> *Once unions organize a workplace, the workers are essentially trapped inside the union.*

A union can hold elections every year to unionize a workplace if they can show enough interest by the workers; but once the union is certified, the workers can only throw out the union with great difficulty. Actually kicking the union out of a workplace is called "decertification" of the union. If decertification happens at all, it usually occurs to replace one union with another. For example, a rival union may raid the membership of another union, and then try to get the workers to decertify the old union and replace it with the new union. You might be able to trade your union boss for another, but you generally can't throw off the yoke of unionism once it's forced upon you.

Legally speaking, the workers have a contract with their government employer, and the government employer itself has a "union security contract" with the union, which gives the union dues checkoff, the right to use workplace mails, and other valuable rights. But the workers themselves don't contract directly with their union, and this severely limits their rights.

As a result, many union members have little or no control over union dues, despite being given some rights under the Landrum-Griffin Act, as we discussed earlier. The Department of Labor tells workers that "union members have a voice in setting rates of dues, fees, and assessments." Members may have a voice, but they generally don't have a vote. For many unions, dues are approved by vote of the convention of delegates elected by the members, but do not require approval of the members themselves.[30] Additionally, the unions can set special assessments, which is extra dues requirements, used for funding special political activities like voter initiatives—again generally by convention vote. So the union members have little direct control over their dues—and little recourse if they are dissatisfied with their union.

Registering Voters the Easy Way

"Okay," you say, "so what? I'm not a member of a union, and what they do in the privacy of their boardrooms is their business."

There's only one problem: it's your business, too, when they fund political organizations that commit voter fraud to influence elections across the nation.

Government employee unions spend vast amounts of money on voter registration drives around the country. And in at least some cases, this money seems to have been spent on extensive fraudulent registration of voters.

In the U.S. Congress, a report issued by Rep. Darrell Issa's House Oversight Committee explains that the Service Employees International Union (SEIU) worked extremely closely with the now-defunct Association of Community Organizations for Reform Now (ACORN) on voter registration, get-out-the-vote, and other election efforts. The report lists many examples of allegations that ACORN submitted falsified voter registration cards and engaged in various other fraudulent political activities.[31]

The congressional report shows that the SEIU has donated millions of dollars to ACORN across the country to do the political organizing work that it did so well. ACORN and the SEIU even shared office addresses, employees, and leadership in some cases.[32] "SEIU and ACORN are financially and politically codependent," the report stated. "Documents show the clear exchange of funds goes back and forth between the two organizations depending on who needs money at the time."

Although the SEIU is ACORN's most well-known supporter, many of the other government employee unions also gave millions to support ACORN in its heyday—including the teachers unions, which contributed $1.3 million to ACORN since 2005.[33] AFSCME was also an ACORN supporter, although the union's support in one notable case failed to reach ACORN. The head of an AFSCME local union in Milwaukee pleaded guilty to embezzling $180,000 of union funds intended for an ACORN affiliate, which the union official used instead to fund her gambling habit.[34] Our federal government supported ACORN, particularly with respect to its affordable housing subsidiary, Acorn Housing Corporation, to which it gave a reported $16 million from 1997 to 2007.[35]

You will recall that the SEIU is probably the government employee union that is closest to President Obama. He has appointed numerous SEIU officials to White House jobs and commissions, including former SEIU president Andy Stern to the Deficit Commission, former SEIU associate counsel Craig Becker to the National Labor Relations Board, and former SEIU Local 1199 political director Patrick Gaspard as White House political affairs director.

But Obama was close to ACORN also. Obama worked right out of law school at SEIU Local 880 in Chicago, which just happens to have been founded and run by ACORN. He later brought a lawsuit on ACORN's behalf for increased access to the polls in Illinois. And his 2008 Presidential campaign paid an ACORN umbrella organization a reported $832,000 for get-out-the-vote efforts.[36] So, while the congressional report concludes that "ACORN and SEIU work together as one corporate conglomerate,"[37] we should bear in mind President Obama has worked closely with both organizations on voter registration efforts himself.

Another of the report's principal findings was "ACORN, as a corporation, is responsible for thousands of fraudulent voter registrations throughout the United States."[38] As the report strongly pointed out, "Responses from various state election offices show that ACORN's late filings of voter registration cards and the sheer amount of fraudulent cards obstructed election administration efforts in many states." The report emphasizes, "Fraudulent voter registrations are not isolated incidents; they reflect ACORN's criminal motive to compromise the system of free and fair elections promised in the Constitution of the United States."[39]

ACORN in Action

ACORN was a big player in the 2008 elections. After all, it had a big stake in Barack Obama's election. Obama certainly didn't forget his earlier benefactors when he geared up to run for president. In a speech to ACORN leaders in 2007, Obama gushed: "I come out of a grass-roots organizing background...I know personally, the work you do, the importance of it. I've been fighting alongside of ACORN on issues you care about my entire career. Even before I was an elected official, when I ran Project Vote in Illinois, ACORN was smack dab in the middle of it, and we appreciate your work."[40]

ACORN became important to voter turnout in many states in the 2008 elections. One key state was Nevada, a swing state. In 2008, the police received reports that there was fraudulent voter registration emanating from the ACORN Las Vegas offices. So they raided it. Clark County Registrar of Voters Larry Lomax said he saw "rampant fraud in the 2,000 to 3,000 registrations ACORN turns in every week," with nearly half of those forms being "clearly fraudulent."[41]

Soon, local election officials noticed strange names cropping up in voter registration forms submitted by ACORN, including the entire starting lineup of the Dallas Cowboys. It turned out that ACORN had hired prison inmates, some of whom had been convicted of identity theft, to supervise the voter registration effort. Some joked that ACORN was doing election fraud right—they had specialists doing the work.[42] In April 2010, two top ACORN officials pleaded guilty to conspiracy in the Nevada case.[43] It is reported that at least fifty-four ACORN officials have been convicted of voter fraud across the nation.[44]

Senator Harry Reid, the Senate Majority Leader, declined to hold hearings on ACORN voter fraud, stating that he did not want to distract lawmakers from more important priorities, specifically passing health-care reform. The *Las Vegas Review-Journal* was scathing in its denunciation of Reid's action: "Do Sen. Reid and congressional Democrats really believe that if they just ignore the big mess their pet bear has dumped in the middle of the room, it'll somehow stop stinking?"[45]

ACORN went belly-up before the 2010 elections—thanks to independent journalist James O'Keefe. O'Keefe busted ACORN in a sting operation in which he and colleague Hannah Giles posed as a pimp and a prostitute and visited ACORN offices all over the country. At almost every ACORN office they visited, the ACORN officials offered them advice on how to hide their income and set up a house of prostitution using underage Latin American girls. In the ensuing furor,

Congress voted to cut off millions in federal funding to ACORN and related groups, and ACORN declared bankruptcy. Within a year, the former leadership of ACORN had reportedly set up new front groups to carry on its mission under different names.[46]

Conclusion

The labor movement has a much longer and stronger tradition of questionable governance practices than corporations and other organizations. The Association for Union Democracy, a pro-union group aimed at protecting democracy within unions, explains, "In many unions democratic rights are as real and unquestioned as in most of American society. They are written into federal law, enshrined in union tradition, extolled by union leaders. But in large sections of the American labor movement these rights are trampled upon and must be restored."[47]

Securing the right of union members to control the governance of their union and eliminating the culture of corruption in the union movement should be the goals of any true friend of the labor movement, but this does not seem to be the direction in which the movement is headed.

Unions remain some of the most secretive organizations in America. And the Democrats consistently protect union secrecy—keeping important information from union members and from the public. During the Bush Administration, then secretary of labor Elaine Chao increased financial reporting requirements for union officials, requiring them to report how much they received from the union and union trust funds.[48] She also required shop stewards, union officials in the workplace, to file financial disclosures so that rank-and-file members could see how much stewards were getting paid for their union work. But President Obama's Department of Labor halted these types of disclosures.[49] Soon after President Obama entered office, Chao explained, "the new leadership at the Labor Department moved to delay implementing a regulation...that would have shed much-needed light on how union managers compensate themselves with union dues."[50] The regulations were designed to promote greater transparency and stop union fraud and embezzlement—and the Obama Administration stopped those regulations dead. Things are so much simpler and cleaner for the Democrat-Shadowboss complex when the little people and the taxpayers don't know what's up.

But what about you? Yes, you, the nonunion member. The person who doesn't work for the government, or even aspire to work for the government. Should you worry about any of this? Absolutely. The government employee unions have plans for you, too, as we'll see next.

Chapter 7 Summary Points

- Unions are secretive and undemocratic organizations.
- Numerous unions have been found to have irregularities in their internal election processes, usually designed to keep the existing leadership in place against a challenger.
- Very low percentages of union members actually vote in union elections, making it easier for incumbent union bosses to turn out the vote for themselves and stay in power.
- Decertification of an existing union is extremely difficult, so union members don't generally have the chance to get rid of the union if they don't like how their union is handling matters.
- There are numerous documented cases of union officials and others engaging in embezzlement from unions, even involving tens of millions of dollars, which reveals not only corruption but also the huge sums of money that are run through unions.
- Congress has documented extensive financial and organizational ties between the SEIU and the now-discredited ACORN, which was involved in fraudulent registration of voters in the 2008 elections. President Obama, too, has extensive ties to both the SEIU and ACORN.

CHAPTER 8

Shadowboss Battle Plan

So what?" you ask. "What's the difference? I'm not a union member; if the unions get some tax dollars, good for them. If they control some politicians, that's their prerogative. I'm not paying dues."

Well, Virginia, get ready. Soon you, too, may be a member of a government employee union. You're not a government employee? Don't worry—the unions have a fix for that. The unions are reaching far and wide to organize the unorganizable, and to force people under union control who can't be unionized under current law.

We've seen again and again how government employee unions have been able to get political favors and special treatment from government that ordinary Americans aren't able to win for themselves. But now, in their relentless quest to increase their membership and the amount of dues they collect, government employee union officials are doing the unthinkable—they're targeting citizens who aren't even government employees for forced unionization and calling in political favors to get it done.

Government Employee Unions 2.0

The mechanism for this latest union power grab is extremely clever. First, unions work with friendly politicians to relabel groups of independent workers as "government employees." Then, with a few tweaks of the law, they unionize them.[1] With favors from government officials, the unions can unionize *almost anyone.*

Union growth has exploded thanks to this new model for

organizing—which we will call Government Employee Unions 2.0. As we will see in this chapter, government employee unions have already captured home health-care workers and home child-care providers— who are often just parents receiving government benefits to take care of their disabled children or people taking care of their own elderly parents.

But the government employee unions have bigger plans—to unionize other groups that receive payments from the government related to their work. Unions have their sights set on the millions of health-care workers who will receive government funds under Obamacare and the large groups of Americans that receive government benefits.

No doubt unions will try to extend the model as far as possible, since it's filling their bank accounts with additional union dues.

But first, let's look at what the government employee unions have already done to home-care providers in many states across the nation.

Union Boss 2.0

Andy Stern, the SEIU's president until 2010, is widely considered a union visionary. During his tenure, Stern is credited with developing the new strategy for unionizing whole new groups of workers.[2]

Stern always has seemed a little too white collar to be a hard-elbowed union official—he is the son of a lawyer from New Jersey. Unlike labor leaders of old, "Stern was part of a generation of idealistic union leaders who came to organized labor from college, not the factory floor," the New Republic reports.[3] Stern went to the Ivy League University of Pennsylvania, where he started at the Wharton School of Business, but finished up with a degree in education and urban planning.[4] He quickly climbed the ladder of success, finally taking over the presidency of the SEIU in 1996.

Stern and the new generation of labor officials like him, referred to sometimes as the "Ivy League Amigos,"[5] used their business training to turn their unions into competitive and growing enterprises. Stern cleaned house, merged many local affiliates, and centralized power in the SEIU Washington headquarters. The result has been a more modern and efficient union that stays on message. But Stern has many critics within the union movement, who say that Stern operated his union like a dictatorship and didn't pay enough attention to the interests of rank-and-file members.[6]

Stern has a history of innovative union tactics. In one case, after trying aggressive tactics to unionize nursing homes owned by Beverly Enterprises in the 1980s and early 1990s, Stern tried a new strategy— selling the employer on the SEIU's value as a political operative and lobbyist. Stern explained, "With Beverly, we could both appreciate that there were certain things we did better together—lobbying for more staffing and higher wages. That was the basis of our partnership."[7] Once Stern explained to employers the benefit of partnering with the SEIU—that the union could call in its political clout on the *employer's* behalf—employers often chose to let the SEIU unionize their workforces without a fight. The SEIU's move deeper into lobbying was a win-win for unions and employers. Of course, it was a loss for taxpayers, who had to pay for the government largesse lobbied for by the SEIU— but Stern and Co. weren't exactly concerned about those poor souls.

In 2005, Stern pulled the SEIU out of the AFL-CIO federation of labor unions and founded a new rival union federation called Change to Win. The Teamsters, United Food and Commercial Workers, and several other unions joined him. This break with the AFL-CIO was good for the SEIU for two reasons. First, the SEIU saved paying the considerable annual fees to the AFL-CIO by opening its own umbrella group, which it controlled. Second, the SEIU was no longer bound by AFL-CIO anti-raiding policies, which would have prevented it from trying to attract members of other AFL-CIO–affiliated unions to switch to SEIU unions. Once it dropped out of the AFL-CIO, the SEIU was free to raid the memberships of AFL-CIO–affiliated unions, which it has done from time to time.[8]

The SEIU's new labor federation, Change to Win, focused on searching for new groups to unionize. It's also shifted the union business model from collective bargaining toward lobbying. In Stern's own words, "We have to be a voice for something much bigger than our own members." The *New Republic* explained Stern's vision: "The role of a union is not simply to represent its workers, but to fight for *all* workers— including those who are not unionized themselves—by pushing for social and political changes that benefit laborers across the country." In other words, Change to Win was going to be a broad lobbying organization for America's workers.

On its website, Change to Win proclaims, "If corporations can join together to hire an army of lobbyists, working and middle-class Americans must also band together and restore balance by making sure we have a strong voice and a seat at the table again."[9]

Stern had grand plans for Change to Win and the SEIU, but the SEIU would need more dues income to implement them. That meant looking for new groups to unionize. So Stern led the SEIU headfirst into a huge campaign to unionize a new group of self-employed workers, home-care providers. To do this, the SEIU would have to put into place special legal arrangements to transform these independent care providers into state "employees" so they could be unionized. It required a big leap, but nothing that the union couldn't clear.

For Their Own Good

The unions' plan was cleverly planned and conceived: they preyed on two groups of self-employed workers who received funds from the state but were not themselves government workers. First, unions targeted care providers who took care of the elderly, infirm, and disabled in their homes. Then, they selected child-care providers who care for children in their own homes as their second target. The SEIU seems to have planned on completing a unionization drive without the providers having time to organize a resistance movement against them. But they had one obstacle—these providers didn't work for a common employer and weren't government employees, either, so they couldn't be unionized under current law.[10] But the unions always find a way.

The SEIU faced competition from other unions, who were fighting for the same turf for their dues-collection business. The American Federation of State, County and Municipal Employees (AFSCME), and later some other unions, tried to muscle in on the care providers. The SEIU and AFSCME rival local unions even took their fight to the sandbox, badgering child-care providers to sign cards for the union on the playground while they were tending children.[11] Finally, the SEIU and AFSCME reached an agreement to divide up the states between them instead of fighting over the same territory—a union version of the Missouri Compromise, which divided up America's Western territories into free and slave territories to avoid civil war.[12] In this same way, by minimizing noisy union skirmishes and identifying their turf, both unions could pursue their goals quickly and stealthily.

But how could Stern sell this power grab to the public? The SEIU developed a terrific story: the union was taking these poor, downtrodden care providers into their membership for their own good, creating a humanitarian movement to help this "traditionally poorly paid and isolated workforce" find a voice.[13]

Women, minorities, and immigrants are heavily represented in these groups of care providers. Because liberals paternalistically think that these populations need special representatives to defend their interests, liberals buy into forced representation of those populations by unions. Pro–labor union academics, for example, call these drives "social movement organizing," as if somehow a social justice movement and a union movement came together in harmony. Just coincidentally, of course, this new unionizing movement just happens to be the most successful and lucrative drive in decades for the unions.[14] But that couldn't be the SEIU's whole purpose, could it?

Blago Chronicles

Let's look at how the SEIU plan played out in Illinois in 2002.

Democrat governor Rod Blagojevich, who would later go to jail for trying to sell Barack Obama's Senate seat, helped out his good buddies and political supporters at the SEIU. Chicago SEIU Local 880, the local union that Barack Obama worked for, had proclaimed that it stood for tens of thousands of Illinois home-care providers. But in reality, these workers couldn't actually be unionized under the law. Until Governor Blagojevich made it possible.

SEIU Local 880 wasn't just any local union. Local 880 had deep ties with the now-defunct scandalous political organization ACORN. And as the union's association with ACORN might suggest, Local 880 union officials certainly weren't going to let a little thing like federal or state labor law get between them and all those juicy union dues.

And so, the union found a political way in. SEIU Local 880's first drive was for 20,000 "personal assistants" of severely disabled people in Illinois. Personal assistants work for the disabled people themselves, not the state, but are partially or fully paid for with government programs that pay for their care.[15] Many of the personal assistants are actually close relatives of the people for whom they care. But because the providers were at least partially paid using government money, the union claimed that the assistants were "state employees" and could be unionized.

In order to get them unionized, the union needed the governor's help. Fortunately, the SEIU had supported his campaigns for years. In his race for governor, Blagojevich reportedly received $800,000 in cash from SEIU entities, plus huge amounts of soft-dollar support such as union phone bank support, mailings, and get-out-the-vote drives.[16] The SEIU had delivered the election for Blagojevich. Now, it was the new governor's turn to deliver the personal assistants over to the union.

In March 2003, just a few weeks after his inauguration, Governor Blagojevich issued an executive order allowing the SEIU to unionize these personal assistants.[17] The executive order put the legal structure in place to allow these assistants to be unionized—and to allow SEIU Local 880 to be recognized as the collective bargaining agent for all such assistants in Illinois.[18]

Unbelievably, the state of Illinois certified the union as the exclusive representative for personal assistants despite the fact that *personal assistants had never had the opportunity to vote* on whether or not they wanted to be under control of the union. The SEIU bosses didn't even conduct a perfunctory card check to show that the personal assistants were interested in being unionized, let alone win a secret-ballot election. Instead, Governor Blagojevich took the SEIU officials' word that the union was supported by a majority of personal assistants and unionized the whole lot of them.[19] As Andy Stern later admitted, Governor Blagojevich's personal support for this campaign to unionize personal assistants was pivotal to its success.[20] Shortly after certifying the union, the state of Illinois notified personal assistants that they would have to pay dues to the SEIU local affiliate to keep their jobs.[21]

Let's let Rush Limbaugh recap. "It's not complicated, it just sounds unbelievable," Rush told his audience in November 2011. "You are a parent, Joe Schmo, and your wife, Molly Schmo, and you have a mentally disabled adult child, and so you accept Medicaid payment. Guess what? You are now a member of the SEIU. You have no choice, and a portion of what Medicaid gives you to care for your child now gets thrown back to SEIU in the form of union dues. That money then ends up back in the traditional money laundering operation, the Democrat Party."[22]

The personal-care assistants may have lost out from this backroom deal, but the SEIU came out way ahead. The SEIU local union that represents Illinois's twenty thousand personal assistants rakes in at least $3.6 million a year in forced dues from these workers.[23]

Next Steps

While former SEIU president Andy Stern can rightfully take the credit for pioneering the Government Employee Unions 2.0 strategy, others have caught on, including AFSCME and the United Auto Workers (UAW). The UAW is a hybrid private sector/government employee union that now represents fifty thousand government employees, with home-care workers a significant and growing part of its business. And there is some serious dues income available to unions in this market. Fourteen states have authorized unions to represent home-care providers, almost all with forced-dues provisions.[24]

An SEIU local affiliate in Los Angeles County forcibly unionized seventy-four thousand local workers caring for elderly and disabled residents in their homes. To pull off this feat, the SEIU had "poured millions" into the campaigns of politicians for ten years beforehand.[25] The SEIU local union was certified as the workers' representative even though barely more than 20 percent of the eligible voters actually mailed in a ballot in the union election.[26] Many personal assistants reported that they had never even heard of this union until it began confiscating dues from them. That's union democracy in action, folks!

In Michigan, AFSCME and the UAW launched a similar campaign to unionize home-based day-care providers statewide.[27] Just like the personal assistants, Michigan's home day-care providers set their own hours, work at home, and even negotiate their own rates with the families of the children they care for. The providers are partially or fully paid from the families' government subsidies for child care.

Again, political allies gave the unions the creative legal structures needed to convert these care providers into "government employees" who could be unionized. In Michigan, for example, Democrat governor Jennifer Granholm was ready to pull as many strings as necessary for the unions to make this happen. In July 2006, Michigan created a shell corporation that would be the "employer" of the day-care providers so that they could be considered "state employees" for the limited purposes of unionizing them. A mail-in ballot union election was held. Fewer than 15 percent of the day-care providers voted in favor of the union, but the union won the election and was certified as the representative of all 40,500 providers. After the state started deducting union dues out of their reimbursement checks, many providers reported that they had never previously heard about any election or even about a unionization drive.[28]

Michigan home child-care provider Peggy Mashke explained how she learned about the unionization scheme: "I received a notice in the mail from the UAW congratulating me on my new membership. I was kind of shocked." Peggy's husband is a retired Ford worker, but she was confused when she received a letter telling her that she would now be paying dues to the UAW. Peggy explains, "I don't have a problem with the union. Just not in my home."[29] Sadly, the union unionized her home business whether she wanted it to or not.

Another Michigan child-care provider, Carrie Schlaud, explained her decision to fight being forced into a union on *Fox & Friends*. "You know," said Schlaud, "I'm just a mom who decided to care for children in my home. I provide a good service, and I'm able to contribute to the household income, while caring for my own children. And never did I dream I would have to fight the UAW out of my living room."[30]

Both Mashke and Schlaud fought in court to be free of UAW control of their home-based business. Amazingly, they actually won in a settlement with the state of Michigan. But this is a rare victory in an unrelenting wave of similar unionization drives across the nation.[31]

How It Works

But how do states turn independent care providers into government workers so that unions could organize them?

University professors have an interesting way of describing what states have done to convert unorganizable self-employed care providers into union members. A history professor and a feminist studies professor wrote an article together praising the "unusual creativity" that was required to unionize home-based child-care workers. "Workers and their unions," they write, "also had to compel innovations in labor law and labor policy."[32] The unions certainly had to "compel innovations" in the law, but it wasn't the workers doing it—many of those workers didn't find out that they were represented by a union until after the unionizing election had been held.

A law professor explains that labor unions "perfected a new model of organizing, one capable of representing the workers even as the law views many of them as independent contractors" who couldn't be organized under current law.[33] We might say instead: it took quite a lot of finagling and political favors to convert a bunch of people who work for themselves into government employees so they could be unionized.

A law professor explains that labor unions "perfected a new model of organizing, one capable of representing the workers even as the law views many of them as independent contractors" who couldn't be organized under current law. We might say instead: it took quite a lot of finagling and political favors to convert a bunch of people who work for themselves into government employees so they could be unionized.

States generally formed a commission, or a government shell entity, to serve as the "employer of record" for the independent care providers.[34] If these government shell entities remind you of shell companies that enabled the Enron accounting scandal, you are not far off. This is a legal fiction designed to paper over a union power play. It is cooking the government books. But of course, it's never a problem when the government cooks its own books.

Once this commission or shell entity was in place, providers were then considered "employees" of this entity.[35] The workers could be unionized and the unions could avail themselves of both dues checkoff and forced-dues collection if legal in that state. Thereafter, the fictitious employer would also sit on the other side of the table from the union in any negotiations.[36]

Union Legal Genius

How did unions figure out these clever legal fictions to make independent care providers into fake government workers? They used lawyers, of course, and one in particular—Craig Becker, SEIU former counsel and Andy Stern's go-to guy on complex legal machinations.[37] Becker is no schlub—he is a Yale College and Yale Law School educated super-union lawyer and was the legal mastermind behind the SEIU's plan to unionize the world. The radical founder of the discredited and disbanded political organization ACORN, Wade Rathke, praised Becker for "crafting and executing the legal strategies and protections which have allowed the effective organization of informal workers."[38]

Becker's writings indicate he has lots of other creative plans for advancing the interests of labor unions. Becker wants to take away workers' rights to vote for "no union" in elections to unionize their workplace; that way, workers will only be able to choose which union will represent them, not whether they want to be unionized at all.[39] Becker also wants to use National Labor Relations Board rule making and decisions to implement pro-labor "reforms" rather than actually changing our nation's laws through a vote of Congress.[40]

Becker had so many good ideas that President Obama appointed him to his Presidential Transition Team when he got elected. Then, he appointed Becker to the National Labor Relations Board (NLRB), where Becker would have a chance to tilt the playing field in favor of unions himself. President Obama appointed Becker to the NLRB in a controversial "recess appointment" when Congress was out of session. Apparently, Becker was far too radical to be confirmed by Congress. Then, President Obama pulled his nomination of Becker in late 2011 because Congress was unwilling to approve him.[41] Becker still managed to serve on the NLRB for a year and a half under his recess appointment and probably accomplished quite a lot of mischief there during his tenure.[42]

Becker's clever legal structuring led to increases in union membership of "perhaps a half-million such workers" and untold millions in new dues income for the SEIU.[43]

Robbing Peter to Pay the Unions

What does the union do for its dues income? It lobbies the legislature on behalf of the providers for increased payments and other improvements for the care providers. But in many cases, the union scheme actually reduces the amount of money available to the elderly, disabled, and poor families that receive assistance under the government programs.

Let's take the example of a mother who serves as a "personal assistant" to her adult disabled son and has been unionized in Illinois. Before the unionization drive, her son received a subsidy from the government that he could use to pay for care or other expenses—say $1,000 a month. Because the son required personal care, his mother forgoes other employment to act as his "personal assistant" and uses his subsidy to defray the cost of his care. His subsidy doesn't cover all the expenses of caring for her son or all of her hours taking care of him, but the $1,000 helps the family stay afloat.

But one day, Mom is told she is now part of a labor union and that her dues will be automatically deducted from the government subsidy. This means that the family's subsidy for care of their disabled son is now reduced by union dues—say $95 per month, the current dues rate for care providers in Washington State.[44] This simply reduces the amount of money the family has to take care of their disabled son by $95 a month and gives it to the union.

Many other "benefits" that unions lobby for help the union more than the care providers they represent. A perfect example is that unions often demand "training opportunities" for providers—but this training is provided by the union.[45] So whether or not providers themselves actually want or benefit from the training, the union receives additional income for conducting training, which increases its bottom line just a little bit more at state expense.

Stealth Unionization

The unions are able to organize care providers in a state by convincing a pro-union governor to issue an executive order or a state legislature to pass a law imposing forced unionism on care providers. But usually an election is held to give the government action a false air of legitimacy. In many cases, a stealth election is held quickly and quietly to certify the union before the providers have time to organize a resistance or to start a media campaign against unionization.

It's in the union's interest to conduct a stealth unionization drive. The union needs to win a majority of the votes cast, not a majority from all the workers eligible to vote in the election. So the union may try to get only providers likely to favor unionization to vote in the election. By notifying as few care providers as possible about the election, the union may be able to get enough yes votes from its supporters to be certified, without encountering resistance from dissenting providers.[46] Of course, the union is required to notify all eligible voters. But in many cases, care providers seem not to have received notice of the vote and to have been surprised when they learned they had been unionized.

Once the union is certified, providers would have to go through the draconian process of decertification to get rid of the union. Each state has its own procedure for decertification, but all of them are extremely difficult to accomplish. In fact, the procedure is so difficult that no group of care providers has ever achieved decertification.[47]

Where It Ends

Who knows?

If the state can recast independent care providers as "government employees," give them all the burdens of unionization but none of the privileges of government employment, then what can't they do? Who are unions going to go after next?

The Government Employee Unions 2.0 model opens up new groups of people to unionization, people who are not actually government work-

Government officials can probably unionize any group of people who are compensated for their work through a government program—as long as the government officials can argue it is in the public interest to unionize them.

ers but who receive funds from the government in relation to their work. Unions will probably expand this model to other groups of workers that receive government funds in connection with their work.

In our age of increasing government intervention in the

economy, almost anyone could potentially be unionized. Union bosses realize this. One union lawyer in a case challenging the unionization of care providers in Michigan admitted in open court that unionizing these care providers was a "slippery slope."[48] He reportedly admitted to the judge that "unionization of any group that accepted state subsidies would be within the state's authority if it had 'added value' to the state or the public's interest."[49] The union lawyer was simply pointing out that it is a slippery slope when states start handing over independent workers to the unions. Government officials can probably unionize any group of people who are compensated for their work through a government program—as long as the government officials can argue it is in the public interest to unionize them. And what Shadowboss-supported politician wouldn't agree that unionizing more Americans is in the public interest?

Hunting Big Game

The unions' next target group may be the over 21 million health-care workers who will be needed to implement Obamacare. New opportunities to unionize health-care workers are probably the key reason the unions supported Obamacare so ardently.[50] Once Obamacare is implemented, most health-care workers in America will receive government funds and will be regulated by the government in connection with their work. Health-care workers currently serving Medicare and Medicaid patients also receive government funds. Because only about 14 percent of our nation's health-care workers are unionized, this represents a huge growth market for the unions.[51] What is to stop the unions trying to unionize them all?

The unions' next target group may be the estimated 21 million health-care workers who will be required to implement Obamacare. New opportunities to unionize health-care workers are probably the key reason the unions supported Obamacare so ardently.

Next, unions may be emboldened enough to expand their organizing efforts to groups receiving government funds that have less of a connection to work or employment. This could include people receiving Social Security or Medicare payments, or even veterans—after all, these groups of people worked once to earn their government benefits.

Labor lawyer William Messenger, who represents some groups of care providers in their legal battles to throw off the union mantle, explains, "The representation imposed upon providers is no different than the government designating the American Association of Retired Persons as the mandatory representative of all senior citizens on Medicare;...or the American Banking Association as the mandatory trade association for all financial institutions receiving Troubled Asset Relief Program funds..."[52] It is possible that associations like the American Association of Retired Persons (AARP), a lobbying organization for people over fifty years old, could actually morph into a union representing the aged. After all, the National Education Association (NEA) started as a teachers association and then turned into a labor union later in the 1950s when government employee unionism was on the rise.

If this seems farfetched to you—that in your golden years, the state could appoint the AARP or a union as your representative to argue for increases to your Social Security benefits or Medicare benefits—think again. We should never suffer a failure of imagination about what government employee unions are capable of doing; they are far more innovative than we give them credit for.

If this seems farfetched to you—that in your golden years, the state could appoint the AARP or a union as your representative to argue for increases to your Social Security benefits or Medicare benefits—think again. We should never suffer a failure of imagination about what government employee unions are capable of doing; they are far more innovative than we give them credit for.

Then there are enormous and growing groups of recipients of public assistance, Medicaid, and electronic benefit transfer (EBT) cards, which we used to call food stamps. Many people receive government aid under programs for parents with dependent children. Surely, these parents work as caregivers to their dependent children, just as parents of disabled people work as caregivers to their children. Similarly, unions might suggest reforming the public assistance programs to require recipients to perform some sort of work in exchange for their benefits. While this may seem like a good idea at first, this change could make it easier to treat welfare recipients as "government employees" and then to unionize them.

And what if we don't stop unions from forcing all the different groups of people who receive public monies under their control? What would come next? The next step could be to unionize people who have other relationships with the government—like people whose work is regulated by the state. Once we are used to Government Employee Unions 2.0, couldn't the Shadowbosses take it one step further and ask the government to treat these people as "government employees" also? Think forced unionization of Realtors, insurance agents, "nail technicians," and anyone else who requires a license to conduct his livelihood. Of course, that's virtually everyone. Any type of self-employed workers who are regulated by the state or federal government—which now regulates almost every type of profession or business—could also be forced under union representation.[53] Based on how the unions conducted the campaigns over care workers, they would probably start with the least educated, most isolated groups, whom they would unionize "for their own good," then expand outward from there. We need to stop them now, before this plan goes any further.

For now, we know that government cash is the worm on the hook. We're the fish. The moment we snap up that juicy worm, we're caught by the gills and thrown in the union net. Really, who knows what the unions will think of next?

Conclusion

Who is going to stop the unions from rolling out their next wave of organizing the unorganizable?

Our current federal government is chock-full of former union officials and pro-unionists who won't stop unions from overreaching in their organizing efforts. Secretary of Health and Human Services Kathleen Sebelius certainly won't step in—she actually issued an executive order to forcibly unionize seven thousand child-care workers while she was governor of Kansas in 2007.[54]

What about the First Amendment to our Constitution and our free speech rights? By forcing groups of people who receive all or part of their compensation from the government into unions, the states are foisting an exclusive lobbyist on these people. Once unionized, these people can petition, or speak, with state government only through a single, exclusive voice—their union. Their independent right to political speech, guaranteed by our Constitution, has been taken away.[55]

The First Amendment guarantees that you have the right to "petition the Government for a redress of grievances"—that is, without the union getting between you and your government.[56] Unions do precisely this when they forcibly unionize Americans, unrestrained by our Constitution.

Governor Rod Blagojevich and his successor, Governor Pat Quinn, in their executive orders unionizing personal assistants, claimed that care providers "cannot effectively voice their concerns...without [union] representation."[57] As the nanny state grows under President Obama, these patronizing viewpoints will become more commonplace, and the left will decide that we all need union masters to help us petition our government. But don't we all have elected representatives? Isn't that what democracy is all about?

Not anymore. We all still have elected representatives, but many of them have been co-opted by the Shadowbosses. The unions are working with union-supported government officials to expand the groups of people whom they can organize. Remember, union power ratchets up, never down. It may take them a few years to get all the right politicians in place, but they will likely get there—step by step, according to their latest Shadowboss battle plan.

What's our plan? In the next chapter, we will see how some Americans are fighting back against growing government employee union power, and winning some important early battles. But will we win the war? For that, we will need your help.

Chapter 8 Summary Points

- Government employee unions are working to recast anyone who receives benefits or compensation from the government and does some work for the funds as a government employee who can be forcibly unionized.
- Parents taking care of their disabled children, people taking care of their elderly parents, and other caregivers who are compensated under government programs have been the first targets for forced unionization.

- Many care providers never even heard about the election putting them under union control until they received notice that they had been unionized and that they owe as much as $95 in union dues per month.
- Ivy League union bosses like Andy Stern and his successors at the SEIU and Change to Win have focused on organizing ever larger groups of American workers who were previously considered unorganizable.
- "Organizing the unorganizable" is a lucrative growth plan for government employee unions. SEIU Local 880, the notorious ACORN-dominated Chicago local that Obama worked for, unionized twenty thousand personal-care assistants, generating at least $3.6 million a year in forced dues.
- With a few tweaks of the law and help from pro-union politicians, Social Security recipients, welfare moms, food stamp recipients, veterans, and even the self-employed could be forcibly unionized.

CHAPTER 9

Insurrection

IN the original *Star Wars* movie, the shadowy forces of the Empire reign over the galaxy with the Emperor, via his henchman Darth Vader and his stormtroopers, controlling every element of citizen life. As the movie opens, the Empire is nearing completion of the Death Star—a battle station capable of destroying entire planets and crushing the Rebel Alliance.

That's when our hero, Luke Skywalker, stumbles upon an old Jedi Knight, Obi-Wan Kenobi. After receiving an urgent message from Princess Leia, Obi-Wan explains to Luke the importance of getting involved in the rebellion against the Empire. But Luke resists. Only when Luke finds his village in ruins, his uncle and aunt killed, does he decide to take up his lightsaber to use the Force to fight back against the Empire.

In 2011, Americans across the nation realized that the government employee union Empire had left their fiscal village in ruins. And they decided to join the rebellion.

The Rebellion Begins

A Luke Skywalker of this new rebellion is Wisconsin governor Scott Walker. Governor Walker's state was in dire trouble. Wisconsin had been the first state to permit collective bargaining over government employees in 1959. After more than fifty years of government employee unionism, government growth was out of control at the state and local level. As an example, government employee compensation had grown nearly *three times* as fast as private sector worker compensation over the previous decade.[1]

In his 2010 campaign, Walker had promised to reverse Wisconsin's disastrous financial situation. He meant to do it by curbing the power of the state's government employee unions.

Knowing what Walker would do to them if he were elected, the government employee unions, especially the NEA-affiliated Wisconsin Education Association Council (WEAC) teachers union, spent heavily to defeat Walker. But Walker beat his union-funded opponent by a 52 to 46 percent margin.

Once he was elected, the government employee unions started to panic. If Walker were able to roll back their collective bargaining powers, their dues-funded Empire could collapse.

So the unions acted. In December 2010, Big Labor demanded that the lame-duck Democrat-controlled state Assembly and Senate approve multi-year state union contracts that would extend union benefits into future years. The Assembly passed the measure, but it fell short by just one vote in the Senate.[2] So the unions would be forced to negotiate with the new governor over the terms of their contracts.

Once in office, Walker started out making moderate requests for government workers to contribute to their pensions and increase their contributions to their health-care plans.[3] The *New York Post* reported, "Walker warned that he expects some compromise from unions—and if they weren't cooperative, he'll look at all options, including changing state unionization laws."[4] The state head of American Federation of State, County and Municipal Employees (AFSCME) took offense at Walker's approach, saying "It's like the plantation owner talking to slaves," and the unions rejected his demands.[5] And so, the fight began.

Preparing for Battle

With no compromise forthcoming from the unions, Walker went to battle to save the finances of his state. His first target was Wisconsin's law permitting collective bargaining over government employees. This law had stripped government workers of their freedom to negotiate with employers on their own behalf for over fifty years. And because Wisconsin was a forced-dues state with dues checkoff, union dues were automatically deducted from government employee paychecks as a condition of their employment.

Walker framed his challenge to union power in moral terms. He explained that collective bargaining laws are just plain immoral. "The unions like to talk about collective bargaining," Walker stated. "Collective bargaining is not a right, collective bargaining is an expensive entitlement and it's time we put the power back in the hands of the people."[6] Walker is correct, of course—as we've seen, collective bargaining puts money and power in the hands of the Shadowbosses, and it takes away a fundamental right from workers: the right to bargain over their own labor. And of course, forced-dues provisions are even worse.

On February 11, 2011, Walker laid his cards on the table. His budget reform package abolished forced dues for teachers and many other public employees, and also prevented unions from bargaining over these employees' pensions, benefits, and work rules. Union bosses could still bargain over government employee wages, but "raises could not exceed the increase in the Consumer Price Index unless approved by a referendum"[7]—which effectively meant not much bargaining over wages, either. And also harmful to union power, Wisconsin was going to get out of the dues checkoff business—so no more collecting dues for the union.

A final reform was that government employee unions would have to be recertified by the workers that they represent every year. So workers would now be able to throw off the mantle of the union if enough of them voted against recertification. This proposal scared the unions to death, because for the first time in generations their stranglehold over Wisconsin government employees was actually at risk.

And this meant war.

Walker retained collective bargaining for police and firefighters. Why? Because, after looking at the long, dirty history of union violence, Walker believed that police and fire union chiefs would have fought him by launching illegal strikes.

Walker retained collective bargaining for police and firefighters. Why? Because, after looking at the long, dirty history of union violence, Walker believed that police and fire union chiefs would have fought him by launching illegal strikes. He didn't want burning houses or looting in the streets.[8]

Instead, he got the next best thing.

Battle of the Death Star

With union dues income under serious threat, the Empire took action. The government employee unions targeted the rebel base: Madison, the capital of Wisconsin.

Threats of violence immediately took center stage. One government union militant, a thirty-seven-year-old correctional officer, was arrested for disorderly conduct after allegedly making a verbal threat to shoot Walker.[9]

A Republican Wisconsin state senator received an e-mail stating: "We will hunt you down. We will slit your throats. We will drink your blood. I will have your decapitated head on a pike in the Madison town square. This is your last warning."[10] Another e-mail sent around the same time to fifteen GOP state senators was nearly as lurid: "Please put your

> *A Republican Wisconsin state senator received an e-mail stating: "We will hunt you down. We will slit your throats. We will drink your blood. I will have your decapitated head on a pike in the Madison town square. This is your last warning." Another e-mail sent around the same time to fifteen GOP state senators was nearly as lurid: "Please put your things in order because you will be killed and your families will also be killed due to your actions in the last eight weeks."*

things in order because you will be killed and your families will also be killed due to your actions in the last eight weeks...I hope you have a good time in hell." The author of the second e-mail, a twenty-six-year-old day-care worker and forced-unionism zealot, was later identified and arrested on two felony bomb-scare counts and two misdemeanor counts.[11] She pleaded guilty and avoided jail time by enrolling in a first-offenders program.[12] Welcome to the world of the government employee unions—even if you threaten someone with death, you're usually off the hook. Violence is not necessarily illegal, as we explained in chapter 2, if you're a member of a union and you were doing it for the cause!

Businesses were faced with boycott—and worse—if they did not support the unions. The CEO of a chain of convenience stores located in Wisconsin and Minnesota received a letter from four union officials. The letter told him to support their actions against Walker, and warned, "In the event that you do not respond to this request by that date, we will assume you stand...against the teachers, nurses, police officers, fire fighters, and other dedicated public employees who serve our communities." The letter was clear: it wasn't enough to stay out of the fight. The unions wanted everyone to explicitly endorse their side or face boycotts. That particular letter was signed by a police union official and two firefighters union chiefs. Their signatures created at least the implication that businesses might not be protected by the police and fire departments if they failed to support the unions.[13]

Teachers union bosses, first in Madison and then in Milwaukee and other cities, called teachers out on illegal strikes and staged angry protests at the state capitol and at legislators' residences. Within a few days, at least fifteen school districts across the state were forced to cancel classes as teachers called in "sick." These rallies were chock full of evocative signs: "Why Do Republicans Hate People?" "Scott Walker = Adolf Hitler," "Midwest Mussolini," and "Walker Terrorizes Families."[14]

David A. Keene, the president of the National Rifle Association and a former chairman of the American Conservative Union, summed up the teacher revolt in Wisconsin where he went to college and law school: "Many of my old radical friends are back now in all their glory. Many of those camped out in the state capitol building and carrying signs declaring their support of 'workers' rights' while comparing their state's newly elected governor to Hosni Mubarak and Adolf Hitler are gray pony-tailed remnants of a culture most of us thought had vanished into the mists of history. But here they are again, defying orders to clear the capitol grounds while swaying to the folk music of Peter, Paul & Mary's Peter Yarrow, who can only otherwise be seen on PBS folk revivals with other nearly forgotten guitar-strumming veterans of the '60s protest movement."[15] While Keene's description of old radicals again in their glory is amusing, the protestors were deadly serious about stopping Walker cold in his tracks.

Supporters Line Up

The pro-Walker rebel forces gained supporters across America. Bill O'Reilly cited a Quinnipiac poll showing that 42 percent of Americans think unionized government employees make too much money, and that 63 percent think these employees should pay more for their benefits and retirement. "The left-wing media in America will not give you the straight story," O'Reilly said.[16] A former advisor to President Bill Clinton, Dick Morris, agreed: "The liberal media has tried to sell the myth that the public is siding with the unions in these battles. This poll shows the opposite. They largely agree with the restrictions the governors are trying to impose."[17] To make it look better for television, however, the unions quickly assembled some "grassroots" supporters, some of which the unions may have paid to protest. "The left wing radicals in Wisconsin from the unions have mobbed the capital with rent-a-mobs," noted radio host Michael Savage.[18]

Leading the pro-Walker supporters in person was the late activist-journalist Andrew Breitbart, who spoke before a massive Tea Party rally in Madison along with Sarah Palin. "The Wisconsin Tea Party supporters made it all worthwhile," Breitbart related. "But there was another group also there to greet us; the shock troops sent by Richard Trumka and President Obama's Organizing for America. This was my second trip to Madison in the last couple of months and the defeats that the union's leadership have suffered in that time have plunged these losers into an even more animalistic state of frenzy. It was a mob, whipped up by the divider-in-chief and his cronies who live off of union dues and taxpayer funded handouts."[19]

And the unions weren't backing down. The day after at least fifteen Wisconsin school districts were shut down by wildcat strikes—strikes called without explicit union authorization—union radicals got a thumbs-up from the White House. President Obama actually invited a reporter and camera crew from a Milwaukee TV station to sit down with him for an interview. Obama suggested that the right-to-work and monopoly bargaining rollback provisions in the package were "an assault on unions." *Washington Post* columnist Charles Krauthammer aptly summed up the rationale behind Obama's sudden involvement: "He's facing re-election next year. And Democrats need unions."[20]

Obama's rhetoric was in line with a shift in the union strategy against Walker. For weeks, government union bosses had publically opposed increased public employee contributions to their pension and health-care plans. But once it became clear to Big Labor that the Assembly and Senate majorities were poised to pass the bill, union spokesmen and their allies changed their tune. Suddenly, union officials were all compromising sweetness and light. They were ready to go along with benefit reforms just so long as they "were allowed to keep all of their collective bargaining rights."[21]

The new tack was savvy public relations. Big Labor wanted Wisconsin citizens and residents of other states to believe that public employees' right to join a union was at stake. That wasn't the case. They would retain the right to join a union voluntarily. What was really at stake was monopoly bargaining and forced dues, the two pillars needed to prop up the government employee unions.

Furthermore, even as the government employee union bosses proclaimed they were finally ready to come to the table, many local government union chiefs were doing everything they could to frustrate any actual compromise. Unions were trying to push through contract extensions that would exempt them from having to pay more toward their benefits even as they claimed they wanted to negotiate. In some areas, unions tried to push through *raises* even as they claimed they were willing to negotiate.

Unions Sink Democracy

Despite these disingenuous public relations tactics, the unions couldn't stop the Senate or Assembly from passing the bill. Or could they? Six days after Walker unveiled his Budget Repair Act, Wisconsin's fourteen Democrat senators fled to Illinois to deny the Republican majority in their chamber the quorum it needed to pass legislation requiring appropriations.

With the Senate stalled, GOP leaders in the Assembly decided to take up the Budget Repair Act there. On February 25, 2011, the Assembly voted on the bill. As the Assembly was poised to cast its final vote on Walker's law, one Democrat representative reportedly shouted "You are f—ing dead" at a Republican colleague. A few minutes later, after the Assembly adopted the bill, the Democrats went wild in the chamber. A Democrat representative threw papers and a cup of water at his opponents across the aisle.[22]

Then after three weeks in hiding, the Democrat Senators returned to the statehouse, and the Senate passed the bill, which Governor Walker signed into law on March 11.

It was time for Plan B. If they couldn't stop the bill by preventing a quorum or intimidating elected Wisconsin officials, the unions had another plan: go to court to prevent the Act from going into effect. Using the courts is always a favorite union tactic— unions know that the courts can be used to overrule the will of the people and accomplish what our democratic process will not. And the plan was initially successful—

> *If they couldn't stop the bill by preventing a quorum or intimidating elected Wisconsin officials, the unions had another plan: go to court to prevent the Act from going into effect. Using the courts is always a favorite union tactic—unions know that the courts can be used to overrule the will of the people and accomplish what our democratic process will not.*

a Wisconsin circuit court judge issued a temporary restraining order preventing the law from going into effect. Wisconsin's Justice Department appealed, and the law's fate would be decided by the Wisconsin Supreme Court.

To get the outcome that they were looking for in the Supreme Court, the unions would need to change the composition of the Court in their favor. So, they tried to unseat conservative-leaning state Supreme Court justice David Prosser in an April 2011 election, and replace him with a labor-friendly judge.[23] Despite throwing $3 million into the race against him, the unions were unable to defeat Prosser at the polls. And in June 2011, the Supreme Court ruled to reinstate Walker's reforms.[24]

Finally, the unions led a recall vote on six GOP state senators in August 2011, needing to recall three senators to give the Senate back to the Democrats. But although the unions poured $30 million into the recall election, only two GOP state senators were recalled by the voters.

The unions lost. And, as George Will points out, the unions demonstrated the "limited utility of money when backing a bankrupt agenda: Only two Republicans were recalled—one was in a heavily Democratic district, the other is a married man playing house with a young girlfriend."[25] And the people of Wisconsin sided with the rebellion.

Wisconsin Takeaway

Not surprisingly, Walker's dramatic action achieved its economic purpose—it put Wisconsin back on a track to fiscal sanity. Even Democrats sort of "got it." Milwaukee mayor Tom Barrett, a bitter foe of the bill, admitted that thanks to the legislation, his city would save "at least $25 million a year—and potentially as much as $36 million in 2012."[26] By the summer of 2011, localities and school districts across the state were reporting that despite the economic recession, they were able to balance their budgets without firings. Layoffs were occurring *only* in jurisdictions that didn't take advantage of the bill's reforms.[27] Not only that, 94 percent of business owners in Wisconsin think the state is on the right track, whereas only 10 percent believed that before the reforms were passed.[28]

School districts in particular are benefiting from Walker's bill. One important aspect of the bill was that school districts no longer had to abide by union-negotiated "single-salary schedules," which lock districts into paying teachers by seniority and degrees earned. Instead, the districts are now allowed to give raises to deserving teachers. Reportedly, teacher morale and collegiality have improved, since nobody is forced into a union.

Predictably, too, the Wisconsin unions took an immediate hit to their bank account. The teachers unions in Wisconsin had to lay off 40 percent of their staff.[29] As George Will reported, when Colorado did something similar in 2001, union membership in the government employee union declined 70 percent. "In 2005, Indiana stopped collecting dues from unionized public employees; in 2011, there are 90 percent fewer dues-paying members," Will noted.[30]

Steve Moore of the *Wall Street Journal* summed up the effect of Walker's reforms: "Last year's $3 billion deficit is now a $300 million surplus—and it was accomplished without the new taxes that unions favored."[31] The *Journal* also reported recently that the Wisconsin state budget office estimates that the typical homeowner's property tax bill would be some "$700 higher without Mr. Walker's collective-bargaining overhaul and budget cuts."[32] Hallelujah!

Some of the reforms in the Budget Repair Act were struck down by a federal court judge in March 2012, precisely because these reforms applied to some government employees but not to public safety workers, which Walker had excluded.[33] While the rest of the law was upheld, union recertification and the elimination of dues checkoff were struck down. The law had provided for annual recertification of the unions based on a majority vote of all eligible voters (not just people actually voting in the election). The court suggested that this recertification provision and the prohibition against the state collecting dues on behalf of unions directly from employees' paychecks, or dues checkoff, would have been upheld if it had applied to all government employee unions equally. For fairness's sake alone, more states need to adopt regular recertification so that workers have a real choice as to whether or not to be represented by a union and aren't just stuck with a union certified long ago. Likewise, more states should get out of the business of collecting dues on behalf of government employee unions, which are private organizations.

The battle raged on in Wisconsin, with the unions attempting to recall Governor Walker. On June 5, 2012, Walker became the first governor in American history to survive a recall election. Walker's victory in this key battle may encourage leaders in other states to curb union power and increase prosperity and workers' freedoms. But the war against the Shadowbosses will be long and hard-fought.

Empire Strikes Back

While the unions let Pandora out of the box in Wisconsin, they kept her locked securely inside in Ohio.

In March 2011, Ohio governor John Kasich rammed through a bill similar to the Wisconsin law. It reduced some of the unions' collective bargaining power over public workers and got rid of binding arbitration in labor disputes. Public workers were banned from striking and teachers' salaries were tied to test scores. The bill passed narrowly in the State Senate, by a vote of 17–16.[34]

But there was a difference. In Wisconsin, the reform law actually went into effect—and the people of Wisconsin saw its benefits. As the *Wall Street Journal* explains about the Wisconsin reforms: "Attempts to modernize government are always controversial, but support usually builds over time as the public comes to appreciate the benefits of structural change."[35] But in Ohio, the law never did go into effect—and so the citizens of Ohio never got to experience the benefits that the law would bring.

What else was different in Ohio? First, Kasich didn't make the moral case for curtailing collective bargaining. He focused instead on budgetary issues, a crucial public relations mistake on his part. Second, Kasich's job-approval rating was already low. Third, Kasich didn't exclude public safety workers from his reforms, like Walker had. The people were afraid of being left unprotected by striking police and firefighters.[36] Finally, the unions spent more than $40 million on the repeal effort, outspending the pro-bill forces 3 to 1.[37]

For all these reasons, the government employee unions quickly gathered enough signatures to start a referendum on the law. And predictably, in November 2011, the bill was recalled by a wide margin, 61–39.

Since the law was repealed, Ohio has continued to sink into an economic morass. Firings are the order of the day. In Marion, Ohio, the budget situation caused the firing of fifteen police officers, delaying response times to emergency 911 calls. Teachers unions are threatening to strike for higher pay, even as the teachers themselves are getting the ax.[38] As *Red State* reported, "Ohio's public workers are enjoying the sort of union victory that's often accompanied by a pink slip."[39]

Return of the Jedi

The battle continues in New Jersey. Chris Christie is the Han Solo of this story, fighting the Imperial forces once again.[40]

In a memorable speech to the New Jersey legislature, Mr. Christie branded "pensions and benefits" as "the major driver of our spending increases at all levels of government—state, county, municipal, and school board." And, like Walker, he made the moral case against the government employee unions: "Is it 'fair,'" he asked, "for all of us and our children to pay for this excess?"

During 2010, Christie convinced his Democrat-controlled legislature to pass a budget for the year that closed the state deficit without raising taxes.[41] Christie admits that he has further to go before New Jersey could be considered in good financial shape. As Christie has pointed out, New Jersey is "never going to have enough money to pay that $50 billion" shortfall that it needs to pay future government employee pensions. The same is true for its $67 billion shortfall for funding retiree health-care costs.[42] To bring New Jersey's government spending in line, Christie ultimately will have to lay off many government employees. This is what happens when government employee unions come into conflict with reality: jobs get lost.

Other rebel forces are beginning to get it, too. North Carolina recently passed a law over Democrat governor Bev Perdue's veto, barring the state from collecting dues automatically from teachers' paychecks on behalf of teachers unions—the dues checkoff provision that unions value so much.[43] Governor Perdue, who took $1.8 million from the unions in her 2008 governor's race and benefited from another $1.7 million in campaign ads paid for by the unions, complained that the vote took place "in the dark of night," because it was passed at 1 a.m.[44] Nonetheless, repealing dues checkoff is likely to substantially curb teachers union membership in the state of North Carolina as in other states where it has been repealed.

Other states, too, are swarming to the anti–government employee union rebel cause. Tennessee, a right-to-work state, ended collective bargaining for teachers. Under the new law, the districts will sit down to discuss working conditions with the teachers unions, a process called "collaborative conferencing." But the school board, not the teachers unions, will ultimately be responsible for decisions about how the district's schools are run.[45]

Meanwhile, in Oklahoma, the legislature repealed a law that had required Oklahoma cities with populations of over thirty-five thousand to impose collective bargaining on certain types of city workers.[46] A number of other states, including Indiana, Idaho, Florida, and even

Massachusetts, passed laws in 2011 that cut into union collective bargaining power over government employees by limiting the issues over which the unions can bargain with the government.

The tide is turning now.

Writing on the Wall

When do you know the government employee unions are in trouble? When Darth Vader begins to turn on the Emperor—when the government officials that the unions helped elect begin to bail on government employee unions, and when even their private sector union brethren begin to disassociate from them.

In Massachusetts, some Democrat politicians have attempted to curtail collective bargaining. In April 2011, the Democrat-led Massachusetts House voted to limit collective bargaining for municipal employees over health care. The bill was specifically aimed at reducing runaway health-care costs for municipal workers by giving city governments the right to set health-care co-pays and deductibles for their workers unilaterally, saving an estimated $100 million in the first year alone.[47] The unions went on the offensive to prevent passage of this bill in the Senate. One union official complained, "These are the same Democrats that all these labor unions elected. The same Democrats who we contributed to in their campaigns."[48] In other words, the Democrat legislators, whom the unions had supported, were not staying bought. Another union official hit this same point, "All votes relating to the matters discussed in this letter may be considered Labor Votes and calculated into Labor Voting Records upon which endorsements and levels of support are determined."[49] In other words, look out, labor-supported Democrats—the unions are keeping careful score of your vote on these matters. Eventually, the unions reached a compromise agreement with the Democrat governor to maintain a large role for the unions in negotiating health-care terms, while still holding out a hope of reducing municipal health-care costs. And the change was passed into law as part of the 2012 budget.[50]

Similar small steps are occurring in Connecticut and New York. In Connecticut, the Democrat governor Dannel Malloy forced through

$1 billion in wage and benefits concessions and cuts from the state employees union. He said, "I am attempting to bring the benefits enjoyed by state employees—wages, healthcare, and pension benefits— more in line with those enjoyed by their counterparts in the private sector and federal workforce."[51] It's a good move and about time.

New York Democrat governor Andrew Cuomo forced state agencies to cut spending by 10 percent, or $1.5 billion, and cut $1 billion from Medicaid and $1.5 billion from education. Cuomo has pushed for pension reform, raising minimum retirement age to sixty-five and cutting benefits for newly employed state workers. Mayor Michael Bloomberg of New York City has also cut $4.6 billion from the budget that would largely impact the unions, including pensions.[52]

Democrat strategist Pat Caddell sees the writing on the wall for the Democrats and unions. Caddell explains that the Democrats are "asking taxpayers, asking ordinary people, to pay for people who make twice as much as they make…"[53] He concluded that "the public unions are going to take the country and the Democratic party down the tubes." How will we know that we are winning? We will see more and more Shadowboss-supported politicians pulling away from the unions' agenda to save their own political hides, as we are starting to see in a small way with politicians like Governors Malloy and Cuomo.

A House Divided

In theory, unions of all kinds are supposed to be united in fraternal solidarity. Indeed, for many years, private sector unions fought to extend collective bargaining over government workers, while public employee unions supported their private sector brethren in their opposition to treaties such as the North American Free Trade Agreement in the 1990s.

Suddenly, it's a different world. In the current tough economic times, construction workers are suffering from unemployment levels double the national rate, according to the Associated General Contractors of America. They are relearning the hard way that without a growing economy, all the labor-friendly laws and regulations in the world won't create new jobs for them. And many private sector workers, including union members, are starting to resent paying for government employee union members' large paychecks and benefits.

Democrat Stephen Sweeney, the president of the New Jersey State Senate and an ironworkers union boss, drew a sharp distinction between private sector unions and government employee unions. He could fix things, he said, "if the unions were willing to work and basically stand up and tell their members the truth like I do in the private sector." But the government employee unions instead "keep telling their members the sun's shining when it's raining. Well, we got a monsoon right now and my job is to do the right things for the people of this state."[54]

Not only are private and government union members starting to pull away from each other on issues, but also there is a growing gap between their rates of unionization. Even in heavily unionized New York, private sector union membership continues to decline whereas government sector union membership continues to rise. A recent article in *Crain's New York Business* noted that in New York State, "Unionization in the private sector last year fell to 13.5% from 13.7% in 2010, while the rate in the public sector rose to 72.2% from 70.5%."[55] In the hard hit construction industry, unionization rates fell from 27.5 percent to 23.7 percent in a single year, from 2010 to 2011. Of course, New York is a forced-dues state, so private sector union members are not leaving the unions voluntarily (because they can't). But new businesses that replace failing businesses are not being unionized as quickly as previously, showing that unions are increasingly falling out of favor with private sector workers.

When the Obama Administration first delayed building the Keystone Pipeline, a massive infrastructure project that would have employed thousands of union members, the decision was met with disbelief by the president of the Laborers International Union: "The administration chose to support environmentalists over jobs. Job-killers win, American workers lose." Privately, union officials whose members would have gotten jobs from the project express bitterness that the government employee unions sided with the environmentalists against them, and that the Obama Administration took the government employee union/environmentalist side. One unnamed official told Politico about his outrage and his disappointment, "People are p——d. The emotions are really, really raw right now. This is a big deal."[56] Another private sector union boss echoed the sense of betrayal felt by some private sector union members: "Unions...have kicked our members in the teeth."[57]

Union bosses divided, and a group of unions openly criticizing the Obama Administration? This *is* something new. But it is not surprising that Obama went with the government employee unions and the environmentalists against the private sector unions. After all, it is the government employee unions that devote their resources to political activities and campaign giving, because their dues income depends on it. Private sector unions have been dwindling in importance for decades and are not as politically important as government employee unions. So we should expect to see a lot more issues on which President Obama and other Democrats come down on the side of the government employee unions against the private sector unions. After all, you get what you pay for.

As all taxpayers, including private sector union members, find themselves unable to support the growing numbers of net tax receivers, particularly government employees, the wedge between private sector and government employee union members will grow deeper.

When the Obama Administration first delayed building the Keystone Pipeline, a massive infrastructure project that would have employed thousands of union members, the decision was met with disbelief by the president of the Laborers International Union: "The administration chose to support environmentalists over jobs. Job-killers win, American workers lose." Privately, union officials whose members would have gotten jobs from the project express bitterness that the government employee unions sided with the environmentalists against them, and that the Obama Administration took the government employee union/ environmentalist side.

As all taxpayers, including private sector union members, find themselves unable to support the growing numbers of net tax receivers, particularly government employees, the wedge between private sector and government employee union members will grow deeper.

Conclusion

Our country is at a turning point. Americans will either follow the Shadowbosses and our nation will decline steadily, or they will embrace the rebellion.

The good news is that more and more Americans seem to be joining the rebellion. In January 2012, the Indiana legislature passed a right-to-work bill. Governor Mitch Daniels signed the bill into law, calling it a "bold stroke." The law makes Indiana the first new right-to-work state in ten years—and in doing so, frees two hundred thousand workers from forced unionism.[58]

The great battle has begun. Will you join? To paraphrase Princess Leia, you—the taxpayers of the United States, the pie makers—are our only hope.

Chapter 9 Summary Points

- Americans are fighting back against government employee unions. One leader of this movement is Governor Scott Walker of Wisconsin, who has significantly curbed government employee union power in his state and recently won a bitter recall election.
- Unions still wield tremendous power, as shown by their defeat of Ohio's union reform bill, which the unions spent over $40 million to recall.
- Governors and state legislatures in New Jersey, North Carolina, Tennessee, Oklahoma, Indiana, Idaho, Florida, Massachusetts, and other states are working to curb the runaway powers of the government employee unions.
- Some Democrat politicians are beginning to turn against their Shadowbosses in small ways in order to improve their state's fiscal future—and save their own political careers.
- There is a growing divide between private sector union members and government employee union members, because their interests are diverging.

- Private sector union members have interests that are more aligned with taxpayers than with their government employee union brethren. Private sector union members and other taxpayers both become frustrated when government employee unions refuse to make small concessions on their retirement and health-care benefits to bring state and local budgets into line.

Conclusion

Consider our version of Aesop's fable of the Three Tradesmen:

It once happened that a large walled city came under attack from raiders. The inhabitants came to a public meeting to decide how best to defend their city from invasion.

At the meeting, the head of the Bricklayer's Union stood up. "Bricks!" he thundered. "They're the best way to defend against invasion. Build walls full of 'em. And it won't cost you too much."

"No, no!" interjected the head of the Carpenter's Guild. "Timber, sharpened to points, makes an excellent defense! And wood is even cheaper and stronger than bricks."

"I beg to differ," the head of the Leatherman's Local cried to the crowd. "Leather will provide the best resistance for our city, far better than sticks or bricks."

LEATHER obviously wouldn't do much to protect the city from attack, but that didn't stop the leather tradesman from making his pitch. This fable has been used for thousands of years to teach children a simple truth: every man is out for his own trade, even when their city's future rests in the balance. And America's future certainly does rest in the balance.

But unlike the walled city in the fable, our celebrated "city on a hill" is threatened from within. America is under attack. Our nation's finances are ruinous. We face out-of-control government spending and deficits. Our states are going bankrupt. And instead of working on defending us against these calamities, our government is making the problem worse by following the advice of tradesmen out for their own trades. Our government keeps buying government union bricks, hand over fist. It purchases and stockpiles government union wood. And our government has signed a long-term contract with government union leather merchants. Yet our government is quickly running out of money and borrows from foreign nations to pay its bills. Meanwhile, our undefended city walls are weak and starting to crumble. When outside forces come to threaten us again, we will no longer have the resources to mount an adequate defense to save our people. And our very American way of life will be threatened.

The biggest issues of our time are tied up with the growth of government employee unions and the resulting growth of government. When people talk about America borrowing more than it can pay back, the growth of government is the cause. When people warn us that America is becoming reliant on foreign lenders like China and oil-rich Arab states, excessive government spending is really to blame. When people worry about our states and municipalities nearing insolvency, government employee unions are again at the root.

The growth of our government may be in the unions' interest, but it endangers us as a nation. Growing government hurts all the taxpayers— the people who make our nation's pie. The losers include private sector union members who are also pie makers and don't share the same interest in growing our government as government employee union members.

Government employee unions and politicians have been working on growing our government for decades. The growth of our government may be in the unions' interest, but it endangers us as a nation. Growing government hurts all the taxpayers—the people who make our nation's pie. The losers include private sector union members who are also pie makers and don't share the same interest in growing our government as government employee union members.

Government employee unions dug us a deep hole, threw us in, and pushed us back down when we tried to climb out. Now, they are handing us a shovel and telling us to dig deeper. Our government can no longer reform, streamline, and improve itself because government employee unions stand in the way. From our schools to our skies, government employee unions hold our nation back from all the greatness that we could achieve and drag our nation closer and closer to the abyss.

End of Common Sense in America

For far too long, Americans have been blind and deaf to the threat of the government employee unions. The level of control that these Shadowbosses now exert over the lives of everyday Americans is increasing and approaching the absurd.

Just ask eighty-six-year-old Pennsylvania volunteer crossing guard Warren Eschenbach. When a nearby school built an area for parents to pick up their children from school near his house, Eschenbach, trying to be a good citizen, volunteered to control traffic.[1] He had retired a few years before from a crossing guard position at another school and wanted to protect the schoolchildren in his own neighborhood.

But then a local union representative for AFSCME heard about this helpful citizen. AFSCME then insisted that Eschenbach be canned—from a *volunteer position*—because he was "undermining the union" and that he be replaced with a $12.65-an-hour unionized, dues-paying crossing guard.[2]

The elementary school principal couldn't believe it: "Here we have a community member who's giving back to the community and offering something to the children to keep them safe and so I just view it as a good thing and I'm not sure why someone would find fault with that but obviously somebody has." Somebody did—a government employee union official. And when the city denied the union's formal grievance, the union threatened to take the case to arbitration.[3]

Of course unions would find fault with Eschenbach—he's showing that there are people who are willing to actually work for free for the good of their community—to volunteer. And we don't mean *volunteer* in the union sense of the word, as in getting a stipend, meal, and T-shirt for "volunteering" at a get-out-the-vote phone bank for a few hours.

The Manhattan Institute's *City Journal* recently broke a story about how parents volunteering in their children's schools to help in the library or answer phones were being challenged by the teachers unions, who claimed that the parents were taking jobs that should have been performed by union workers.[4] In America today, it starts to seem almost logical to ask: why should parents be able to volunteer at their kids' schools, when we can hire dues-paying union members to do the work instead?

Or ask seventeen-year-old Eagle Scout Kevin Anderson, also of Pennsylvania. This hardworking teenager voluntarily cleared a walking trail in his local park, not realizing that the local SEIU affiliate would threaten to file a grievance against him for doing work that could have been done by a dues-paying union member. Only after the story broke nationwide did the SEIU back down.[5]

These crazy stories aren't the exception; they're becoming the rule in America today. And unless we fight back, government employee unions will bankrupt our country, morally and financially, and destroy our nation's future.

Future in the Balance

Our future *does* hang in the balance, and still the government employee unions press for every advantage, ignoring the looming fact that the walls will soon come tumbling down upon us.

The lasting legacy of our government employee unions is the corruption of our political system. Once unions shifted to representing government employees, they became intensely political because their growth depended on the largesse of government. As we have seen, these unions use money and manpower to elect government officials. These government officials pass legislation enshrining pro-union measures and negotiate favorable contracts with the unions that helped elect them. The unions then earn more forced-dues income as a result—which they redeploy to reelect pro-union politicians. It is a perfect cycle of corruption because the only people in a position to end the cycle actually get a piece of the graft and don't want to stop the flow of free money.

We must always keep in mind that government employee unions are private entities; their business is maximizing dues income. Generating more benefits for the workers already in the union is a secondary priority. That means that they won't make deals allowing the government to reward better workers. They won't make deals that benefit their members if it means that the unions make less cash. The union's interests always come first. The workers' interests

Although government jobs seem to be where it's at in America today, we can't all go to work for the government. If we do, our nation will be a lot like the former Soviet Union—everybody will have a job, but nobody will have a potato.

come second. And the taxpayers' interests come a distant last place.

The Shadowbosses need taxpayers for one important thing: our tax dollars pay for our ever-expanding government. The government employee unions create no wealth; they merely feed from the public trough. Although government jobs seem to be where it's at in America today, we can't all go to work for the government. If we do, our nation will be a lot like the former Soviet Union—everybody will have a job, but nobody will have a potato.

Many government employees make more than private sector workers; they get better benefits; they get better retirement packages. While it's great to be a government employee these days, at least in comparison to a private sector worker, government employee union bosses have taken important rights away from government employees, too.

Few workers ever had the opportunity to vote for or against their union. It was just there when they got there, and it will likely be there forever, thanks to laws favoring the establishment of unions. And once workers are represented by a union, the workers lose their rights to sell their own labor and to petition their government employer on their own behalf.

Union bosses trade top jobs among themselves and take the cream off the top. And they do it on the backs of America's workers, who are often denied a real voice in union governance. These same workers have to pay substantial union dues, generally without their consent. "Taxation without representation" was the rallying cry of the American revolutionaries. Today, union members should think about beginning their revolution to reclaim their right to control their own labor, to be free from coercive forced-dues obligations, and to speak with their own voice.

Looming Dangers

Not only do we pay for these unions, we also have to worry about what happens when they strike. We have seen that making strikes illegal for critical public safety workers doesn't mean that strikes don't happen. According to one union boss, it just means that the strikes will be *more* effective because illegal strikes are more alarming to ordinary citizens. And government employee strikes are far more dangerous than private sector strikes—surely if the functions of government are too vital to be transferred to the private sector, they're too important to be handed over to the Shadowbosses. Police unions have gone on strike and allowed crime to go unpoliced; firefighting unions have gone on strike and committed arson in order to make their point. Tacit acceptance of union violence isn't just for old-time private sector union thugs like Jimmy Hoffa—it's for government employee union bosses like James Hoffa Jr. And, unbelievably, the Supreme Court itself has all but declared that kneecapping can be legal if in the pursuit of a legitimate union interest.[6] Apparently, your right to swing your fist *doesn't* end where my nose begins—at least not if you've got your union card in your fist.

The possibility of unions striking led even FDR to denounce the notion of government employee unions. But it didn't stop his ideological heirs from expanding unionism into the government sector. FDR knew that union support was crucial to his election efforts; his political heirs knew that government employee union support could pave a path to permanent majority status for Democrats.

Government employee unions know what a fantastic deal they have, and so they spend vast sums of money to keep pro-union politicians in power. These unions create massive political organizations that work hand in glove with the vast left-wing conspiracy, sometimes called the Shadow Democrat Party.

This process resulted in 2008 in the election of the unions' ally, Barack Obama, a man with deep experience with the SEIU, AFSCME, and the rest of the government employee union movement, but no experience with the challenges of business or actually making the pie. He promptly signed a stimulus bill that handed out millions in grants to his union supporters. He rammed through Obamacare, which renders millions more health-care workers ripe for unionization, all while issuing waivers for union members so they could keep their own insurance plans. He sanctioned unionizing national security workers. He appointed union officials to the National Labor Relations Board and much, much more. And he's not done yet.

The reelection of President Obama would be the greatest victory in American history for the Shadowbosses. If the first term was a disaster for American taxpayers, a second term will push America over the edge.

Our children, who are our nation's future, are literally playing the lottery to determine whether they will receive a decent education. The teachers unions are keeping our school system disastrously bad, because the current system works fine for the unions. The teachers unions won't allow bad teachers to be fired. The teachers unions insist on arbitrary standards for pay, like years at the desk and degrees achieved, and won't allow teachers to be paid for merit and performance. Worst of all, the teachers unions indoctrinate our students with a leftist agenda, creating new unionists in the process.

Greater unionization leads to greater decline. The stats bear this out: the states that have the most heavily unionized government workforce are the states most in debt. These states also have the highest tax burden. Meanwhile, these states are losing the capacity to fix themselves, thanks to union contracts that include arbitration clauses—making political disputes into legal ones, and letting arbitrators rather than legislatures decide whether taxes ought to be raised.

For all these reasons, taxpayers are fleeing the Union states and running to the Free states, reshaping the demographic map of the country. But the unions are powerful in the Free states, too, and we will all pay the price when the Union states go belly-up and the federal government bails them out.

Make no mistake—the government employee unions have bigger plans still. They're already pushing into new areas, achieving forced unionization of people who are paid through government programs but who don't even work for the government, like care providers. By extension, if you receive government funds in connection with your work, you may soon find that a union can be appointed to represent you. And if government employee unions are able to expand their model to Social Security recipients, veterans, welfare recipients, and other people who receive government benefits, these unions will lobby for increases to social spending and entitlement programs. And that will pretty much be the end of America as we know it. We're not there yet, but we're close.

Join the Fight

There is good news, however: America is fighting back. The battle has begun in states across our nation, where good politicians have decided to stop letting union bosses hold the future hostage. But the government employee unions won't go down without a fight. In Ohio, unions were able to roll back a major pro-taxpayer bill. In Wisconsin, unions pushed for the recall of Governor Scott Walker to punish him for reforming collective bargaining of government workers in that state, but lost the recall election. But in Indiana, unions have encountered a big setback and lost their power to forcibly collect dues there. In February 2012, Indiana became our nation's twenty-third right-to-work state, returning to workers in that state their right to decide whether or not to support a union financially.

This is the great battle of our time. It is a battle for the heart and soul of our country. It's not merely a question of fiscal responsibility. It's a question of freedom. Will taxpayers have the freedom to control their political process, or will the Shadowbosses usurp that power? Will workers control their own labor, or will they be forced to give away their rights simply in order to work? How will we fight the next government employee union power grab—when unions try to continue to expand their power over our nation's workers? What will happen when there are not enough hardworking Americans willing to keep making the pie and just too many pie eaters?

This is the great battle of our time. It is a battle for the heart and soul of our country. It's not merely a question of fiscal responsibility. It's a question of freedom. Will taxpayers have the freedom to control their political process, or will the Shadowbosses usurp that power?

Government employee unions are a threat not only to our economy, but to our fundamental American way of life—our respect for workers' freedoms, our right to petition our government, our free and fair elections, and at the very heart of the matter—our democracy.

In 1981, the Professional Air Traffic Controllers Organization proclaimed a strike against the government, hoping for a huge increase in pay and a thirty-two-hour workweek. President Ronald Reagan responded: "Let me make one thing plain. I respect the right of workers in the private sector to strike. Indeed, as president of my own union, I led the first strike ever called by that union. I guess I'm maybe the first one to ever hold this office who is a lifetime member of an AFL-CIO union. But we cannot compare labor-management relations in the private sector with government. Government cannot close down the assembly line. It has to provide without interruption the protective services which are government's reason for being."[7]

President Reagan fired the striking workers—over 11,300 of them. Replacement workers were found, and American air travel went on uninterrupted. The air traffic controllers union was disbanded, only to be formed again a few years later.

But today, we must all remember the words—and the actions—of President Reagan. The Shadowbosses must be toppled.

Now is the time.

Let's get started.

Acknowledgments

My wife, Elizabeth, and I came to this project after years of interest in how labor unions affect our nation and with a sinking feeling that our nation was heading in the wrong direction. But we had no idea when we started where the project would lead and what it would uncover.

A million thanks to our terrific editor, Kate Hartson, who had faith in the idea of publishing a book on government employee unions for a general audience and in us to write it. Thanks, Kate, for expertly guiding us through the publishing process and producing this beautiful book. Thanks to our esteemed publisher, Rolf Zettersten, who saw the wisdom of publishing titles like this one and who supported our vision for this project. Thanks to our wonderful team at Hachette who saw this project through to fruition and taught us a lot about publishing—especially Harry Helm, Andrea Glickson and Shanon Stowe. We also greatly appreciate the help of our agent, Gene Brissie, who helped us find the right publisher for this project and gave us wise counsel at every turn. We really appreciate Nancy Mace for bringing my website, www.MalloryFactor.com, to life. I also want to thank Keith Urbahn of Javelin, and Matthew Swift and Nicholas Logothetis of Legacy Management Group for bringing *Shadowbosses* to a greater audience.

This book could not have been written without the help of a number of people to whom we are greatly indebted. We have been blessed with help from Stanley Greer and Don Loos, who were critical to this project and who work tirelessly to bring right-to-work freedoms to all workers. Thank you both for always being available to answer our questions and tracking down every lead, no matter how late at night we asked you. We are extremely grateful for the legal expertise of Milton Chappell and William Messenger, who were extremely generous with their time for this project. We thank each of you for your life's work in defense of workers' freedoms.

Ben Shapiro was absolutely critical to this project and a pleasure to work with. Ben, thanks for bringing your intelligence and commitment to *Shadowbosses*. We can't wait to see what you will do next with your immense talent.

We also want to sincerely thank Joe Ricketts for inspiring work in this area and for his efforts to bring attention to many of the problems we discuss in this book. Thanks also to Brian Baker for his valuable insights. We thank you both for your continued interest in bringing the important subject of government employee unions to a wider audience and for all you do for our nation.

Thanks to our trusted friend Mark W. Smith, who gave us an honest appraisal of our work and helped us to shape this book. And to Donna Wiesner Keene and David A. Keene, who have been so instrumental in this and many of our other projects, we thank you for your friendship. And thanks to John Fund, who helped us understand how unions steal elections and for his excellent work on voter fraud.

Many knowledgeable experts offered their own insights and research on the subjects covered in our book: Steve Forbes; Pat Pizzella, former assistant secretary of labor for administration and management; John Tamny of Real Clear Markets and Forbes.com; Daniel DiSalvo of the Manhattan Institute; Don Todd; Mike Antonucci of Education Intelligence Agency; Barry Hirsch of Georgia State University; David Macpherson of Trinity University; Vincent Vernuccio of the Competitive Enterprise Institute; Pat Caddell of Fox News; James Sherk of the Heritage Foundation; Terry Moe of Stanford University; and Art Laffer. We are so much richer for your insights and your work, although any errors in this book remain our own.

We also want to thank the many, many people who shared with us their own experiences with government employee unions, but who wished to remain anonymous for reasons that we understand too well.

I want to thank Mia Haugen for her support of my interview series with leading conservatives at TheStreet.com, which gave me many of the ideas that I develop in this book. I am extremely grateful to Bill Shine of Fox News for his guidance on the media and also to Eric Shawn of Fox News for his insights.

I am grateful for my association with The Citadel, South Carolina's military college. It has been one of the greatest honors of my life to serve as the John C. West Professor of International Politics and American Government at The Citadel. Although I am not a graduate, I am a huge believer in the power of a Citadel education to transform the lives of young men and women. I want to thank everyone at The Citadel for their support of all my endeavors, particularly Lt. Gen. John W. Rosa, Brig. Gen. Sam Hines, Brig. Gen. Thomas J. Elzey, Dean Bo Moore, Col. Gardel Feurtado, Col. Jeffrey Perez, DeBose Kapeluck, Brad Collins, Gary Hassen, my other colleagues, and the wonderful alumni.

I want to thank each and every student that I have worked with at The Citadel, the fine young men and women who will be our future leaders. Thanks specifically to all the wonderful students who have journeyed with me through my course on The Conservative Intellectual Tradition in America. I want to acknowledge my honored guest lecturers for the course, many of whom offered their thoughts and suggestions for *Shadowbosses*: Alfred S. Regnery, David A. Norcross, Speaker Newt Gingrich, Michael Barone, Burton Folsom Jr., David A. Keene, Douglas J. Feith, Gen. Edwin Meese, Ken Cribb, Daniel J. Mitchell, Phyllis Schlafly, Secretary Donald Rumsfeld, Senator Rand Paul, Ralph Reed, and Director R. James Woolsey. I also want to thank Christopher Long and Jeffrey Nelson of the Intercollegiate Studies Institute, Alan R. Crippen and Doug Minson of the John Jay Institute, and Susan Burdock and Ellen Schweiger of C-SPAN for their support of my course and for bringing it to America.

I am indebted to James Higgins, with whom I started The Monday Meeting in New York City over ten years ago. And also to Grover Norquist, who gave us the inspiration for the meeting, and O'B Murray and Andrew Boucher, who have helped us run it all these years. And to the participants of The Monday Meeting, thanks for your support and continued interest in conservative politics election cycle after election cycle. Thanks also to Senators Jim DeMint and Lindsey Graham, Representatives Tim Scott and Joe Wilson, Governor Nikki Haley, Lt. Governor Glenn McConnell, Speaker Bobby Harrell, and Representative Chip Limehouse for their leadership on right-to-work issues and legislation against union violence.

Special thanks are required for all the wonderful friends, family, and colleagues who support us in our life. And to our friends who carefully read our manuscript and gave us their comments, we owe you our special gratitude. We particularly appreciate the careful review and help of Tommy McQueeney, Steve Matthews, Mary Ann and Eddie Taylor, Pamela Meisel, Michelle Condon, Dede Waring, Margaret Brockinton, Chris Yegen, Herb Kozlov, Carol Stewart, Rhonda Steinfeld, Julie Groves, Nicole Papst, and the initial read by John Gardner. And for other friends who guided us through the process of writing and launching a book, including Judge Andrew Napolitano, Frank Abagnale, Sally Pipes, Max Boot, Rich Miniter, Frank Miniter, Matt Kibbe, Elizabeth and Jim Pinkerton, Jack Hunter, Jameson Campaigne, Ellen Ratner, Anita and Burt Folsom, Colleen Holmes, Lynn Bradshaw, Doug Stafford and many others.

Finally, we want to thank our five children who graciously allowed us to devote so much time and effort to this project. Thanks to them also for testing out the fables peppered throughout our book. And hopefully, we will someday be able to write the children's book that they have asked us to tackle next, an illustrated tale of the "big bad Shadowbosses who are blowing our fiscal house down," one of their favorite bedtime stories.

Notes

Introduction

1 Briefing by White House Press Secretary Robert Gibbs, January 11, 2010, http://www.whitehouse.gov/the-press-office/briefing-white-house-press-secretary-robert-gibbs-11110, accessed April 2012; "POTUS Meeting With Labor Leaders, Monday, January 11, 2010," internal White House document, https://www.judicialwatch.org/files/documents/2010/HHS_combined-3.pdf, accessed April 2012. Additional labor union bosses who attended this meeting were: Anna Burger, chair of Change to Win (now retired); Joe Hansen, president of United Food and Commercial Workers; Terry O'Sullivan, president of Laborers International Union of North America; Leo Gerard, president of United Steelworkers; Ed Hill, president of International Brotherhood of Electrical Workers; and Larry Cohen, president of Communications Workers of America. Every single union at this meeting represents some government employees (most in addition to private sector workers).

2 Andrew Kreig, "AFL-CIO President Says Courage Missing in Health Care Debate," The National Press Club, January 12, 2010, http://press.org/news-multimedia/news/afl-cio-president-says-courage-missing-health-care-debate, accessed January 2012.

3 Sheryl Gay Stolberg and Steven Greenhouse, "President Signals Flexibility on Health Plan Tax," New York Times, January 12, 2010, http://www.nytimes.com/2010/01/12/health/policy/12health.html, accessed February 2012.

4 Erica Werner, "Labor Leaders Fight White House, Senate Democrats on Plan to Tax Workers' Insurance Plans," Associated Press, January 12, 2010, http://cnsnews.com/news/article/labor-leaders-fight-white-house-senate-democrats-plan-tax-workers-insurance-plans, accessed February 2012.

5 As an extra bonus, the Administration would waive the burdensome new requirements of Obamacare for many unionized workers. In May 2011, it was reported that of all 3.1 million people for whom Obamacare waivers applied, over half were union members. Mark Hemingway, "Over Half of All Obamacare Waivers Given to Union Members," Weekly Standard, May 16, 2011, http://www.weeklystandard.com/blogs/over-half-all-obamacare-waivers-given-union-members_561115.html, accessed November 2011.

6 "Cadillac Plans," editorial, *New York Times*, January 15, 2010, http://www .nytimes.com/2010/01/16/opinion/16sat1.html, accessed February 2012.

7 In 2011, there were 477,000 unionized post office workers and only 219,000 unionized workers in the entire domestic auto industry, according to James Sherk of the Heritage Foundation.

8 Charles Krauthammer, "'Magnificent Turmoil' Threatens Union Privilege," Full Comment, *National Post*, February 25, 2011, http://fullcomment .nationalpost.com/2011/02/25/charles-krauthammer-magnificent-turmoil -threatens-union-power/, accessed January 2012.

9 Larry Margasak, "STOCK Act: Senate Passes Insider Trading Ban Bill," *Huffington Post*, March 21, 2012, http://www.huffingtonpost.com/2012/03/22/ stock-act-senate-insider-trading-ban_n_1373081.html, accessed April 2012.

10 "Where Is the Civility?" transcript, *Sean Hannity Show*, February 25, 2011, http://www.hannity.com/article/where-is-the-civility/12769, accessed March 2012.

11 See Steve Moore, "We've Become a Nation of Takers, Not Makers," *Wall Street Journal*, April 1, 2011, http://online.wsj.com/article/SB1000142405274 8704050204576219073867182108.html, accessed April 2012.

12 John C. Henry, "Fat Cat Union Salaries Exposed!" Fox Nation, *Fox News*, March 3, 2011, http://nation.foxnews.com/politics/2011/03/03/fat-cat-union -salaries-exposed, accessed March 2012.

13 Matthew Kaminski, "'The New Tammany Hall,'" *Wall Street Journal*, November 26, 2011, http://online.wsj.com/article/SB1000142405297020371 6204577016092542307600.html?mod=WSJ_Opinion_LEADTop, accessed November 2011.

14 Michael O'Brien, "DeMint: Collective Bargaining Has No Place in Government," *The Hill*, March 2, 2011, http://thehill.com/blogs/blog-briefing-room/ news/146927-demint-collective-bargaining-has-no-place-in-representative -government, accessed January 2012.

15 Both quotes cited in James Sherk, "Majority of Union Members Now Work for the Government," WebMemo #2773, Heritage Foundation, January 22, 2010, http://www.heritage.org/Research/Labor/wm2773.cfm, accessed January 2012.

16 Arthur Laffer, "The States are Leading a Pro-Growth Rebellion," *Wall Street Journal*, February 11, 2012, http://online.wsj.com/article/SB100014240529702 0371110457720139135473460.html, accessed April 2012.

17 Joel Klein, "The Failure of American Schools," *Atlantic*, May 10, 2011, available at http://www.nationaljournal.com/the-failure-of-american-schools -20110510, accessed April 2012.

18 "Can I Be Required to Be a Union Member or Pay Dues to a Union?" National Right to Work Legal Defense Foundation, http://www.nrtw.org/a/a_1_r.htm, accessed March 2012.

19 Technically, workers covered by collective bargaining agreements in forced-dues states have the option of not joining the union and paying agency fees to the union (instead of joining the union and paying dues). But agency fees are generally set at the same amount as union dues (or slightly less than union

dues), so there is generally not much practical difference between paying *dues* or *fees* to a union.

20 Already, unions like the American Federation of State, County and Municipal Employees (AFSCME) promote "retirement unions," which lobby the government to increase and protect retiree benefits including Social Security and Medicare. See http://www.afscme.org/union/retirees. People join these unions voluntarily, but future organizing efforts may force retirees and other groups into unions under a new organizing model discussed in chapter 8.

21 Bureau of Labor Statistics, Union Member Survey 2011, table 3, http://www .bls.gov/news.release/union2.t03.htm, accessed April 2012.

22 "State Debt Per Capita, Fiscal Year 2010," Tax Foundation, February 16, 2012, http://www.taxfoundation.org/research/show/268.html, accessed March 2012 (latest data is from 2010). Two right-to-work states are among the top twenty states in terms of debt per capita as a percentage of GDP: #14, South Dakota; and #20, Louisiana.

23 "Testimony of Mark A. Mix, President, National Right to Work Committee," House Committee on Oversight and Government Reform, April 14, 2011, p. 3, http://oversight.house.gov/wp-content/uploads/2012/01/4-14-11_Mix _Testimony_full_hearing.pdf.

24 "Back to School Statistics," U.S. Department of Education, National Center for Education Statistics, http://nces.ed.gov/fastfacts/display.asp?id=372.

25 Jason Riley, "Was the $5 Billion Worth It?" *Wall Street Journal*, July 23, 2011, http://online.wsj.com/article/SB10001424053111903554904576461571362279 948.html. "'The overall impact of the intervention, particularly the measure we care most about—whether you go to college—it didn't move the needle much,' he says. 'Maybe 10% more kids, but it wasn't dramatic...We didn't see a path to having a big impact, so we did a mea culpa on that.'"

26 Walter Isaacson, *Steve Jobs* (New York: Simon & Schuster, 2011).

27 Sid Johnston, "Teacher of the Year Fired in Lincoln Park Due to Budget Issues," Newjersey.com, June 13, 2010; Mary Ellen Flannery, "I Thought I'd Stay Forever," NEA *Today*, January 23, 2010. New Jersey is not the only state to fire promising young teachers ahead of all older teachers—almost all states do the same. See, e.g., Erin Richards and Amy Hetzner, "Seniority System Cuts Fresh MPS Teachers amid Budget Crunch," *Milwaukee Wisconsin Journal Sentinel*, June 14, 2010, http://www.jsonline.com/news/education/96349689 .html, accessed April 2012.

28 Bureau of Labor Statistics, Union Member Summary, January 21, 2011; Steven Greenhouse, "Union Membership in U.S. Fell to a 70-Year Low Last Year," *New York Times*, January 21, 2011.

29 Mark Mix, "Public Unions Seek National Monopoly," *Washington Times*, September 3, 2010.

30 Reed Larson, quoted in "Passage of Civil Service Reform Reconfirms Union Clout," *National Right to Work Newsletter*, October 13, 1978, p. 5.

31 Quoted in Neil MacNeil and Amy Wilentz, "I Will Veto Again and Again," *Time*, March 18, 1985.

Chapter 1. Meet the Shadowbosses

1   As we discuss elsewhere in this book, some government employee unions don't have the power to negotiate over wages and benefits. For example, unions cannot generally bargain for increased wages for most federal employees, which are set by Congress according to government pay schedules, and the same is true in some states. These unions, however, do lobby Congress (for federal workers) or the state legislature (for state workers) to increase the compensation of their members, and the unions handle workplace evaluations and grievances and provide other worksite representation.

2   Donna Wiesner Keene, e-mail to the author, January 30, 2012.

3   Byron York, "Michelle Obama: 'Don't Go into Corporate America,'" *National Review Online*, February 29, 2008, http://www.nationalreview.com/corner/159678/michelle-obama-dont-go-corporate-america/byron-york, accessed January 2012.

4   Chris Edwards, "Overpaid Federal Workers," Downsizing the Federal Government website, February 2012, http://www.downsizinggovernment.org/overpaid-federal-workers, accessed March 2012. This report states, "In 2010, federal worker compensation averaged $126,141, or double the private-sector average of $62,757."

5   "Mitt Romney Says 500,000 Federal Workers Earn More Than $100,000 a Year," *Tampa Bay Times Politifact.com*, September 3, 2011, http://www.politifact.com/truth-o-meter/statements/2011/sep/03/mitt-romney/mitt-romney-says-500000-federal-workers-earn-more-/, accessed April 2012; Dennis Cauchon, "Some Federal Workers More Likely to Die Than Lose Jobs," *USA Today*, July 19, 2011, http://www.usatoday.com/news/washington/2011-07-18-fderal-job-security_n.htm, accessed January 2012.

6   James Sherk, "Inflated Federal Pay: How Americans Are Overtaxed to Overpay the Civil Service," Center for Data Analysis Report #10-05, Heritage Foundation, July 7, 2010, http://www.heritage.org/research/reports/2010/07/inflated-federal-pay-how-americans-are-overtaxed-to-overpay-the-civil-service, accessed December 2011. See also Andrew J. Biggs and Jason Richwine, "The Public Worker Gravy Train," *Wall Street Journal*, February 24, 2011.

7   Sherk, "Inflated Federal Pay: How Americans Are Overtaxed to Overpay the Civil Service."

8   For a thorough analysis of studies of government versus private sector compensation, see Daniel DiSalvo, "What's the Evidence on Comparative Compensation?" Public Sector Inc., February 13, 2012, http://www.publicsectorinc.com/forum/2012/02/whats-the-evidence-on-comparative-compensation.html, accessed February 2012. See also Jason Richwine, James Sherk, and Andrew Biggs, "Federal Pay is Out of Line with Private Sector Pay: CBO Supports Heritage, AEI Conclusions," Backgrounder #2653, Heritage Foundation, February 15, 2012, http://www.heritage.org/research/reports/2012/02/federal-pay-is-out-of-line-with-private-sector-pay-cbo-supports-heritage-aei-conclusions, accessed March 2012.

9 Chris Edwards, "Employee Compensation in State and Local Governments," *Cato Institute Tax and Budget Bulletin*, January 2010, http://www.cato.org/pubs/tbb/tbb-59.pdf, accessed January 2012; Chris Edwards, "Public Sector Unions and the Rising Cost of Employee Compensation," *Cato Journal*, Winter 2010, pp. 87–115, http://www.cato.org/pubs/journal/cj30n1/cj30n1.html, accessed February 2012.

   Other reports show the state and local employees don't necessarily make more in salary alone than private sector workers, but when both salary and benefits are considered, they can make as much as 30 percent more than private sector workers. See Biggs and Richwine, "The Public Worker Gravy Train."

10 Tad De Haven, "Federal Employees Continue to Prosper," *Cato @ Liberty* (blog), August 10, 2010, http://www.cato-at-liberty.org/federal-employees-continue-to-prosper/, accessed April 2012.

11 Cauchon, "Some Federal Workers More Likely to Die Than Lose Jobs."

12 See Edwards, "Public Sector Unions and the Rising Cost of Employee Compensation."

13 Edwards, "Employee Compensation in State and Local Governments."

14 DeHaven, "Federal Employees Continue to Prosper."

15 Lachlan Markay, "CFPB 'Invitations Coordinator' May Get More Than $100,000 Per Year," *The Foundry* (blog), Heritage Foundation, January 6, 2012, http://blog.heritage.org/2012/01/06/cfpb-invitations-coordinator-may-get-more-than-100000-per-year/, accessed March 2012; "Job title: Invitations Coordinator," USA Jobs, http://www.usajobs.gov/GetJob/ViewDetails/306225500, accessed March 2012.

16 Edwards, "Employee Compensation in State and Local Governments."

17 Barbara A. Butrica et al., "The Disappearing Defined Benefit Pension and Its Potential Impact on the Retirement Incomes of Baby Boomers," *Social Security Bulletin* 69, no. 3 (2009), http://www.ssa.gov/policy/docs/ssb/v69n3/v69n3p1.html, accessed March 2012.

18 Only one in ten private sector workers receives employer contributions to his pension exceeding 6 percent of his salary. Andrew Biggs and Jason Richwine, "Why Public Pensions Are Too Rich," *Wall Street Journal*, January 4, 2012.

19 Shane Dixon Kavanaugh, "Fire Department Pensions Near $90,000, Data Show," *Crain's New York Business*, October 6, 2011, http://www.crainsnewyork.com/article/20111006/POLITICS/111009924, accessed January 2012.

20 "Calculate Your Public Pension," http://www.calculateyourpublicpension.com/.

21 See Frederic U. Dicker, "Andy Rocks the 'Bloat,'" *New York Post*, March 19, 2010, http://www.nypost.com/p/news/local/andy_rocks_the_bloat_with_budget_1NwYmtYfeNXlApwskbEV7J, accessed March 2012.

22 Edwards, "Employee Compensation in State and Local Governments"; Brad Heath, "States Act to Curb Double Dipping," *USA Today*, December 3, 2009, http://www.usatoday.com/news/nation/2009-12-03-states-double-dipping_N.htm, accessed March 2012.

23 Paul Van Osdol, "Team 4: See How Govt. Employees Waste Time On Web," WTAE.com, February 1, 2008, http://www.wtae.com/r/15197025/detail.html, accessed January 2012.

24 Lily Garcia, "Weighing the Pros and Cons of a Federal Job," *Washington Post*, June 4, 2009; Lily Garcia, "Uncle Sam Is a Boss You Can Rely On," *Washington Post*, June 21, 2009. The union approach to sick days is that they represent extra paid time off. For example, the NY-NJ Port Authority Police Union forced an agreement that management could not check on "sick" employees until after several days.

25 Steven Greenhut, *Plunder!* (Santa Ana, Calif.: Forum Press, 2009), p. 101.

26 Performance awards were changed under the Obama Administration to be limited to 5 percent of salary for senior executives and professionals, and 1 percent of salary for other employees. See "Administration Limits Performance Award Spending," *Federal Computer Week*, June 13, 2011, http://fcw.com/articles/2011/06/13/administration-announces-limits-on-performance-award-spending.aspx, accessed January 2012.

27 Bureau of Labor Statistics, "Union Affiliation of Employed Wage and Salary Workers by Occupation and Industry," table, January 27, 2012, http://www.bls.gov/news.release/union2.t03.htm, accessed January 2012.

28 Barry T. Hirsch and David A. Macpherson, "Union Membership, Coverage, Density and Employment by Occupation, 2010," chart, Unionstats.com, http://www.unionstats.com/Occ_U_2010.htm, accessed January 2012. See also Bureau of Labor Statistics, "Percent Distribution of Workers in Service Occupations by Bargaining Status, 1997," chart, January 27, 2012, http://www.bls.gov/opub/cwc/tables/cm20030623ar01t3.htm (the latest data available are from 1997).

29 Bureau of Labor Statistics, "Union Members—2011," press release, January 27, 2012, http://www.bls.gov/news.release/union2.nr0.htm, accessed January 2012.

30 Bureau of Labor Statistics, "Union Affiliation of Employed Wage and Salary Workers."

31 "Some Postal Jobs Open," Federal Jobs, http://www.jobsfed.com/fjdpaper/Jumps4_11_03/JumpSpec1_4_11.htm, accessed January 2012.

32 Eighty-five percent of career postal workers are unionized. Postal workers are represented by different unions depending on their job function, but their rate of unionization is very high across the board. The American Postal Workers Union represents clerks, maintenance employees, and motor vehicle service employees; the National Postal Mail Handlers Union represents mail handlers and processors; the National Association of Letter Carriers represents letter carriers; and the National Rural Letter Carriers' Association represents rural mail carriers.

33 Douglas A. McIntyre and Charles Stockdale, "America's Ten Largest Employers," 24/7 *Wall Street* (blog), April 24, 2011, http://247wallst.com/2011/04/24/americas-ten-largest-employers/2/, accessed March 2012.

34 "Postal Facts," U.S. Postal Service, http://about.usps.com/future-postal-service/postalfacts-2011.pdf, accessed January 2012.

35 A recent report on privatizing the Postal Service notes, "Although the USPS is structured to operate like a self-supporting business, this model is on borrowed time." Tad DeHaven, "Privatizing the U.S. Postal Service," *Downsizing the Federal Government* (blog), Cato Institute, November 2010, http://www .downsizinggovernment.org/usps, accessed March 2012.

36 U.S. Government Accountability Office, "United States Postal Service: Strategy Needed to Address Aging Delivery Fleet," report no. GAO-11-386, May 17, 2011. The report states, "Over the past 4 years, capital investments declined from $2.7 billion in fiscal year 2007 to $1.4 billion in fiscal year 2010. According to USPS officials, most capital expenditures since fiscal year 2008 have been for investments that are expected to provide cost savings, such as automated mail sorting equipment..." http://www.gao.gov/htext/d11386 .html.

37 Bill McAllister, "Postal Service Seen as Crippled by Animosity," *Washington Post*, October 28, 1994.

38 Tad DeHaven, "USPS Sinking under Union's Weight," *Downsizing the Federal Government* (blog), Cato Institute, October 19, 2010, http://www .downsizinggovernment.org/postal-service-sinking-under-unions-weight.

39 Tad DeHaven, "Postal Union Wants More," *Cato @ Liberty* (blog), September 7, 2010, http://www.cato-at-liberty.org/postal-union-wants-more/, accessed January 2012. And the postal union demands for greater compensation for postal workers seems to have borne fruit. James Sherk of the Heritage Foundation concluded that in addition to earning 15–20 percent more than comparable workers in the private sector, postal workers earn greater benefits than other federal workers in some regards. Sherk, "Inflated Federal Pay: How Americans Are Overtaxed to Overpay the Civil Service," p. 30.

40 Iain Murray, "Air Traffic Control Reform: Good for You, Good for the Planet, Bad for Bureaucrats," *Washington Examiner*, May 15, 2009, http:// washingtonexaminer.com/blogs/examiner-opinion-zone/2009/05/air-traffic -control-reform-good-you-good-planet-bad-bureaucrats, accessed January 2012. While this book was being written, the President signed a bill authorizing conversion of some existing radar-based systems of air traffic control to GPS at some of the nation's busiest airports, but this is just a modest step down the path toward a national GPS-based air traffic control system.

41 And apparently, NATCA has also done a great job for them in negotiation— the contract that union negotiated for the air traffic controllers was so rich that the president of NATCA gloated, the contract "is such thievery we should all pick up our pay checks with a mask and a gun." Quoted in "FAA Responds to NATCA's False Claims about Controller Pay," Aero News Network, aero news.net/ANNTicker.cfm?do=main.textpost&id=c5e2958f-2329-4057-8f2f -a2c94774c78a, January 27, 2006.

42 Murray, "Air Traffic Control Reform."

43 Marcus Baram, "FAA Launches New Plan to Keep Air Traffic Controllers from Sleeping on the Job," *Huffington Post*, July 14, 2011, http://www.huffingtonpost .com/2011/07/14/faa-air-traffic-controller_n_898830.html, accessed January 2012.

44 Steven Greenhouse, "The Labor Movement's Eager Risk-Taker Hits Another Jackpot," *New York Times*, February 27, 1999.

45 Kyle Olson, "Sunlight on SEIU Part I: Marxist Andy Stern's Compensation Would Have Karl Marx Spinning in His Grave," BigGovernment.com, April 12, 2010, http://biggovernment.com/kolson/2010/04/12/sunlight-on-seiu-part-i-marxist-andy-sterns-compensation-would-have-karl-marx-spinning-in-his-grave/, accessed January 2012.

46 All union official salary figures are from the Center for Union Facts, accessible at http://www.unionfacts.org, which summarizes data from union financial disclosure.

47 "Public Employee Pay, Pensions and Collective Bargaining," AFSCME, http://www.afscme.org/issues/workers-rights/resources/document/AFSCME-FactSheet_PublicEmployeePayPensionsBargaining.pdf, accessed November 2011.

48 See James Sherk, "What Do Union Members Want? What Paycheck Protection Laws Show About How Well Unions Reflect Their Members' Priorities," Center For Data Analysis Report #06-08, Heritage Foundation, August 30, 2006, footnote 7, http://www.heritage.org/research/reports/2006/08/what-do-union-members-want-what-paycheck-protection-laws-show-about-how-well-unions-reflect-their-members-priorities, accessed January 2012.

49 Mark Brenner, "Bloated Salaries Limit Organizing, Leave Members Cynical," Labor Notes, January 25, 2007, http://labornotes.org/node/513, accessed November 2011.

50 Technically, the union is not operating either a closed shop or a union shop over government workers, but this is really a distinction without much of a difference. A *closed shop* is when the employer agrees to hire only union workers and was made illegal under the Taft-Hartley Act in 1947. Similarly, a *union shop*, which is a workplace requiring employees to join the union when they are hired, is considered to violate the U.S. Constitution. But in reality, government employee unions in non-right-to-work states are usually basically union shops. The slight difference is that the workers are not required to join the union—just to pay agency fees more or less equivalent to union dues for representation. And they can be fired for refusing to pay them.

51 The federal government and thirty-four states expressly allow unions to create monopoly bargaining arrangements over some or all of their government workers and require the government employer to negotiate with the union in good faith. Nine additional states allow the government employer to certify a union to represent government workers, but do not require the government employer to bargain with the union.

52 Forced-dues collection is expressly prohibited only in the twenty-three right-to-work states, but for various reasons it is also not practiced in several of the remaining states.

53 Bureau of Labor Statistics, "Union Members—2011." From official figures, we know that half of all union members, public and private, come from these six states. It follows that at least half of all union dues comes from these states. In fact, since salaries are higher in these states than in the other forty-four states

and dues are based on income, probably much more than 50 percent of dues income is collected from these states.

54 For example, bathroom breaks are covered on page 24 of the Collective Bargaining Agreement Between Stockton Unified School District and Stockton Teachers Association, 2002–2005, on file with the authors.

55 When union members vote to ratify their employment contract, they will also generally confirm their union's representation of them at the same time. Once a group of workers is unionized, they almost never organize themselves to decertify their union. When a union is decertified, it is usually because a well-funded and well-organized rival union comes in and poaches workers, causing a union turf battle. Sometimes, the upstart union will be able to replace the existing union through decertification.

56 James Sherk, "Who Pays for 'Official Time' and Why Americans Should Be Concerned," WebMemo #3447, Heritage Foundation, January 12, 2012, http://www.heritage.org/research/reports/2012/01/official-time-of-federal -employees, accessed January 2012.

57 Ibid. Figures for 2010 can be found in the U.S. Office of Personnel Management's "Official Time Usage in the Federal Government Fiscal Year 2010 Survey Responses," http://www.opm.gov/LaborManagementRelations/Official Time/OfficialTime2010.asp, accessed March 2012.

58 We are not aware of any comprehensive accounting for "official" time at the state and local level, although individual cities and states have made calculations. For example, the city of Phoenix has estimated that the city pays for 73,000 hours of "release time" for city workers annually, at an estimated cost of $3.7 million each year. Mark Flatten, "Phoenix Sued over Paying for Union Leaders' Release Time," Watchdog,org, December 7, 2011, http:// watchdog.org/12289/phoenix-sued-over-paying-for-union-leaders%E2%80%99 -%E2%80%98release-time%E2%80%99/. To estimate the total amount of official time at the combined federal, state, and local levels, we used data for union representation from the Bureau of Labor Statistics for 2010, and we assumed that the rate of official time per union member is the same at the state and local levels as it is at the federal level (for which we have official time data for 2010). See Bureau of Labor Statistics, "Union Affiliation of Employed Wage and Salary Workers," http://www.bls.gov/opub/ted/2011/ted_20110125 _data.htm.

59 Vincent Vernuccio and Trey Kovacs, "Official Time: Government Workers Perform Union Duties on the Taxpayers' Dime," *Labor Watch* (blog), Capital Research Center, November 1, 2011, https://www.capitalresearch.org/ 2011/11/official-time-government-workers-perform-union-duties-on-the -taxpayers%E2%80%99-dime/, accessed March 2012.

60 Sylvester Petro, "Sovereignty and Compulsory Public-Sector Bargaining," *Wake Forest Law Review* 10 (1974): pp. 79–81.

61 Ibid., p. 47.

62 It's already happening around the country. In Englewood, New Jersey, an arbitrator ruled in January 2012 that the borough would have to give raises to police officers—even though in order to do so, the borough would need to raise taxes.

Amanda Baskind, "Englewood Cliffs Appealing Arbitration Decision to Raise Police Salaries," NorthJersey.com, January 5, 2012, http://www.northjersey.com/news/136718013_Borough_appealing_arbitration_decision_to_raise_police_salaries__.html, accessed January 2012. In Roscoe, Illinois, arbitrators have consistently favored unions. "Arbitrators are binding the village to long-term debt, and their attitude is that we can just raise property taxes to pay for it," lamented village president Dave Krienke. "Well, guess what: A lot of families can't afford any more taxes." Between 2006 and 2010, arbitrators in Illinois ruled on 433 issues between unions and the state municipalities; they found for the municipalities 217 times and the unions 216 times. But from January to October 2011, arbitrators ruled on 83 contract issues—and ruled for the unions 73 percent of the time, and 80 percent of the time on wage disputes. Greg Stanley, "State Interest Arbitration Favoring Unions in 2011," *Rockford Register Star*, October 22, 2011, http://www.rrstar.com/news/x888174344/In-Sundays-paper-State-interest-arbitration-favoring-unions-in-2011, accessed January 2012.

63 Charles W. Baird, "How Bad Can It Get?" *The Freeman* 59, no. 1 (January/February 2009), http://www.thefreemanonline.org/columns/pursuit-of-happiness/how-bad-can-it-get/, accessed January 2012.

64 To avoid arbitration altogether, government officials can sign so-called consent decrees with unions—essentially a settlement agreement. These decrees are used frequently by liberal groups like the American Civil Liberties Union to lock in funding for, say, a certain number of beds in homeless shelters in a city, into the future. But government employee unions can also use consent decrees to preserve spending on government employees that they represent. For example, a teachers union or related pro-education group can sue a district to require a certain teacher-student ratio, say 1 to 12, to prevent "school overcrowding." Once the city signs a consent decree over the matter, future mayors will be bound by the decree and can be brought to court if they don't hire enough teachers to keep the agreed upon teacher-student ratio. In this way, teachers unions protect against future reform-minded mayors coming in and changing hiring practices that could adversely impact the union. These decrees are great for the union, but terrible for voters and the taxpayers. Because consent decrees are such an effective way to keep government spending high into the future, we can expect unions to make more and more use of them in the future.

65 PATCO president Robert Poli told this to *Businessweek* at the time of the PATCO strike in 1981. It was quoted in Richard Reeves, *President Reagan: The Triumph of Imagination* (New York: Simon and Schuster, 2005), p. 63.

66 The Employee Rights Act, which was introduced in Congress in 2011 by Orrin Hatch in the Senate and Tim Scott in the House of Representatives, would give union members the right to vote before their union calls a strike. James Sherk, "Employee Rights Act Empowers Workers," Backgrounder #2667, Heritage Foundation, March 19, 2012, http://www.heritage.org/research/reports/2012/03/the-employee-rights-act-empowers-workers

#_ftnref19, accessed April 2012; see also the Employee Rights Act website, http://employeerightsact.com/.

67 Petro, p.80.

68 "Domestic Policy: Labor & Workplace," Issues 2012, Heritage Foundation, http://www.candidatebriefing.com/labor-workplace/, accessed January 2012.

69 Jason Miller, "TSA Workers Granted Collective Bargaining Rights," Federal NewsRadio.com, February 4, 2011, http://www.federalnewsradio.com/?nid= 697&sid=2259846, accessed January 2012. Collective bargaining over agencies related to national security is generally prohibited under Section 16 of President Kennedy's Executive Order No. 10,988, which provides: "The order (except section 14 [giving rights to employees prescribed by the Civil Service Commission]) shall not apply to the Federal Bureau of Investigation, the Central Intelligence Agency, or any other agency, or to any office, bureau or entity within an agency, primarily performing intelligence, investigative, or security functions if the head of the agency determines that the provisions of this order cannot be applied in a manner consistent with national security requirements and considerations." This order can be found at https://www.flra.gov/ webfm_send/563.

70 States were granted permission to pass right-to-work laws by the Taft-Hartley Act of 1947, which added this protection to the National Labor Relations Act, Section 14(b). Note that state right-to-work laws generally only protect *private sector* workers in those states from being forced to pay dues or fees to a union. In practice, though, most government workers are also protected against being forced to pay dues to a union in right-to-work states. The right-to-work laws of Arizona, Florida, Idaho, Iowa, Kansas, Nevada, North Dakota, Oklahoma, Texas, Utah, and Virginia explicitly cover state and local government employees in addition to private sector workers. The right-to-work laws of Arkansas, Louisiana, Nebraska, and South Dakota have been interpreted by state courts to also cover government employees. The right-to-work laws of Georgia, Indiana, and North Carolina explicitly exclude government employees from their coverage. Both Georgia and North Carolina ban public sector monopoly bargaining, so there is no forced-dues issue in those states. But in Indiana, the nation's newest right-to-work state, state troopers, public college employees, and non-teacher public school employees can be forced to pay union dues and fees. The right-to-work laws of Alabama, South Carolina, Tennessee, and Wyoming have been construed by courts or the attorney general not to cover public employees. But of these states, only Tennessee has any type of monopoly bargaining laws for some public employees, and so some limited forced-dues issues may arise there. The right-to-work law of Mississippi is silent on whether it covers government employees, and no court has ruled on it.

  The right-to-work states are mostly found in the South and West, and are: Alabama, Arizona, Arkansas, Florida, Georgia, Idaho, Iowa, Kansas, Louisiana, Mississippi, Nebraska, North Carolina, North Dakota, Oklahoma, South Carolina, South Dakota, Tennessee, Texas, Utah, Virginia, and Wyoming. In addition, the U.S. territory of Guam and federal workers have right-to-work protections. Some states have right-to-work protections granted under their state constitutions instead of their laws.

Chapter 2. The Union Fist

1 U.S. v. Larson, et al., May 2007 Grand Jury Superseding Indictment, http://www.nrtw.org/files/nrtw/IUOE17INDICTMENT.pdf; see also U.S. v. Larson, 07-CR-304S, NYLJ 1202511598699, at *1 (WDNY, Decided August 10, 2011); Carl Horowitz, "Buffalo Local Members Arrested for Conducting Reign of Terror," National Legal and Policy Center, April 21, 2008, http://nlpc.org/stories/2008/04/21/buffalo-local-members-arrested-conducting-reign-terror, accessed March 2012.

2 U.S. v. Larson, et al., May 2007 Grand Jury Superseding Indictment; Alan Farnham, "How Nasty Can Union Violence Get and Still Be Legal?," *ABC News*, September 22, 2011, http://abcnews.go.com/Business/nasty-union-violence-legal/story?id=14572790#.Txyfg6VPssY, accessed January 2012; NRTW Committee Staff, "Hobbs Act Loophole Legitimizes Union Violence," *National Right to Work Committee* (blog), February 14, 2012, http://www.nrtwc.org/hobbs-act-loophole-legitimizes-union-violence/, accessed March 2012.

3 U.S. v. Larson, et al., May 2007 Grand Jury Superseding Indictment, pp. 37-38; Horowitz, "Buffalo Local Members Arrested."

4 Gerald Friedman, "Labor Unions in the United States," *EH.Net Encyclopedia*, ed. Robert Whaples, February 1, 2010, http://eh.net/encyclopedia/article/friedman.unions.us, accessed January 2012.

5 Samuel Gompers, Address to the American Federation of Labor Convention, 1924, quoted in National Institute for Labor Relations Research, *Coercive Union Power in Union Officials' Own Words* (1985), on file with the authors. Gompers said further, "The rules and regulations of trade unionism should not be extended so that the action of a majority could force a minority to vote for or give financial support to any political candidate or party to whom they are opposed." Note that the American Federation of Labor later joined with the Congress of Industrial Organizations to become the powerful AFL-CIO.

6 *American Federationist*, February 1913, quoted in Samuel Gompers, *Labor and the Employer*, ed. Hayes Robbins (New York: E. P. Dutton, 1920), p. 267.

7 Burton Folsom, *New Deal or Raw Deal?* paperback ed. (New York: Simon and Schuster, 2008), p. 121.

8 Steven Greenhouse, "Labor Board Drops Suit Against Boeing After Union Reaches Accord," *New York Times*, December 9, 2011, http://www.nytimes.com/2011/12/10/business/labor-board-drops-case-against-boeing.html, accessed May 2012.

9 FDR and his allies criticized the 1930s Supreme Court decisions overturning New Deal policies. Historians hold differing opinions over whether Justice Owen Roberts's sudden change to supporting New Deal policies starting in March 1937 was the result of intimidation. This was the fabled "switch in time, saved nine" because it ended FDR's efforts to add additional Justices to the

Supreme Court in order to get a Court that would uphold his New Deal legislation. For a brief, even-handed account of the ongoing controversy, see Christopher Shea, "Supreme Switch: Did FDR's Threat to 'Pack' the Court in 1937 Really Change the Course of Constitutional History?" *Boston Globe*, December 4, 2005, http://www.boston.com/news/globe/ideas/articles/2005/12/04/supreme_switch/, accessed January 2012.

10 Amity Shlaes, *The Forgotten Man: A New History of the Great Depression*, paperback ed. (New York: HarperCollins, 2007), especially p. 310.

11 U.S. Bureau of Labor Statistics, *Employment and Earnings, United States, 1909–75*, (Washington, D.C., Dept. of Labor, Bureau of Labor Statistics, 1976). From 1937 to 1938, the unemployment rate skyrocketed from 14.3 to 19.0 percent. Manufacturing dropped by 37 percent; industrial production plummeted 30 percent.

12 Sean J. Savage, *Roosevelt: The Party Leader 1932–1945* (Lexington, Ky.: University Press of Kentucky, 1991), pp. 89–90. In 1936, 10.2 percent of the Democratic National Committee's campaign cash came from labor unions; by 1940, it came to 16 percent. And this is just recorded cash. "Throughout Roosevelt's presidency," writes Savage, "organized labor steadily strengthened its position as a major source of Democratic campaign funds and thus strengthened its position in national Party affairs, solidifying the Party's commitment to social welfare and labor reform legislation favored by labor unions."

13 *Federal Times*, April 2, 1979, quoted in *Coercive Union Power in Union Officials' Own Words*.

14 William W. Winpisinger, president, International Association of Machinists, *Richmond (Va.) News Leader*, September 4, 1978, quoted in *Coercive Union Power in Union Officials' Own Words*.

15 On August 16, 1937, President Roosevelt wrote to the National Federation of Federal Employees, a labor union that later joined the International Association of Machinists. In his letter, he supported the rights of federal employees to unionize, but clarified that collective bargaining and strikes are impermissible in the government sector. "All Government employees should realize that the process of collective bargaining, as usually understood, cannot be transplanted into the public service...The employer is the whole people, who speak by means of laws enacted by their representatives in Congress...Particularly, I want to emphasize my conviction that militant tactics have no place in the functions of any organization of Government employees. Upon employees in the Federal service rests the obligation to serve the whole people, whose interests and welfare require orderliness and continuity in the conduct of Government activities. This obligation is paramount. Since their own services have to do with the functioning of the Government, a strike of public employees manifests nothing less than an intent on their part to prevent or obstruct the operations of Government until their demands are satisfied. Such action, looking toward the paralysis of Government by those who have sworn to support it, is unthinkable and intolerable." See Franklin D. Roosevelt, "Letter on the Resolution

of Federation of Federal Employees Against Strikes in Federal Service," The American Presidency Project, August 16, 1937, http://www.presidency .ucsb.edu/ws/index.php?pid=15445#axzz1igz8J9XP, accessed January 2012.

16 Executive Order No. 10,988, available at the Federal Labor Relations Authority website, https://www.flra.gov/webfm_send/563, accessed January 2012.

17 Ibid.

18 "About NTEU," National Treasury Employees Union, http://www.nteu.org/ NTEU/, accessed January 2012.

19 "About AFGE," American Federation of Government Employees, http://www .afge.org/Index.cfm?Page=AboutAFGE, accessed January 2012.

20 "What Is AFSA?" American Foreign Service Association, http://www.afsa .org/what_is_afsa, accessed January 2012.

21 These protections were first granted in the Executive Order and then were codified into law. See 5 U.S.C. § 7102 (2011) (federal employees generally); 39 U.S.C. § 1209(c) (2011) (postal employees).

22 Unions still earn plenty of dues from federal employees and state and local employees in right-to-work states who join the union because of union control over their workplaces.

23 Daniel DiSalvo, "Storm Clouds Ahead: Why Conflict with Public Unions Will Continue," Issue Brief no. 13, Manhattan Institute for Policy Research, November 2011, http://www.manhattan-institute.org/html/ib_13.htm.

24 The key to monopoly bargaining is not that these states allow unions to engage in it, but that they require the government to bargain "in good faith" with the certified or recognized monopoly and exclusive bargaining representative. In thirty-four states, the government employer is required to negotiate in good faith with unions representing government workers. This means basically that the government employer cannot walk away from the bargaining table and is forced to continue negotiating and continue offering concessions until a deal is reached. In nine other states, unions can and do collectively bargain on behalf of at least some state and/or local government workers, although not all the other states require the government to bargain in good faith with unions. In contrast, seven states either expressly forbid unions from engaging in collective bargaining over state and local workers or don't accept it. These states are Arizona, Georgia, Mississippi, North Carolina, South Carolina, Texas, and Virginia.

25 While the twenty-seven states that are not right-to-work states don't prohibit forced-dues provisions, a few of them do not currently have forced-dues provisions in their contracts with government employee unions. Wisconsin, for example, now prohibits most public sector forced-dues contracts. Several other states that are not right-to-work states may or may not have forced-dues contracts but don't prohibit them. This leaves twenty-two states that specifically permit forced-dues contracts over state and/or local government employees.

26 Joseph C. Goulden, *Jerry Wurf: Labor's Last Angry Man* (New York: Atheneum, 1982), pp. 14–17.

27 Ibid.

28 Ibid., pp. 18–24.

29 Wagner ultimately delivered on his promises to Wurf, but it took him several years. In 1958, Wagner issued Executive Order 49, which extended collective bargaining over about 100,000 city employees. See Ken Auletta, *The Streets Were Paved with Gold* (New York: Random House, 1975); Goulden, pp. 45–47. And in 1977, state and local employees under collective bargaining agreements were forced to pay union dues as a condition of their employment. "New York's Gov. Carey Signs Agency Shop Bill," *National Right to Work Newsletter*, September 28, 1977.

Government payrolls shot up even as private employment declined. "By the end of 1975," write E. J. McMahon and Fred Siegel, "the city directly employed an astonishing 340,000 workers, an increase of 100,000 since 1959 alone. And that didn't include the 80,000 people who worked for the state Metropolitan Transportation Authority (which had absorbed the city-run transit system in 1969) or the bi-state Port Authority of New York and New Jersey, or the bevy of private firms supporting themselves almost solely on government contracts." In 1975, New York stood on "the brink of ruin," with "city politics (and politicians)...dominated by extraordinarily large municipal unions." E. J. McMahon and Fred Siegel, "Gotham's Fiscal Crisis: Lessons Unlearned," *Public Interest* 158 (Winter 2005), pp. 96–110.

30 Reed Larson, *Stranglehold* (Ottawa, Ill.: Jameson Books, 1999), chapter 1. AFSCME's own website acknowledged how the union relies on political activity to further its own activities: "In the 1970s and 80s, AFSCME members increased their efforts politically in order to win collective bargaining laws, organize new members, and wield clout on behalf of existing members. All across the country, at every level of government, candidates for public office learned they had to pay attention to AFSCME's political muscle." "AFSCME: 75 Years of History," AFSCME, http://www.afscme.org/union/history/afscme-75-years-of-history, accessed January 2012.

31 Goulden, pp. 142–143.

32 Morris Thomson, "In Memphis, Progress and Poverty," *Washington Post*, April 4, 1988; Goulden, p. 147.

33 Goulden, p. 143.

34 "Coming: Unionized Government," *U.S. News & World Report*, September 26, 1966.

35 According to Goulden, the sanitation workers went on strike for two reasons. On January 30, 1968, two black sanitation workers had been crushed to death in trash compactor trucks, after the workers had warned supervisors about defective "off-on" switches on the trucks. The next day, the black sanitation workers were told to go home because of rainy conditions and received only their two-hour "call-up pay," while the white supervisors waited until the rain cleared and went out for a full day's work (and pay). After they complained to the city without redress, the consensus among the black sanitation workers was that "the city's actions had been racist, and that the sanitation men had had enough of it." Goulden, p. 147.

36 Goulden, p. 149.

37 Ibid.

38 Ibid., p. 169.

39 See, for example, Paul Moreno, *Black Americans and Organized Labor: A New History* (Baton Rouge: Louisiana State University Press, 2006), especially pp. 259–276.

40 Goulden, pp. 169–170.

41 Ibid., pp. 173–175.

42 See Hampton Sides, *Hellhound on His Trail: The Stalking of Martin Luther King Jr. and the International Hunt for His Assassin,* Kindle ed. (New York: Doubleday, 2010), locations 1548–1563, 1579–1610, and 1760–1900.

43 Goulden, pp. 176–177.

44 "Rahm Emanuel: You Never Want a Serious Crisis to Go to Waste," video, YouTube, http://www.youtube.com/watch?v=1yeA_kHHLow, accessed March 2012.

45 Goulden, p. 178.

46 Ibid. In fact, Memphis experienced only scattered riots during that time, although Washington, D.C., and several other major cities did experience severe riots after King's assassination.

47 Ibid., pp. 178–182.

48 Ibid., p. 181.

49 Ibid., p. 182.

50 "AFSCME: 75 Years of History."

51 Information taken from "City of Memphis—Solid Waste History," City of Memphis, http://www.cityofmemphis.org/statistics/2000/sw_history.htm.

52 Armand Thieblot and Thomas Haggard, *Union Violence: The Record and the Response by Courts, Legislatures, and the NLRB* (Philadelphia: University of Pennsylvania, 1983), p. 124.

53 This issue is covered very well in John Berlau, "The Firemen Next Time," *National Review Online,* October 14, 2010, http://www.nationalreview.com/articles/249701/fire-next-time-john-berlau, accessed January 2012.

54 Thieblot and Haggard, p. 125.

55 Ibid., p. 126.

56 Ibid., pp. 125–127.

57 Ibid., p. 132.

58 Ibid., pp. 129–135.

59 Ibid., p.135.

60 Joseph McCartin, "A Wagner Act for Public Employees: Labor's Deferred Dream and the Rise of Conservatism, 1970–1976," *Journal of American History* (June 2008), pp. 123–148, especially pp. 137, 139.

61 "Union-Ruled City," *New York Times,* July 8, 1975.

62 E. Cahill Maloney, "Strikers Sabotage Working Cops," *Progress Bulletin* (Pomona, Calif.), August 22, 1975.

63 "Alioto House Bombed," *Oakland Tribune,* August 20, 1975.

64 Steve Konicki, "Firemen Watch Homes Burn," *Dayton Daily News,* August 9, 1977.

65 Albert Schweitzer and John C. Shelton, "Firemen Turn Backs, U. City Plant Burns," *St. Louis Globe-Democrat,* July 25, 1977.

66 Thieblot and Haggard, pp. 136–142.

67 Quoted in "A Clear and Avoidable Danger: Daschle Amend. Could Lead to Firefighter, Police Strikes During a Terrorist Attack," U.S. Senate Republican Policy Committee, November 1, 2001, p. 2, http://rpc.senate.gov/public/_files/DEFENSEjt110103.pdf, accessed April 2012.

68 Thieblot and Haggard, p. 120.

69 Ibid.

70 "Freedom from Union Violence Act," Fact Sheet, National Right to Work, http://www.right-to-work.org/FactSheets/ViolenceFactSheet.pdf, accessed January 2012.

71 U.S. v. Larson, 07-CR-304S, NYLJ 1202511598699, at *1 (WDNY, Decided August 10, 2011).

72 NRTW Committee Staff, "Hobbs Act Loophole Legitimizes Union Violence," February 14, 2012, http://www.nrtwc.org/hobbs-act-loophole-legitimizes-union-violence/, accessed April 2012.

73 U.S. v. Enmons, 410 U.S. 396 (1973). In-depth treatment of this case and attempts to change the underlying law to remedy the situation can be found in David Kendrick, "Freedom from Union Violence," Policy Analysis no. 316, Cato Institute, September 9, 1998.

74 "Freedom from Union Violence Act."

75 Kendrick, pp. 28–29.

76 Freedom from Union Violence Act of 2012, H.R. 4074, 112th Cong. (2012). Similar acts have been introduced in the House by different House members numerous times but have never made it out of committee. The Freedom from Union Violence Act of 2005 had the most cosponsors—twenty-eight—but none of them were Democrats. This information was obtained via the THOMAS search engine at the Library of Congress website, http://thomas.loc.gov/home/thomas.php.

77 Kris Maher, "SEIU to End Sodexo Campaign," *Wall Street Journal*, September 15, 2011, http://online.wsj.com/article/SB10001424053111904491704576573074162700598.html?_nocache=1326060998873&user=welcome&mg=id-wsj, accessed January 2012.

78 "Sodexo USA Files RICO Lawsuit against SEIU," Sodexo USA press release, PR Newswire, March 17, 2011, http://www.prnewswire.com/news-releases/sodexo-usa-files-rico-lawsuit-against-seiu-118204534.html, accessed March 2012.

79 Sodexo, Inc. v. S.E.I.U. et al., Case No. 1:20 11-cv-00276 (E.D. Va.), complaint, p. 8.

80 Ibid.

81 Sodexo, Inc. v. S.E.I.U. et al., Case No. 1:20 11-cv-00276 (E.D. Va.), complaint, p. 5.

82 "SEIU Contract Campaign Manual—Pressuring the Employer," Scribd, http://www.scribd.com/doc/60893001/SEIU-Contract-Campaign-Manual-Pressuring-the-Employer, accessed March 2012.

83 F. Vincent Vernuccio, "Labor's New Strategy: Intimidation for Dummies," *Washington Times*, July 15, 2011, http://www.washingtontimes.com/

news/2011/jul/15/labors-new-strategy-intimidation-for-dummies/, accessed January 2012.

84 Ibid.

85 Nina Easton, "What's Really behind the SEIU's Bank of America Protests?" Power Play, *CNNMoney*, May 19, 2010, http://money.cnn.com/2010/05/19/news/companies/SEIU_Bank_of_America_protest.fortune/, accessed March 2012.

86 About 75 percent of reported union violence occurs in the twenty-seven states that do not have right-to-work laws, based on reported state-by-state counts from the National Institute for Labor Relations Research.

87 *Hearing on "Open Shops in the 21st Century Workplace," Before the U.S. House Subcommittee on Oversight and Investigations Committee on Education and the Workforce*, 106th Cong. (May 3, 2000) (written statement of Reed Larson, president of the National Right to Work Committee), http://archives.republicans.edlabor.house.gov/archive/hearings/106th/oi/openshop5300/larson.htm, accessed April 2012.

Chapter 3. Follow the Money

1 "Labor Unions Receive $14 Billion in Dues Per Year from CBAs," Fact Sheets, National Institute for Labor Relations Research, March 30, 2012, http://www.nilrr.org/2012/03/31/unions-rake-in-over-14-9-billion-in-dues-per-year-from-cbas/, accessed April 2012. We are basing the assumption that over half of union dues are from government workers on the fact that 51 percent of all union members in America are government workers. See Bureau of Labor Statistics, "Union Members–2011," January 27, 2012, http://www.bls.gov/news/release/union2.nr0.htm, accessed March 2012.

2 See Michael Beckel and Seth Cline, "Labor Lobbying, Union PAC Contributions and More in Capital Eye Opener: Sept. 5," *OpenSecrets*(blog), http://www.opensecrets.org/news/2011/09/labor-lobbying-union-pac-money.html, accessed February 2012.

3 "2.2 Billion Political Outlaws," research paper, National Institute for Labor Relations Research, September 1, 2011, http://www.nilrr.org/files/2011%20NILRR%20Big%20Labor%20Politcal%20Spending%20Preliminary%20Report.pdf, accessed January 2012.

4 Steven Greenhouse, "Union Spends $91 Million on Midterms," *The Caucus* (blog), *New York Times*, October 26, 2010, http://thecaucus.blogs.nytimes.com/2010/10/26/union-spends-91-million-on-midterms/.

5 Brody Mullins and John D. McKinnon, "Campaign's Big Spender," Politics, *Wall Street Journal*, October 21, 2010, http://online.wsj.com/article/SB10001424052702303339504575566481761790288.html

6 A Fox News poll conducted by Anderson Robbins Research (D) and Shaw & Company Research (R), March 14–16, 2011, quoted in "Use of Dues for Politics," UnionFacts.com, http://www.unionfacts.com/political-money/, accessed February 2012.

7 For example, a 2008 report found that the teachers unions collected 83 percent of their dues income from the twenty-four states that allowed forced dues

at that time, even though only 52 percent of teachers worked in those states. See "Two Million K–12 Teachers Are Now Corralled into Unions," Fact Sheet, National Institute for Labor Relations Research, August 28, 2008, http://www .nilrr.org/files/How%20Many%20Teachers%20Fact%20Sheet.pdf.

8 "Political Power," Teachers Union Exposed, http://teachersunionexposed .com/dues.cfm, accessed January 2012.

9 The national right-to-work law would not prevent states from giving unions collective bargaining power over government workers. Union collective bargaining power has a pernicious effect on public policy but does not affect the unions' income as much as forced-dues provisions do.

10 "Republican Senators Introduce National Right to Work Act," Senator Jim DeMint (U.S. Senate website), March 8, 2011, http://demint.senate.gov/ public/index.cfm?p=PressReleases&ContentRecord_id=6c97e4c4-a31f -4636-8fe2-6ffdf625b2d5, accessed January 2012.

11 Letter from Senator Rand Paul, National Right to Work Committee, http:// righttoworkcommittee.org/rprtwa_petition.aspx, accessed January 2012.

12 Lowell Ponte, "How Socialist Unions Rule the Democratic Party," *Front-Page Magazine*, July 14, 2004, http://archive.frontpagemag.com/readArticle .aspx?ARTID=12216, accessed January 2012.

13 Most, but not all, unions are "labor organizations" under section 501(c)(5) of the IRS Code. The income of labor organizations is generally nontaxable, except for certain express political spending. However, labor organizations are given wide latitude to engage in political activities, as long as these are not directed at particular candidates. For this reason, unions engage in more general political organizing rather than working directly for campaigns for particular candidates, although they seem to be getting closer and closer to the line with each election cycle. The IRS explains the permissible political activities of labor organizations as follows: "Seeking legislation germane to the labor or agricultural organization's programs is recognized as a permissible means of attaining its exempt purposes. Thus, a section 501(c)(5) organization may further its exempt purposes through lobbying as its primary activity without jeopardizing its exempt status." With respect to political activities, the IRS clarifies, "The exempt purposes of a labor or agricultural organization do not include direct or indirect participation or intervention in political campaigns on behalf of or in opposition to any candidate for public office. A section 501(c) (5) labor . . . organization may engage in some political activities, however, so long as that is not its primary activity. However, any expenditures it makes for political activities may be subject to tax under section 527(f)." See http://www .irs.gov/charities/nonprofits/article/0,,id=96169,00.html. The unions' financial disclosure is crafted to conform to these limitations. Not all unions are labor organizations. The most notable exception is the National Education Association, which is a federally chartered corporation. Unlike most other federally chartered corporations (like the Red Cross, for example), the National Education Association is specifically excluded from submitting annual audited financial statements to Congress. See 36 U.S.C. §151108 (2011). See http://uscode.house.gov/download/pls/36C1511.txt.

14 Elaine Chao, "Obama Tries to Stop Union Disclosure," *Wall Street Journal*, May 6, 2009, http://online.wsj.com/article/SB124157604375290453.html, accessed January 2012.

15 Unions also have some other expenses on their LM-2 statements, their financial disclosures to the federal government. These LM-2 statements allow for some creative accounting of expenses and are not highly transparent. In addition to the expenses discussed in the body of this chapter, the LM-2 also shows payments for taxes, holding meetings, strike benefits, and other miscellaneous expenses.

16 This is based on our analysis of union financial disclosure, which is limited and tends to understate political spending, as we have discussed. For example, in 2010 AFSCME disclosed 32 percent of the spending of its national organization (not including state and local affiliates) was political spending. The SEIU's national headquarters disclosed that 18 percent of its spending was political in 2010. If you assume some other gray-area spending is allocated to other categories, the SEIU's political spending falls squarely within the 20–30 percent range. The NEA disclosed in 2011 that only 13 percent of its spending that year was political, but an additional 22 percent of its spending was for gifts and contributions to other organizations, which includes its spending to put political operatives in every congressional district in America. If you assume that one-third of its gifts and contributions are political in nature (which seems a conservative estimate), then the NEA's political spending is just under 20 percent of its total spending. And none of these percentages include union PAC spending on political campaigns, which constitutes additional direct political spending. Labor economist Daniel DiSalvo suggests that a rough rule of thumb is that government employee unions spend 20 percent of their revenues on "lobbying and electioneering." See Daniel DiSalvo, "Dues and Deep Pockets: Public-Sector Unions' Money Machine," Civic Report no. 67, Manhattan Institute for Policy Research, March 2012, http://www.manhattan-institute.org/html/cr_67.htm#notes, accessed April 2012.

17 The categories of spending included in "union administration" are very specific and don't seem to include this type of spending, which seems more political in nature: "Union administration includes disbursements relating to the nomination and election of union officers, the union's regular membership meetings, intermediate, national and international meetings, union disciplinary proceedings, the administration of trusteeships, and the administration of apprenticeship and member education programs (not including political education which should be reported in Schedule 16)." National Education Association, national headquarters, Form LM-2, November 29, 2011, covering the period September 1, 2010, to August 31, 2011, p. 376, available at http://rishawnbiddle.org/outsidereports/nea_dol_filing_2011.pdf, accessed April 2012; U.S. Department of Labor, *Instructions for Form LM-2 Labor Organization Annual Report*, http://www.dol.gov/olms/regs/compliance/EFS/LM-2 InstructionsEFS.pdf, accessed April 2012, pp. 30–31.

18 Steven Greenhouse, "Labor Leaders Plan to Apply New Clout in Effort for Obama," *New York Times*, March 11, 2012, http://www.nytimes.com/

2012/03/12/us/politics/unions-plan-a-door-to-door-effort-for-2012-election .html?_r=2&ref=us, accessed March 2012.

19 Unions offer stipends for volunteer expenses. For example, one union offered a $25 stipend for two hours of phone bank work. See "Volunteer for Phone Banks; Earn $25 Stipend," Ohio Civil Service Employees Association (OCSEA), October 6, 2004, http://www.ocsea.org/news/story.asp?sid=58, accessed January 2012. The same union offered $50 for "voter protection" on election day. The website states, "Shifts of 4½ hours are available from 6:00 a.m. to 7:30 p.m. Volunteers will receive a cell phone, money for mileage, and meals. OCSEA members will receive a $50 stipend." See "It's Not Over Yet; Help GOTV Nov. 4–7 to Turn Around Ohio," OCSEA, November 2, 2006, http://www.ocsea.org/politicalaction/news110206.asp. AFSCME Ohio 8 offered $25 gift cards to people who got out the vote. Its website reported, "Members of Local 1846 Athens Public School Employees, Local 1699 Ohio University Employees, and Local 1252 members from O'Bleness Hospital are doing their part to get people to the polls—and receive a $25 'Turkey' gift card." See http://www.afscmecouncil8.org/node/1075. The AFT affiliate the Union of Rutgers Administrators posted the following "volunteer" opportunity on its website for participating in Committee on Political Education labor to labor walk during the 2010 election season:

"* Breakfast provided
  * URA members receive $50 stipend per walk
  * URA t-shirts will be given to each participant
  * URA members that participate in any combination of two or more labor walks or phone banks will be invited to the annual COPE Volunteer/ Steward Appreciation event
  * Any member of a union who walks will get 1 ticket for each time they do a Labor Walk for a raffle to be held on Election Night after Get Out To Vote is done. (Sponsored by the Middlesex & Somerset Central Labor Council) This year they are raffling off a 42" flat screen TV and a Garmin GPS."

See "COPE Committee Get Out the Vote Campaign...Starting Sept. 25," Union of Rutgers Administrators, http://www.ura-aft.org/node/541, accessed January 2012. See also the Health Professionals and Allied Employees website at http://www.hpae.org/carousel/3. For more about the FEC and its rules, see http://www.fec.gov/.

20 Greenhouse, "Labor Leaders Plan to Apply New Clout."

21 See Beckel and Cline, "Labor Lobbying"; "2010 Outside Spending, by Donors' Industries," *OpenSecrets*(blog), http://www.opensecrets.org/outside spending/summ.php?cycle=2010&disp=I&type=A.

22 Paul Blumenthal, "George Soros, Unions Give to New Democratic Super PAC," *Huffington Post*, June 24, 2011, http://www.huffingtonpost .com/2011/06/24/soros-unions-give-to-new-dem-super-pac_n_884021.html, accessed January 2012.

23 "Andrew Stern," DiscoverTheNetworks.org, http://www.discoverthenetworks .org/individualProfile.asp?indid=1830, accessed January 2012.

24 Knox v. California State Employee Assn., 628 F.3d 1115, 1118 (9th Cir. 2010). This case is currently before the Supreme Court.

25 See Ilya Shapiro, "Unions Can't Force Non-Members to Pay for Political Advocacy," *Cato @ Liberty* (blog), http://www.cato-at-liberty.org/unions-cant-force-non-members-to-pay-for-political-advocacy/, accessed January 2012; Charles W. Baird, "The Permissible Uses of Forced Union Dues: From *Hanson* to *Beck*," Cato Policy Analysis No. 174, Cato Institute, July 24, 1992, http://www.cato.org/pubs/pas/pa-174.html, accessed January 2012; and L. Paige Whitaker, "CRS Report for Congress: The Use of Labor Union Dues For Political Purposes: A Legal Analysis," Library of Congress, Congressional Research Service, August 2, 2000, http://congressionalresearch.com/97-618/document.php?study=The+Use+of+Labor+Union+Dues+for+Political+Purposes+A+Legal+Analysis, accessed January 2012.

26 James Sherk, "The Employee Rights Act Empowers Workers," Backgrounder #2667, Heritage Foundation, March 19, 2012, http://www.heritage.org/research/reports/2012/03/the-employee-rights-act-empowers-workers#_ftnref23, accessed April 2012. Sherk explains, "Under the Supreme Court precedent established in Communications Workers v. Beck in 1988, unions cannot force workers to donate to political causes. However, unions make it very difficult to exercise this right. Unions implement bureaucratic obstacles, such as accepting such requests only 30 days of the year, that make it difficult for workers to formally request a refund of their dues. Often unions refuse to honor those requests unless workers file federal charges."

27 Sherk, "The Employee Rights Act Empowers Workers," citing WordDoctors, "Benchmark Study of Union Employee Election Year Attitudes," Question 41, October 2010 (survey of 760 union members). For an excellent treatment of paycheck protection laws, see James Sherk, "What Do Union Members Want? What Paycheck Protection Laws Show About How Well Unions Reflect Their Members' Priorities," Center for Data Analysis Report #06-08, Heritage Foundation, August 30, 2006, http://www.heritage.org/research/reports/2006/08/what-do-union-members-want-what-paycheck-protection-laws-show-about-how-well-unions-reflect-their-members-priorities, accessed April 2012.

28 National Education Association, national headquarters, Form LM-2; "Union Profiles," Teachers Union Exposed, http://teachersunionexposed.com/unions.cfm, accessed January 2012.

29 Mike Antonucci, "The Long Reach of Teachers Unions," *EducationNext* 10, no. 4 (Fall 2010), http://educationnext.org/the-long-reach-of-teachers-unions/, accessed March 2012.

30 This gift was made in 2010.

31 "UFT President Michael Mulgrew Responds to the Ouster of Occupy Wall Street Protesters," press release, United Federation of Teachers, November 15, 2011, http://www.uft.org/press-releases/uft-president-michael-mulgrew-responds-ouster-occupy-wall-street-protesters, accessed December 2011.

32 Lindsey Burke, "National Education Association Convention Fails to Benefit Teachers or Improve Education," *The Foundry* (blog), Heritage Foundation,

July 8, 2011, http://blog.heritage.org/2011/07/08/national-education-association -convention-fails-to-benefit-teachers-or-improve-education/.

33 This bucket also pays for any necessary insurance and benefits for members.

34 James Sherk, "What Do Union Members Want? What Paycheck Protection Laws Show about How Well Unions Reflect Their Members' Priorities," Center For Data Analysis Report #06-08, Heritage Foundation, August 30, 2006, http://www.heritage.org/research/reports/2006/08/what-do-union-members -want-what-paycheck-protection-laws-show-about-how-well-unions-reflect -their-members-priorities, accessed January 2012.

35 For example, in Communications Workers of America v. Beck, when the union's case depended on it, the Communications Workers of America union could show only 21 percent of its budget actually going toward collective bargaining. Communications Workers of America v. Beck, 487 U.S. 735 (1988).

36 U.S. House of Representatives Subcommittee on Workforce Protections, "The Use of Mandatory Union Dues for Politics: Lessons From Washington State," written testimony by Bob Williams, June 20, 2002, http://archives.republicans .edlabor.house.gov/archive/hearings/107th/wp/uniondues62002/williams .pdf, accessed January 2012.

37 Many federal and some other government workers are compensated according to a government pay scale. Many of these workers are under union collective bargaining representation even though their government employee unions cannot negotiate wages or some benefits on their behalf. But their unions do lobby the government for increases to the workers' pay scale and benefits as well as to expand their collective bargaining power over more government workers.

38 As explained above, some states permit unions to give donations to state and local candidates out of their general treasury, and these funds are in the political activities budget, described above.

39 "Are You Funding Your Union's Federal PAC (Political Action Committee) Unknowingly or against Your Will?" National Right to Work Legal Defense Foundation, http://www.nrtw.org/d/illegalpac.htm, accessed January 2012.

40 See "Service Employees International Union Expenditures," OpenSecrets, http://www.opensecrets.org/pacs/expenditures.php?cmte=C00004036& cycle=2010. See "Big Labor: A $20 Billion-a-Year Business," National Institute for Labor Relations Research, July 19, 2007, http://www.nilrr.org/files/ Big%20Labor%2020%20Billion%20A%20Year%20Business%20Update.pdf, accessed March 2012. While this rule of thumb is difficult to demonstrate for all unions for all years, a comparison of direct campaign contributions by top unions when compared to their disclosed political spending bears this out. For example, the NEA's PAC made $2,083,600 in contributions in 2010, while its national headquarters alone reported spending $29,712,732 on political activity (without taking into account its $91,352,936 in contributions, gifts, and grants, most of which are political as well). Similarly, the SEIU made contributions of $5,563,250 to all candidates in the 2010 cycle, and its national headquarters alone spent $55,108,669 on political activity.

41 Kevin Bogardus, "AFL-CIO Chief Amplifies Warning to Democrats," *The Hill*, June 7, 2011, http://thehill.com/business-a-lobbying/165151-afl-cio-chief-amplifies-warning-to-democrats, accessed January 2012.

42 W. James Antle III, "A Piece of the Action: Labor Expects Much from the Next Congress, New Administration," *Labor Watch*, Capital Research Center, December 2008, http://www.capitalresearch.org/pubs/pdf/v1228146537.pdf, accessed January 2012.

43 Matthew Kaminski, "Let's 'Share the Wealth,'" *Wall Street Journal*, December 6, 2008, http://online.wsj.com/article/SB122852244367484311.html, accessed April 2012.

44 Ann Coulter, "Look For The Union Fable," *Human Events*, February 23, 2011, http://www.humanevents.com/article.php?id=41971, accessed January 2012.

45 Lindsay Renick Mayer, "Labor and Business Spend Big on Looming Unionization Issue," *OpenSecrets*(blog), February 26, 2009, http://www.opensecrets.org/news/2009/02/labor-and-business-spend-big-o.html, accessed December 2011.

46 Jean Merl and Antonio Olivio, "Solis Trounces Martinez in Bitter Race," *Los Angeles Times*, March 8, 2000, http://articles.latimes.com/2000/mar/08/news/mn-6735, accessed January 2012.

47 Jean Merl, "Solis Prepares to Take Another Step Up," *Los Angeles Times*, December 28, 2000, http://articles.latimes.com/2000/dec/28/local/me-5513/2, accessed January 2012.

48 Ezra Klein, "Hardball Time on Health Care Reform," *Washington Post*, March 12, 2010, http://voices.washingtonpost.com/ezra-klein/2010/03/hardball_time_on_health-care_r.html, accessed January 2012.

49 In fact, of the thirty-four Democrats who voted against Obamacare, only thirteen won reelection. But the reasons for this probably have little to do with the withdrawal of union support in this case. It is well known that moderate Democrats in the House of Representatives lost their seats in 2010 in far greater numbers than for Democrats generally. About one in four Democrats in the House lost his seat in 2010 generally, whereas 62 percent of the Democrats who voted against Obamacare lost their seats.

50 Daniel DiSalvo and Fred Siegel, "The New Tammany Hall," *Weekly Standard*, October 12, 2009, http://www.weeklystandard.com/Content/Public/Articles/000/000/017/031citja.asp?page=2, accessed January 2012.

51 David Postman, "Gephardt Gives Boeing Advice," *Seattle Times*, September 23, 2005, http://seattletimes.nwsource.com/html/businesstechnology/2002514352_gephardt23.html, accessed January 2012; see also Sebastian Jones, "Dick Gephardt's Spectacular Sellout," *The Nation*, October 19, 2009, http://www.thenation.com/article/dick-gephardts-spectacular-sellout?page=0,1, accessed January 2012.

52 Amanda Ripley, "The Story of Barack Obama's Mother," *Time*, April 9, 2008, http://www.time.com/time/magazine/article/0,9171,1729685-3,00.html, accessed January 2012; Russell Goldman and Devin Dwyer, "Hawaii Gov. Says Proof of Obama's Birth Certificate Exists but Hasn't Produced the Document," *ABC News*, January 20, 2011, http://abcnews.go.com/Politics/

obama-birth-hawaii-gov-proof-presidents-birth-certificate/story?id=12721552, accessed January 2012.

53 DiSalvo and Siegel, "The New Tammany Hall."

54 Ibid.

55 David Postman, "Republicans Say They've Found 249 More Felons Who Voted," *Seattle Times*, January 29, 2005, http://community.seattletimes .nwsource.com/archive/?date=20050129&slug=felons30m, accessed January 2012.

56 Gregory Roberts, "Judge Upholds Gregoire's Election; Rossi Won't Appeal," *Seattle Post-Intelligencer Reporter*, June 5, 2005, http://www.seattlepi.com/ local/article/Judge-upholds-Gregoire-s-election-Rossi-won-t-1175262.php #page-1, accessed April 2012.

57 DiSalvo and Siegel, "The New Tammany Hall."

58 Ibid.

59 Rachel La Corte, "State Workers Sue Gregoire over Canceled Raises," Associated Press, December 23, 2008, http://www.seattlepi.com/local /article/State-workers-sue-Gregoire-over-canceled-raises-1295728.php, accessed January 2012.

60 Mayer, "Labor and Business Spend Big on Looming Unionization Issue."

61 David Catanese, "Romanoff Cans Caddell in Colorado," *Politico*, February 17, 2010, http://www.politico.com/news/stories/0210/33058.html, accessed April 2012.

62 "About," America Votes, http://www.americavotes.org/about, accessed February 2012.

63 Thomas B. Edsall, " '527' legislation would affect Democrats more," *Washington Post*, March 28, 2006, http://www.washingtonpost.com/wp-dyn/content/ article/2006/03/27/AR2006032701386.html, accessed April 2012.

64 Anna Burger, "Catalist Analysis of SEIU's 2008 Voter Contact Programs," SEIU.org, September 16, 2009, http://www.seiu.org/catalistreport-SC3.pdf, accessed January 2012.

65 Ibid.

66 Statement by AFL-CIO President John Sweeney, April 15, 2008, http://www .consumerwatchdog.org/resources/SEIURelease.pdf accessed May 2012. The SEIU itself said that while its members were at the conference to protest, the "protest was mostly peaceful." Jesse J. Holland, "2 Labor Groups Bicker over a Michigan Scuffle," Associated Press, April 16, 2008.

67 Jamie Court, "Will Andy Stern Repudiate Violence in the Union Hall?" *Huffington Post*, April 15, 2008, http://www.huffingtonpost.com/jamie -court/will-andy-stern-repudiate_b_96841.html, accessed January 2012; Deborah Burger, "SEIU's Latest Disgrace: Violent Attack on Michigan Meeting of Union Members and RNs," *Huffington Post*, April 13, 2008, http://www .huffingtonpost.com/deborah-burger/seius-latest-disgrace_b_96399.html, accessed May 2012.

68 Steven Greenhouse, "Two Unions, Once Bitter Rivals, Will Now Work Together," *New York Times*, March 19, 2009, http://www.nytimes.com/ 2009/03/19/health/19union.html, accessed March 2012.

69 Michelle Malkin, "'Brown Shirts' vs. Purple Shirts," Townhall.com, August 12, 2009, http://townhall.com/columnists/michellemalkin/2009/08/12/brown_shirts_vs_purple_shirts, accessed January 2012.

70 A 2005 Zogby poll of likely voters shows that 32 percent of unionized voters said the NRA spoke for them. "Disorganized Labor," Zogby International, August 10, 2005, http://www.ibopezogby.com/news/2005/08/10/disorganized-labor/, accessed April 2012.

71 See http://aftmichigan.org/files/compare_guns-unions.pdf.

72 Jake Tapper, "Obama Explains Why Some Small Town Pennsylvanians Are 'Bitter,'" *Political Punch* (blog), *ABC News*, http://abcnews.go.com/blogs/politics/2008/04/obama-explains-2/.

73 "US Elections: How Groups Voted in 2008," Roper Center, http://www.ropercenter.uconn.edu/elections/how_groups_voted/voted_08.html.

74 John Lott, "President Obama's Anti-Gun Agenda Shows No Sign of Stopping," *Fox News*, December 28, 2011, http://www.foxnews.com/opinion/2011/12/28/president-obamas-anti-gun-agenda-shows-no-sign-stopping/, accessed January 2012.

75 "National Organizations with Anti-Gun Policies," National Rifle Association Institute for Legislative Action, http://www.nraila.org/issues/factsheets/read.aspx?id=15, accessed January 2012. See also "NRA to Promote 'Gun Control' Petition Drive," NRA, http://www.nrawinningteam.com/0007/nea.html. The defunct organization ACORN, which was considered by many to be the political action arm of SEIU, is also antigun. See Dave Kopel, "What's That Smell?" Second Amendment Project, http://davekopel.org/2A/Mags/ACORN.htm.

Chapter 4. Union-Label President

1 William McQuillen, "AFL-CIO Drops Criticism to Endorse Obama, Citing Focus on Jobs," *Bloomberg Businessweek*, March 14, 2012, http://www.businessweek.com/news/2012-03-14/afl-cio-drops-criticism-to-endorse-obama-citing-focus-on-jobs, accessed March 2012; Harold Meyerson, "Under Obama, Labor Should Have Made More Progress," *Washington Post*, February 10, 2010, http://www.washingtonpost.com/wp-dyn/content/article/2010/02/09/AR2010020902465.html, accessed March 2012.

2 "New Leadership on Health Care: A Presidential Forum," transcript, March 24, 2007, http://www.americanprogressaction.org/events/healthforum/fulltranscript.pdf.

3 Peter Nicholas, "Obama's Curiously Close Labor Friendship," *Los Angeles Times*, June 28, 2009, http://articles.latimes.com/2009/jun/28/nation/na-stern28, accessed December 2011.

4 Because of division within the SEIU over endorsing a candidate in the Democrat primary in the 2008 election, Andy Stern let each separate SEIU affiliate make its own endorsement. By January 9, 2008, five SEIU state councils had endorsed Senator Obama. Steven Greenhouse, "Obama Received Union Endorsements," *The Caucus* (blog), *New York Times*, January 9, 2008, http://thecaucus.blogs.nytimes.com/2008/01/09/obama-to-get-union-endorsement/, accessed January 2012.

5 Nicholas, "Obama's Curiously Close Labor Friendship."

6 Steve Early, *The Civil Wars in U.S. Labor* (Chicago: Haymarket Books, 2011), p. 260.

7 "Obama's Remarks to the AFL-CIO," Real Clear Politics, April 2, 2008, http://www.realclearpolitics.com/articles/2008/04/obamas_remarks_to_the_aflcio.html, accessed April 2012.

8 Steven Greenhouse, "AFL-CIO Endorses Obama," *The Caucus* (blog), *New York Times*, June 26, 2008, http://thecaucus.blogs.nytimes.com/2008/06/26/afl-cio-endorses-obama/, accessed December 2011.

9 "The NEA: Organized, Energized and Mobilized for Barack Obama," National Education Association, August 25, 2008, http://www.nea.org/home/11141.htm, accessed March 2012; see also Jason Koebler, "National Education Association To Endorse Obama," High School Notes, *U.S. News & World Report*, May 13, 2011, http://www.usnews.com/education/blogs/high-school-notes/2011/05/13/national-education-association-endorses-obama, accessed March 2012.

10 Barack Obama, "AFSCME National Convention—Challenge for Labor," August 7, 2006, http://obamaspeeches.com/086-AFSCME-National-Convention-Obama-Speech.htm, accessed December 2011.

11 Ibid.

12 Ibid.

13 Peter Wallsten, "AFSCME Votes to Endorse Obama for Reelection," Post Politics, *Washington Post*, December 6, 2011, http://www.washingtonpost.com/blogs/44/post/afscme-votes-to-endorse-obama-for-reelection/2011/12/06/gIQAjJanZO_blog.html, accessed December 2011.

14 Katie Fretland, "John McCain vs. Baby in Anti-War Ad," *The Swamp*, June 18, 2008, http://www.swamppolitics.com/news/politics/blog/2008/06/john_mccain_vs_baby_in_antiwar.html, accessed December 2011.

15 Connie Cass, "Big Donors All around White House," Associated Press, February 24, 1997.

16 Michael O'Brien, "Video seizes on union leader's boast of daily contact with the White House," *The Hill*, March 9, 2011, http://thehill.com/blogs/blog-briefing-room/news/148323-video-seizes-on-trumkas-boast-of-daily-contact-with-white-house, accessed May 2012.

17 Guest List for the First Lady's Box at the President's Address to Congress, White House press release, September 8, 2011, http://www.whitehouse.gov/the-press-office/2011/09/08/guest-list-first-ladys-box-president-s-address-congress, accessed February 2012.

18 Lynn Sweet, "Obama's First State Dinner: The Guest List," *Politics Daily*, November 24, 2009, http://www.politicsdaily.com/2009/11/24/obamas-first-state-dinner-the-guest-list/, accessed May 2012. Anna Burger also served as the chair of the labor union federation, Change to Win, but retired from her posts with both the SEIU and Change to Win in 2010. Steven Greenhouse, "After a life in labor, a union leader retires, frustrated by the movement's troubles," *New York Times*, September 4, 2010, http://www.nytimes.com/2010/09/05/us/05labor.html, accessed April 2012.

19 Carol E. Lee, "State Dinner Guest List: 2012 in Mind?" *Washington Wire* (blog), *Wall Street Journal*, June 7, 2011, http://blogs.wsj.com/washwire/2011/06/07/state-dinner-guest-list-2012-in-mind/, accessed February 2012.

20 "Guest List for the White House State Dinner," *Washington Wire* (blog), *Wall Street Journal*, http://blogs.wsj.com/washwire/2012/03/14/guest-list-for-the-white-house-state-dinner/, accessed April 2012.

21 Jeff Zeleny, "White House Visitor Log Lists Stars and C.E.O.'s," *New York Times*, October 30, 2009, http://www.nytimes.com/2009/10/31/us/politics/31visitor.html, accessed January 2012; Carl Horowitz, "SEIU President Andrew Stern Is Frequent White House Visitor; May Have Violated Lobbying Laws," National Legal and Policy Center, November 18, 2009, http://nlpc.org/stories/2009/11/18/seiu-president-andrew-stern-frequent-white-house-visitor-may-have-violated-lobbyi, accessed January 2012.

22 "Union Leader Says Green Buildings Training Cost-Effective Way to Reduce CO2 Emissions," 32BJ SEIU, press release, November 18, 2009, http://www.seiu32bj.org/au/PR_2009_1118.asp, accessed January 2012.

23 "Federal Grant to Expand Union's 'Green Supers' Program," 32BJ SEIU, press release, January 7, 2010, http://www.seiu32bj.org/au/PR_2010_0107.asp, accessed January 2012.

24 Ibid.

25 Nick Prigo, "Recovery Act Grants Help SEIU Grow Green Training Programs," SEIU, January 12, 2010, http://www.seiu.org/2010/01/recovery-act-grants-help-seiu-grow-green-training-programs.php, accessed December 2011.

26 Ibid.

27 "SEIU 721, Worker Education & Resource Center (WERC) Win $1.2 Million in Funding for Job Training," SEIU721, February 12, 2010, http://www.seiu721.org/2010/02/seiu-721-worker-education-resource-cente.php, accessed December 2011.

28 Daniel Stone, "What Green Jobs?" *Newsweek*, July 27, 2009, http://www.thedailybeast.com/newsweek/2009/07/27/what-green-jobs.html, accessed December 2011.

29 John M. Broder, "White House Official Resigns After G.O.P. Criticism," *New York Times*, September 6, 2009, http://www.nytimes.com/2009/09/07/us/politics/07vanjones.html, accessed April 2012; "Obama and the Left: The Lesson of the Rise and Fall of Van Jones," *Wall Street Journal*, Review and Outlook, September 8, 2009, http://online.wsj.com/article/SB10001424052970203440104574399452969175732.html, accessed April 2012.

30 "The Working for America Institute," WorkingforAmerica.org, http://www.workingforamerica.org/documents/waibrochure.htm, accessed December 2011.

31 Each of these grants is documented at www.recovery.gov.

32 "Crony Contacts: Want Federal Business? Better Be a Union Shop," *Wall Street Journal*, April 14, 2010, http://online.wsj.com/article/SB10001424052702

2303695604575182333308913608.html#articleTabs%3Darticle, accessed February 2012.

33 Executive Order 13,202, February 17, 2001.

34 Vince Vasquez, Dale Glaser, W. Erik Bruvold, "Measuring the Costs of Project Labor Agreements on School Construction in California," National University System Institute for Policy Research, July 2011; Paul Bachman, David Tuerck, "Project Labor Agreements and Public Construction Costs in NY State, Beacon Hill Institute at Suffolk University, April 2006; Paul Bachman, Jonathan Haughton, David G. Tuerck, "Project Labor Agreements and the Cost of Public School Construction in Connecticut," Beacon Hill Institute at Suffolk University, September 2004.

35 Rider, Levett, Bucknall, "Project Labor Agreements—Impact Study for the Department of Veteran Affairs," June 2009, p. 35, http://www.thetruth aboutplas.com/wp-content/uploads/2009/10/PLAs-Impact-Study-for-the -Department-of-Veterans-Affairs-Rider-Levett-Bucknall-060209.pdf, accessed May 2012; David G. Tuerck, Sarah Glassman, Paul Bachman, "Project Labor Agreements on Federal Construction Projects: A Costly Solution in Search of a Problem," Beacon Hill Institute at Suffolk University, August 2009.

36 Daniel Massey, "Ruling: Some WTC Workers Can't Strike," *Crain's New York Business*, August 3, 2011, http://www.crainsnewyork.com/article/20110803/ REAL_ESTATE/110809961, accessed January 2012. Joseph De Avila, "WTC Work Stoppage Continues for Third Day," *Wall Street Journal*, August 3, 2011. In addition to construction delays from work stoppages, some reports show that projects with Project Labor Agreements in place take longer to complete that non-PLA projects. "Annual Report to the Governor and Legislature, use of Project Labor Agreements in Public Works Building Projects in Fiscal Year 2008," New Jersey Department of Labor, October 2010 (concluding PLA projects have a longer duration than non-PLA projects).

37 To an audience of building and construction union members, President Obama stated, "I believe our economy is stronger when workers are getting paid good wages and good benefits...that's why we've reversed the ban on Project Labor Agreements. As long as I serve as your President, I'm going to keep it up." "Remarks of President Obama at Building and Construction Trades Department, AFL-CIO, April 30, 2012," http://www .dailykos.com/story/2012/04/30/1087528/-Remarks-of-President-Obama-at -Building-and-Construction-Trades-Department-AFL-CIO-April-30-2012, accessed May 2012.

38 Steven Greenhut, *Plunder!* (Santa Ana, Calif.: Forum Press, 2009), p. 73.

39 Michelle McNeil, "Education stimulus maintained jobs, didn't grow them," *Edmoney.org* (blog), January 28, 2011, http://edmoney.org/blog/2011/jan/28/ jobs/, accessed January 2012. Assuming that education workers pay an average of $600 a year in union dues, and that 75% of the jobs saved are union jobs (based on the percent of teachers that are unionized), then the stimulus preserves $165 million in teachers union dues annually. And the stimulus bill wasn't the end of channeling money to the teachers unions, of course. In August

2010, Obama pushed through a second stimulus bill, this time focused on education: the Keep Our Educators Working Act, which cost "only" $23 billion.

40 Alyson Klein, "States: Come Get Your EduJobs Money," *Education Week*, August 13, 2010, http://blogs.edweek.org/edweek/campaign-k-12/2010/08/edujobs_guidance_is_available.html, accessed January 2012.

41 Kyle Olson, "Will Third Teachers' Union Bailout Fund Obama's Re-Election?" BigGovernment.com, September 13, 2011, http://biggovernment.com/kolson/2011/09/13/will-third-teachers-union-bailout-fund-obamas-re-election/, accessed December 2011.

42 "Federal Grant Supports Union Initiative," *American Teacher*, October/November 2010, p. 2, http://www.aft.org/pdfs/americanteacher/at_octnov10.pdf, accessed December 2011.

43 Tamar Lewin, "Obama Wades into Issue of Raising Dropout Age," *New York Times*, January 25, 2012, http://www.nytimes.com/2012/01/26/education/obama-wades-into-issue-of-raising-dropout-age.html, accessed January 2012.

44 See "The High Cost of High School Dropouts: What the Nation Pays for Inadequate High Schools," Issue Brief, Alliance for Excellent Education, November 2011, http://www.all4ed.org/files/HighCost.pdf, accessed March 2012.

45 This calculation is based on the current student/school worker ratio of 1:8.

46 "NEA's 12-Point Action Plan for Reducing the School Dropout Rate," National Education Association, http://www.nea.org/home/18106.htm, accessed February 2012.

47 See Rennie Center for Education and Research Policy, "Raise the Age, Lower the Drop Out Rate? Considerations for Policy Makers," April 9, 2009, http://renniecenter.issuelab.org/research/listing/raise_the_age_lower_the_dropout_rate_considerations_for_policymakers, accessed February 2012; and "Raise the Bar, Not the Age," Spotlight no. 321, John Locke Foundation, May 31, 2007, http://www.johnlocke.org/acrobat/spotlights/spotlight_321-compulsiveed.pdf, accessed February 2012.

48 This two-step process of card collection, followed by secret-ballot election, is set forth in the National Labor Relations Act, 29 U.S.C. 159(c) (http://www.nlrb.gov/national-labor-relations-act). Currently, if over 50 percent of the employees in a bargaining unit sign a card requesting a union, the employer can voluntarily choose to waive the secret-ballot election process and recognize the union. The Employee Free Choice Act—the card check legislation—would replace the provision requiring a secret-ballot election with the following provision: "If the Board finds that a majority of the employees in a unit appropriate for bargaining has signed valid authorizations designating the individual or labor organization specified in the petition as their bargaining representative . . . the Board shall not direct an election but shall certify the individual or labor organization as the representative." Employee Free Choice Act of 2009, H.R. 1409, 111th Cong. (2009), http://www.govtrack.us/congress/bills/111/hr1409/text, accessed April 2012.

49 "Union-Controlled NLRB Approves Union Thuggery in Union Elections," RedState, March 13, 2011, http://www.redstate.com/laborunionreport/2011/

03/13/union-controlled-nlrb-approves-union-thuggery-in-union-elections/, accessed December 2011.

50 James Sherk, "Workers Reject Card Checks, Favor Private Ballots in Union Organizing," WebMemo #1363, Heritage Foundation, February 16, 2007, http://www.heritage.org/research/reports/2007/02/workers-reject-card -checks-favor-private-ballots-in-union-organizing, accessed December 2011.

51 Kris Maher, "President Tells Unions Organizing Act Will Pass," *Wall Street Journal*, March 4, 2009, http://online.wsj.com/article/SB123611995496723249 .html, accessed December 2011.

52 Sam Stein, "Obama's Remarks On Employee Free Choice Act Make Labor 'Very Pleased,'" *Huffington Post*, March 15, 2009, http://www.huffington post.com/2009/02/12/obamas-remarks-on-employe_n_166345.html, accessed December 2011.

53 Kyle Olson, "Wisconsin Unions Insurance Scam at Stake in Collective Bargaining Reform," BigGovernment.com, February 23, 2011, http://biggovernment .com/kolson/2011/02/23/wisconsin-unions-insurance-scam-at-stake-in -collective-bargaining-reform/, accessed January 2012.

54 Kimberley A. Strassel, "Union Power for Thee, But Not for Me," *Wall Street Journal*, February 25, 2011, http://online.wsj.com/article/SB100014240527487 03530504576164822561737348.html, accessed December 2011.

55 "SEIU: Building a New American Health Care System," http://www.seiu.org/ SEIUHCstory/SEIU%20healthcare%20reform%20booklet.pdf; Mandy Nagy, "SEIU: Building a New American Health Care Empire?" BigGovernment .com, November 16, 2009, http://biggovernment.com/libertychick/2009/ 11/16/seiu-building-a-new-american-health-care-empire/, accessed December 2011.

56 Don Loos, "21.1 Million Reasons Big Labor Pours Money into Obama-Care," BigGovernment.com, January 7, 2010, http://biggovernment.com/ dloos/2010/01/07/21-1-million-reasons-big-labor-pours-money-into -obamacare/, accessed December 2011.

57 SEIU, "The National Health Care Workforce Enhancement Initiative," December 9, 2008, http://otrans.3cdn.net/eaad856a6456eb4795_i2m6bxlyz .pdf, accessed April 2012. The memo represents proposed stimulus spending initiatives for health-care worker training prepared by the SEIU, and states, "$10 billion in federal funds will be available over two years through the economic stimulus package for use in the health care workforce development initiatives...Priority would be given to joint labor-management training and job placement initiatives, and consortiums involving nursing school, community colleges and worker organizations [i.e., labor unions]." The cover letter from SEIU health-care chair Dennis Rivera states, "We look forward to working closely with you to reform health care in 2009."

58 Don Loos, e-mail to the authors, March 15, 2012.

59 James Sherk, "Labor Unions on Health Care: Their True Motives," Heritage Foundation, September 8, 2009, http://www.heritage.org/research/ commentary/2009/09/labor-unions-on-health-care-their-true-motives, accessed January 2012.

60 Loos, "21.1 Million Reasons."

61 "SEIU: Building a New American Health Care System," booklet, Service Employees International Union, http://www.seiu.org/SEIUHCstory/SEIU %20healthcare%20reform%20booklet.pdf.

62 Mandy Nagy, "SEIU: Building a New American Health Care Empire?"

63 For a detailed discussion of Obamacare's treatment of Cadillac plans, see Jenny Gold, "Cadillac plans explained," *Kaiser Health News*, March 18, 2010, http://www.kaiserhealthnews.org/Stories/2010/March/18/Cadillac-Tax -Explainer-Update.aspx, accessed January 2012.

64 Michelle Malkin, "The Year in Obama Scandals—and Scandal Deniers," MichelleMalkin.com, December 28, 2011, http://michellemalkin.com/2011/ 12/28/the-year-in-obama-scandals-and-scandal-deniers/, accessed January 2012.

65 Dr. Milton R. Wolf, "Obamacare Waiver Corruption Must Stop," *Washington Times*, May 20, 2011, http://www.washingtontimes.com/news/2011/may/20/ obamacare-waiver-corruption-must-stop/, accessed December 2011.

66 "ObamaCare's Billions In Hidden Pork For Unions," *Investor's Business Daily*, November 3, 2011, http://news.investors.com/Article/590517/201111031841/ ObamaCares-Union-Slush-Fund.htm, accessed December 2011.

67 Ibid.

68 Jena Baker McNeill, "TSA Privatization Freeze: More Politics Than Security," WebMemo #3130, Heritage Foundation, February 2, 2011, http://www .heritage.org/research/reports/2011/02/tsa-privatization-freeze-more-politics -than-security, accessed January 2012.

69 "TSA Administrator: 'We Will Not Negotiate on Security,'" press release, Transportation Security Administration, February 4, 2011, http://www.tsa .gov/press/releases/2011/0204.shtm, accessed January 2012.

70 Rory Cooper, "Putting Politics over Security, Obama Moves to Unionize TSA," *The Foundry* (blog), Heritage Foundation, February 16, 2011, http://blog .heritage.org/2011/02/16/morning-bell-putting-politics-over-security-obama -moves-to-unionize-tsa/, accessed January 2012.

71 10 U.S. Code 976. See also 32 CFR 143—DOD Policy on Organizations that Seek to Represent or Organize Members of the Armed Forces in Negotiation or Collective Bargaining.

72 Department of Defense, Implementation Plan for Executive Order 13522— Creating Labor-Management Forums to Improve Delivery of Government Services, May 5, 2010, http://www.cpms.osd.mil/ASSETS/6ED1D73CD AE34512BB14A42C47847921/DOD_ImplementationPlan_EO13522.pdf, accessed May 2012.

73 Implementation Plan for Executive Order 13522, Department of Homeland Security, March 8, 2010, http://www.dhs.gov/xlibrary/assets/mgmt/mgmt _eo_implementation_plan_13522.pdf, accessed May 2012.

74 Ibid. Unionizing these national security workers "reduces the government's flexibility when defending the country," James Sherk writes. James Sherk, "Opportunity, Parity, Choice: A Labor Agenda for the 112th Congress," The Heritage Foundation Center for Data Analysis, Special Report #96, July 14,

2011, http://www.heritage.org/research/reports/2011/07/opportunity-parity -choice-a-labor-agenda-for-the-112th-congress#_ftnref82, accessed April 2012. See also "National ICE Council," http://www.iceunion.org/; "National Border Control Council," http://www.nbpc.net/.

75 See National Collective Bargaining Agreement Between U.S. Customs and Border Protection and National Treasury Union Employees, May 11, 2011, http://www.cbp.gov/linkhandler/cgov/careers/benefits_employees/bargaining _agreement.ctt/bargaining_agreement.pdf, accessed May 2012; Statement of Colleen M. Kelley, National President, National Treasury Employees Union, on Building One DHS: Why is Employee Morale Low?, Testimony before the House Homeland Security Committee, Subcommittee on Oversight, Investigations and Management, March 22, 2012.

76 "AFGE Certified as Exclusive Union at TSA," press release, AFGE, June 29, 2011, http://www.afge.org/Index.cfm?Page=PressReleases&PressReleaseID= 1296, accessed April 2012.

77 Federal employees also aren't compelled to join unions or forced to pay dues, but 1,185,000 federal employees were union members or were represented by a union in 2011. "Table 3. Union affiliation of employed wage and salary workers by occupation and industry, 2010-2011 annual averages," Bureau of Labor Statistics, http://www.bls.gov/news.release/union2.t03.htm, accessed April 2012.

78 Kimberley A. Strassel, "Union Power for Thee, But Not for Me."

79 Executive Order 13,522; "Memorandum for Heads of Executive Departments/Agencies and Labor Management Forums," Unites States Office of Personnel Management, January 19, 2011 http://www.fedsmith.com/articles/ records/file/2011/Pre_Decisional_2011.pdf, accessed May 2012.

80 The UAW was traditionally an industrial union, but it now represents both private employees and government workers.

81 Alex Kellogg and Kris Maher, "UAW to get 55% stake in Chrysler for concessions," *Wall Street Journal*, April 28, 2009, http://online.wsj.com/article/ SB124087751929461535.html, accessed March 2012.

82 Newt Gingrich, "Once, We Would Have Called It a Scandal," Human Events, June 10, 2009, http://www.humanevents.com/article.php?id=32212, accessed December 2011.

83 Ross Kaminsky, "Government Motors," Human Events, June 1, 2009, http:// www.humanevents.com/article.php?id=32085, accessed December 2011.

84 Ashby Jones, "Product Liability Winners Made Losers by Big Auto Bailouts," *Law Blog* (blog), *Wall Street Journal*, May 27, 2011, http://blogs.wsj.com/ law/2011/05/27/product-liability-winners-made-losers-by-big-auto-bailouts/, accessed December 2011.

85 Gingrich, "Once, We Would Have Called It a Scandal."

86 Trumka himself says, "Being called a Socialist is a step up for me." When Trumka ascended to head of the AFL-CIO, he immediately ended the long-standing prohibition on Communist Party members serving in its leadership. The Communist Party of America publically works closely with him, as does our White House. Matthew Vadum, "AFL-CIO's Richard Trumka Is a Thug's Thug," BigGovernment.com, November 3, 2011, http://biggovernment

.com/mvadum/2011/11/03/afl-cios-richard-trumka-is-a-thugs-thug/, accessed January 2012; Nice Deb, "According to AFL-CIO's Trumka, He and White House Are Pretty Darn Tight," NewsRealBlog, February 23, 2011, http://www .newsrealblog.com/2011/02/23/according-to-afl-cio%E2%80%99s-trumka -he-and-white-house-are-pretty-darn-tight/?utm_source=feedburner&utm _medium=feed&utm_campaign=Feed%3A+nrb-feature+%28NewsReal +Blog+%C2%BB+Feature%29, accessed January 2012.

87 Dana Milbank, "Wanted: More Bite from Obama the Great Nibbler," *Washington Post*, August 26, 2011, http://www.washingtonpost.com/opinions/ wanted-more-bite-from-obama-the-great-nibbler/2011/08/25/gIQAigGAgJ _story.html, accessed March 2012.

88 Matea Gold and Melanie Mason, "Unions Return to Democratic Fold for 2012 Election," *Los Angeles Times*, February 19, 2012, http://articles.latimes.com/2012/ feb/19/nation/la-na-labor-politics-20120220, accessed March 2012.

89 Jennifer Liberto, "Obama Council Repeats Job-Creating Ideas," *CNNMoney*, January 17, 2012, http://money.cnn.com/2012/01/17/news/economy/Obama _jobs_council/, accessed January 2012.

90 Michael Warren, "Immelt, Trumka to Join First Lady at Jobs Speech," *The Blog* (blog), *Weekly Standard*, September 8, 2011, http://www.weeklystandard .com/blogs/immelt-trumka-join-first-lady-jobs-speech_592909.html, accessed January 2012.

91 McQuillen, "AFL-CIO Drops Criticism to Endorse Obama."

92 Michael O'Brien and Kevin Bogardus, "AFL-CIO: Labor Will Stand by Obama," *The Hill*, August 18, 2011, http://thehill.com/homenews/campaign/ 177271-afl-cio-labor-will-stand-by-obama-, accessed December 2011.

93 Sam Hananel, "Unions Gearing Up to Spend Big in 2012 Elections," *Huffington Post*, February 22, 2012, http://www.huffingtonpost.com/2012/ 02/22/labor-unions-obama-elections-2012_n_1293173.html, accessed February 2012.

94 Stephen Sawchuck, "NEA's Delegates Approve Obama Endorsement, Dues Increase," *Teacher Beat* (blog), *Education Week*, July 4, 2011, http://blogs .edweek.org/edweek/teacherbeat/2011/07/neas_delegates_approve_obama_e .html, accessed December 2011.

95 Sixty percent of the assessment would fund the Ballot Measure/Legislative Crisis Fund. The other 40 percent would fund media for political campaigns.

96 Kyle Olson, "Will Third Teachers' Union Bailout Fund Obama's Re-Election?" BigGovernment.com, September 13, 2011, http://biggovernment.com/kolson/ 2011/09/13/will-third-teachers-union-bailout-fund-obamas-re-election/, accessed December 2011.

97 Kevin Liptak and Paul Courson, "Endorsing Obama, SEIU Says President for 99%," *Political Ticker* (blog), CNN, November 16, 2011, http://politicalticker .blogs.cnn.com/2011/11/16/endorsing-obama-seiu-says-president-for-99/, accessed April 2012.

98 Ed Barnes, "Obama Draws Fire For Appointing SEIU's Stern to Deficit Panel," *Fox News*, March 6, 2010, http://www.foxnews.com/politics/2010/03/05/ obama-draws-appointing-seius-stern-deficit-panel/, accessed January 2012.

99 Wallsten, "AFSCME Votes to Endorse Obama for Reelection."

100 Various bills have been introduced in Congress to repeal Section 14(b) of the National Labor Relations Act, but none have been successful—yet. See H.R. 6384 (111th Cong.). Section 14(b) states: "Nothing in this Act [subchapter] shall be construed as authorizing the execution or application of agreements requiring membership in a labor organization as a condition of employment in any State or Territory in which such execution or application is prohibited by State or Territorial law." The text is available at https://www.nlrb.gov/national-labor-relations-act.

101 Amanda Palleschi, "Expansion of Federal Collective Bargaining Considered," Government Executive, February 16, 2012, http://www.govexec.com/management/2012/02/expansion-collective-federal-bargaining-considered/41227/, accessed February 2012. It should be noted that President Clinton also mandated that federal agencies had to negotiate these same issues with unions, although Clinton's administration apparently failed to enforce this expansion. President George W. Bush then removed the mandate.

102. See 5 U.S.C. § 7106(b)(1).

Chapter 5. Schoolhouse Shadowbosses

1 Nathan Rabin, "*Waiting for Superman* Director Davis Guggenheim," A.V. Club, October 13, 2010, http://www.avclub.com/articles/waiting-for-superman-director-davis-guggenheim,46295/, accessed January 2012.

2 OECD, *Education at a Glance 2011: OECD Indicators*, table B1.1a, available at http://www.oecd.org/dataoecd/61/18/48630868.pdf.

3 Likewise, we spent in 2008 on secondary students—$12,087 per student. This is 41 percent more spending than Germany, 33 percent more than Japan, 53 percent more than Korea, and 28 percent more than the UK. *Education at a Glance 2011: OECD Indicators*, table B1.1a.

4 OECD, *PISA 2009 Results: Executive Summary*, figure 1, OECD, http://www.oecd.org/dataoecd/34/60/46619703.pdf, accessed December 2011. On the mathematics scale, the United States scored 487; the UK, 492; Germany, 513; Japan, 529; and Korea, 546. On the science scale, the United States scored 502; the UK, 514; Germany, 520; Japan, 539; and Korea, 538.

5 Richard Lee Colvin, "Can Obama Reverse the Dropout Crisis?" Special Report introduction, *Washington Monthly*, July/August 2010, pp. A2–A4.

6 Johanna Sorrentino, "'Waiting for Superman': What it Means for You and Your Child," Education.com, http://www.education.com/magazine/article/waiting-superman-means-parents/, accessed January 2012.

7 "Two Million K–12 Teachers Are Now Corralled into Unions," Fact Sheet, National Institute of Labor Relations Research, August 18, 2008, http://www.nilrr.org/files/How%20Many%20Teachers%20Fact%20Sheet.pdf, accessed December 2011. Terry Moe estimates that the two teachers unions make $2.7 billion a year. Terry M. Moe, *Special Interest: Teachers Unions and America's Public Schools* (Washington, D.C.: Brookings Institution Press, 2011), p. 280. Our own analysis confirms this approximate figure as follows: For 2011, the financial disclosure for the national NEA shows dues and agency fee income of $370,805,951. We know from unified dues examples and other

data that the ratio of NEA income to total dues income at NEA/state/local union level is about 25 percent, so we know that the total income for NEA and its state and local affiliates is approximately $1.48 billion. Similarly, for 2011, the financial disclosure for AFT shows dues and agency fee income of $148,388,677. We know from the unified dues examples that the ratio of national AFT dues income to total AFT/state/local union dues income is in the range of 27 to 32 percent. Accordingly, we can estimate that total AFT/state/local union dues collected are in the range of $458 to $535 million for 2011. Therefore, the total amount of dues collected by both teachers unions at the national, state, and local levels is between $1.9 to $2.0 billion for 2011. The teachers union makes income from other sources, as well, so their total income would be significantly higher.

We can also confirm the $2 billion total dues number by considering data for state affiliates and certain local affiliates of the National Education Association, available on the Education Intelligence Agency website: http://www.eiaonline.com. From this data, we learn that the NEA plus all its state affiliates took in $1.4 billion in dues income alone in the 2009–10 school year. Additionally, the top thirty-six local teachers unions took in over $337 million in dues in the same school year, for a total of $1.73 billion. To this amount, we would need to add all the other local affiliates of the NEA, plus all the national headquarters of the AFT, plus all its state and local affiliates, which would easily result in a total dues number of over $2 billion. See http://www.eiaonline.com/archives/20120312.htm, accessed April 2012.

8 Moe, *Special Interest*, pp. 54–55.

9 Orrin Hatch, "Putting Workers over Union Bosses," *Washington Times*, December 1, 2011, http://www.washingtontimes.com/news/2011/dec/1/putting-workers-over-union-bosses/, accessed February 2012.

10 Moe, *Special Interest*. Terry Moe's book provides an excellent in-depth treatment of the effect of teachers unions on America's public schools. Since the writing of his book, Wisconsin changed its laws so that teachers are not required to pay dues to a union, and so Wisconsin in now a C-grade state.

11 The New Haven, Connecticut, school district's contract with the teachers union provides in Article 3.A: "All teachers in the bargaining unit, as a condition of continued employment shall on the sixtieth (60th) day following the beginning of the school year, beginning of their employment or the execution of this Master Agreement, whichever is later:
1. Become members of the Association, or
2. Pay a service fee, which is equivalent to the amount of dues (including New Haven Education Association, Local 1 MEA and NEA dues) uniformally [*sic*] required of members of the Association." In other words, whether you join or not, you pay the same amount, although a later provision states that the teachers who decide to pay the service fee may file a written objection to the fee under certain conditions for spending of fees on political or ideological causes. See Master Agreement between the New Haven Schools Education Association MEA/NEA/LOCAL 1 and the New Haven Schools Board of Education, 2008–09, 2009–10,

2010–11, http://newhaven.misd.net/uploads/transparency/NHCS%20 Teachers%20Contract%202010-2011.pdf, accessed February 2012.

12 "Two Million K–12 Teachers Are Now Corralled into Unions." The original report found that the twenty-three states at that time with forced unionism (which included Wisconsin, but didn't include D.C. as a state) have less than 52 percent of the teachers but generate about 83 percent of all state and local dues collected by NEA and AFT affiliates. To update this analysis and account for changes in law, we used data from the Education Intelligence Agency on the dues collected by state- and local-level National Education Association affiliates for 2008. We also used data on teacher populations from Moe, p. 54, table 2-2. Our analysis generally confirmed the original report with some differences relating to regrading Wisconsin as a C state. We found that the twenty-two states and D.C. with forced unionism for teachers account for about 49 percent of the teachers but over 77 percent of the total NEA state- and local-level dues collected. Furthermore, the original report found that approximately 15 percent of America's teachers work in C-grade states, but approximately 8 percent of teachers union dues are collected in these states. We found that 17 percent of teachers work in C-grade states (with Wisconsin), and that over 12 percent of dues are collected in these states. Similarly, the earlier report found that teachers in the B-grade states represent approximately 11 percent of all teachers but contribute only 5 percent of the total teachers union dues collected in the United States, while our analysis found that the B states represent 11 percent of teachers and contribute 6 percent of dues. The earlier report also found that teachers in the A-grade states represent approximately 23 percent of public teachers nationwide, but contribute only 4 percent of all teachers union dues, whereas our analysis found that teachers in A states represent 23 percent of teachers, but contribute about 5 percent of dues income.

13 "Two Million K–12 Teachers Are Now Corralled into Unions." These figures show that the B states are on average more than twice as unionized as the A states.

14 Ibid.

15 The percentage of dues income collected in right-to-work states is estimated by analyzing the dues figures for state NEA organizations provided by Mike Antonucci's valuable Education Intelligence Agency website. See http:// www.eiaonline.com/NEAandStateAffiliateFinances2008-09.htm. The percentage of teachers working in right-to-work states is based on Moe, p. 54, table 2-2.

16 Randi Weingarten's exact statement was: "First, the states that actually have lots of teachers in teacher unions tend to be the states that have done the best in terms of academic success in this country. And the states that don't tend to be the worst." "'This Week' transcript: Crisis in the Classroom," ABC News, August 15, 2010, http://abcnews.go.com/ThisWeek/week-transcript-crisis -classroom/story?id=11506701&page=4, accessed May 2012. See also "Randi Weingarten says students in strong union states perform better academically," Politifact.com, September 2, 2010, http://www.politifact.com/truth-o-meter/ statements/2010/sep/02/randi-weingarten/randi-weingarten-says-students -strong-union-states/, accessed May 2012.

17 Kyle Wingfield, "Do Unionized Teachers Really Produce Better Results?" AJC, March 3, 2011, http://blogs.ajc.com/kyle-wingfield/2011/03/03/do-unionized-teachers-really-produce-better-results/, accessed January 2012.

18 Moe, pp. 207–213.

19 Liability insurance is also available to teachers who join the Association of American Education (AAE), the largest national nonunion professional teachers organization, for a fraction of the cost of union dues, but many teachers are not aware of this option.

20 Myron Lieberman, *The Teachers Unions* (New York: Simon & Schuster, 1997), pp. 75–76.

21 Moe explains the different work rules in states with and without collective bargaining in chapter 6 of his book *Special Interest*. Moe, p. 196.

22 "2011-12 Dues," Westport Education Association, http://westportea.org/contracts/salary/dues/, accessed February 2012. Similarly, full time teachers in Union Local 3037 of BOCES Educator of Eastern Suffolk, an AFT affiliate, making at least $30,000 a year pay a total of $738.78 in teacher union dues, broken up as follows: $211.58 to their local union, $322.00 to the state union, and $205.20 to the national AFT, for the 2011–12 school year. "NYSUT/AFT/LOCAL Dues Schedule for 2011-2012 membership year," *The Beacon*, BOCES Educators of Eastern Suffolk, Union Local 3037, http://www.beesbeacon.org/DuesScheduleTemplate%2010-11.pdf, accessed February 2012. Other examples can be found (as of February 2012) at: http://www.ntu1.com/teacher%2011-12%20dues.pdf; http://decaturea.org/pdf/1011dues.pdf; and elsewhere.

23 Charles Sykes, *Dumbing Down Our Kids* (New York: St. Martin's Press, 1995), p. 230.

24 Michael Barbera, "Teachers' Union Fierce Foe of School-Choice," *National Catholic Register*, Oct. 11, 1996.

25 E. J. McMahon, *Obama and America's Public Sector Plague* (New York: Encounter Books, 2010), p. 26.

26 Sykes, *Dumbing Down Our Kids*, p. 230.

27 Moe, p. 113.

28 Ibid.

29 Ibid., 138.

30 Lieberman, pp. 101-103.

31 Ibid.

32 "Teachers Unions Will Target Swing States in '04," *Washington Times*, June 30, 2003.

33 George Archibald, "NEA challenged on political outlays," *Washington Times*, April 7, 2003.

34 Phyllis Schlafly, "Who Is the Biggest Campaign Spender?" *Eagle Forum* (blog), September 3, 2010, http://blog.eagleforum.org/2010/09/who-is-biggest-campaign-spender.html, accessed March 2012.

35 Mike Antonucci, "The Long Reach of Teachers Unions," *EducationNext* 10, no. 4 (Fall 2010), http://educationnext.org/the-long-reach-of-teachers-unions/, accessed March 2012.

36 McKinsey & Company, "How the World's Best Performing School Systems Come Out on Top," September 2007, p. 12, http://mckinseyonsociety.com/downloads/reports/Education/Worlds_School_Systems_Final.pdf, accessed March 2012.

37 Eric A. Hanushek, "Valuing Teachers," *EducationNext* 11, no. 3 (Summer 2011), pp. 40–45, http://educationnext.org/valuing-teachers/, accessed December 2011.

38 Eric Hanushek, "Lifting Student Achievement by Weeding Out Harmful Teachers," personal blog, Hoover Institution, Stanford University, October 31, 2011, http://hanushek.stanford.edu/opinions/lifting-student-achievement-weeding-out-harmful-teachers, accessed March 2012. See also Eric A. Hanushek, "Teacher Deselection," in *Creating a New Teaching Profession*, ed. Dan Goldhaber and Jane Hannaway (Washington, D.C.: Urban Institute Press, 2009), pp. 165–180.

39 McKinsey & Company, p. 20.

40 Moe, p. 21.

41 See ibid., chapter 6.

42 Ibid., p. 180.

43 National Center for Educational Statistics, "Digest of Education Statistics 2010," Table 88, http://nces.ed.gov/programs/digest/d10/tables/dt10_088.asp?referrer=list, accessed April 2012; Andrew J. Coulson, "The Effects of Teachers Unions on American Education," *Cato Journal*, Winter 2010, pp. 160–61, http://www.cato.org/pubs/journal/cj30n1/cj30n1-8.pdf, accessed December 2011.

44 Ibid.

45 McKinsey & Company.

46 Ibid.

47 Karen Matthews, "New York Teachers Paid To Do Nothing: 700 Of Them," Associated Press, June 22, 2009, available at http://www.huffingtonpost.com/2009/06/22/new-york-teachers-paid-to_n_219336.html, accessed December 2011.

48 "Rubber Rooms Gone, But Idle NY Teachers Still Getting Salaries," *Eagle Forum*, February 2011, http://www.eagleforum.org/educate/2011/feb11/rubber-rooms.html, accessed December 2011.

49 Rachel Monahan, "Rubber-room teachers bounce back as city says most have returned to classroom," *Daily News*, March 12, 2011; Karen Matthews, "NYC Teachers To Leave Rubber Rooms," Associated Press, April 15, 2010.

50 Eric A. Hanushek, "Teacher Deselection," Leading Matters, Stanford University, May 2008, http://leadingmatters.stanford.edu/san_francisco/documents/Teacher_Deselection-Hanushek.pdf, accessed January 2012; *PISA 2009 Results: Executive Summary*, figure 1.

51 *PISA 2009 Results: Executive Summary*.

52 Rhee resigned as chancellor of the D.C. School District in 2010 and founded Students First, a non-profit organization that works to achieve meaningful improvements in public K–12 education. "Michelle Rhee, Founder and CEO

of Students First," Students First website, http://www.studentsfirst.org/pages/about-michelle-rhee, accessed May 2012.

53 Sam Dillon, "A School Chief Takes On Tenure, Stirring a Fight," *New York Times*, November 12, 2008, http://www.nytimes.com/2008/11/13/education/13tenure.html?pagewanted=print, accessed January 2012.

54 Jason Riley, "Weingarten for the Union Defense," *Wall Street Journal*, March 26, 2011, http://online.wsj.com/article/SB10001424052748704608504576208443882799456.html, accessed March 2012.

55 Evan Thomas, "School Yard Brawl," *Newsweek*, March 5, 2010, http://www.thedailybeast.com/newsweek/2010/03/05/schoolyard-brawl.html, accessed May 2012; Jason Riley, "Weingarten for the Union Defense."

56 "Timeline: The Winding Road toward DC Schools Deal," *Washington Post*, April 7, 2010, http://www.washingtonpost.com/wp-srv/special/metro/teachers-union-timeline/?tid=grpromo, accessed May 2012; Sam Dillon, "Former Foes Join Forces for Education Reform," *New York Times*, May 20, 2011, http://www.nytimes.com/2011/05/21/education/21rhee.html, accessed May 2012.

57 See Coulson, pp. 162–163.

58 "Union Blasts Jindal's Choice Proposal for Louisiana Students," *Education News*, January 28, 2012, http://www.educationnews.org/education-policy-and-politics/union-blasts-jindals-voucher-proposal-for-louisiana-students/, accessed January 2012.

59 Becket Adams, "Revealed: Michigan Union Manual Instructs Teachers on How to Use Children as 'Propaganda,'" *TheBlaze*, January 24, 2012, http://www.theblaze.com/stories/revealed-michigan-union-manual-instructing-teachers-on-how-to-use-children-as-propoganda/, accessed February 2012.

60 Ibid.

61 Coulson, p. 163, quoting James Cibulka, "The NEA and School Choice," in *Conflicting Missions? Teachers Unions and Educational Reform*, ed. Tom Loveless (Washington, D.C.: Brookings Institution Press, 2000).

62 Kyle Olson, *Indoctrination: How "Useful Idiots" Are Using Our Schools to Subvert American Exceptionalism* (Bloomington, Ill.: AuthorHouse, 2011), p. 97.

63 Nina L. Floro, "Beyond the Convention Hall and into the Classroom: Finding a Lesson at the 2009 CFT Convention," *Advocate*, May 2009, http://www.publicschoolspending.com/wp-content/uploads/2011/06/advo5-09.pdf, accessed March 2012; *Trouble in the Hen House: A Puppet Show*, California Federation of Teachers, http://www.cft.org/uploads/LIS/trouble%20in%20the%20hen%20house.pdf.

64 *Trouble in the Hen House: A Puppet Show.*

65 "Committee Curricula," California Federation of Teachers, http://www.cft.org/index.php/component/content/article/40-uncategorized/309-committee-curricula.html.

66 Olson, p. 160, citing Bob Bigelow and Bob Peterson, *Rethinking Globalization: Teaching for Justice in an Unjust World* (Wisconsin: Rethinking Schools Ltd., 2002).

67 Olson, p. 1.

68 Olson, p. 3.
69 Olson, p. 162. "Labor in the Schools Committee," California Federation of Teachers, http://www.cft.org/index.php/committees/105.html, accessed May 2012.
70 Howard Zinn, *Transforming Teachers Unions: Fighting for Better Schools and Social Justice* (Wisconsin: Rethinking Schools Ltd., 1999).
71 Patrick J. Finn and Mary E. Finn, eds., *Teacher Education with An Attitude* (Albany, N.Y.: State University of New York Press, 2007), p. 5.
72 Denise Konkol, "Muskego-Norway Says Thanks But No Thanks to NEA Grant for Activism," *MuskegoPatch*, October 27, 2011, http://muskego.patch .com/articles/muskego-norway-says-thanks-but-no-thanks-to-nea-grant-for -activism, accessed December 2011.
73 Phyllis Schlafly, "How Did We Get a Federal Curriculum?" *Eagle Forum*, February 13, 2002, http://www.eagleforum.org/column/2002/feb02/02-02-13 .shtml, accessed January 2012.
74 Jonathan M. Seidl, "Shocking Vid: Wis. HS Students Admit Teachers Bringing Them to Protests But Don't Know Why They're There," *TheBlaze*, February 16, 2011, http://www.theblaze.com/stories/shocking-vid-wis-hs-students -admit-teachers-bringing-them-to-protests-but-dont-know-why-theyre-there/, accessed December 2011.
75 Daniel Halper, "In Wisconsin, Teachers Take Students from Class to Protest," *The Blog* (blog), *Weekly Standard*, February 16, 2011, http:// www.weeklystandard.com/blogs/wisconsin-teachers-take-students-class -protest_550230.html, accessed December 2011.
76 Seidl, "Shocking Vid."
77 Sarah Palin, "Union Brothers and Sisters: Seize Opportunity to Show True Solidarity," Sarah Palin's Notes, Facebook, February 18, 2011, http://www .facebook.com/#!/notes/sarah-palin/union-brothers-and-sisters-seize -opportunity-to-show-true-solidarity/10150093967618435, accessed January 2012.
78 "Teachers, Students Protest Cuts to Education," Associated Press, May 13, 2011, available at http://losangeles.cbslocal.com/2011/05/13/teachers-students -protest-cuts-to-education/, accessed December 2011.
79 Katherine Mangu-Ward, "Teachers Unions versus Online Education," *Reason*, August–September 2010, http://reason.com/archives/2010/07/20/ teachers-unions-vs-online-educ/singlepage, accessed February 2012.
80 "CTYOnline Accelerated Math for Elementary Students," Johns Hopkins Center for Talented Youth, http://cty.jhu.edu/ctyonline/information/Elementary _Math_Courses.html.
81 Tamar Lewin, "M.I.T. Expands Its Free Online Courses," *New York Times*, December 19, 2011, http://www.nytimes.com/2011/12/19/education/mit -expands-free-online-courses-offering-certificates.html, accessed February 2012.
82 Stanford on iTunes U can be accessed at http://itunes.stanford.edu/index. html.

83 Mangu-Ward, "Teachers Unions versus Online Education." Several states like Oregon and Wisconsin have already severely capped online virtual charter schooling in their states.

84 "The Condition of Education: Homeschooled Students," National Center for Educational Statistics, April 2011, http://nces.ed.gov/programs/coe/indicator _hsc.asp, accessed December 2011.

85 Brian D. Ray, "Homeschool Population Report 2010: 2.04 Million Homeschooled Students in the United States in 2010," National Home Education Research Institute, http://www.nheri.org/HomeschoolPopulationReport2010 .pdf, accessed February 2012.

86 "The Condition of Education: Private School Enrollment," National Center for Educational Statistics, April 2011, http://nces.ed.gov/programs/coe/ indicator_pri.asp, accessed December 2011.

87 This assumes a 79 percent overall rate of unionization of these workers and dues of $600 to $1200 per worker. Moe, 54–55.

88 Michelle Malkin, "The EduJobs III Bailout," MichelleMalkin.com, October 19, 2011, http://michellemalkin.com/2011/10/19/the-edujobs-iii-bailout/, accessed January 2012.

Chapter 6. Shadowbosses Bankrupt Our States

1 Eileen Norcross, "Public-Sector Unionism: A Review," Working Paper no. 11-26, Mercatus Center, May 2011, http://mercatus.org/sites/default/files/ publication/WP1126-Public-Sector-Unionism.pdf.

2 Many states are looking for ways to declare bankruptcy and get protections against their debts, although current law does not permit it. Mary Williams Walsh, "A Path Is Sought for States to Escape Their Debt Burdens," *New York Times*, January 20, 2011, http://www.nytimes.com/2011/01/21/business/ economy/21bankruptcy.html?_r=1&scp=1&sq=state%20bankruptcy& st=cse, accessed February 2012.

3 Ibid.

4 Gregory White, "Here Are the 10 U.S. States Most Likely to Default," Money Game, *Business Insider*, July 16, 2010, http://www.businessinsider.com/here -are-the-11-us-states-most-likely-to-default-2010-7, accessed January 2012.

5 Tad DeHaven, "State Dependency on the Federal Government," *Cato @ Liberty* (blog), January 23, 2012, http://www.cato-at-liberty.org/state -dependency-on-the-federal-government/.

6 "Country Comparison: Public Debt," 2011 figures, The World Factbook, Central Intelligence Agency, https://www.cia.gov/library/publications/the -world-factbook/rankorder/2186rank.html, accessed February 2012.

7 Steve Forbes, "For Whom The Greek Bell Tolls," Forbes.com, July 18, 2011, http://www.forbes.com/forbes/2011/0718/opinions-steve-forbes-fact-comment -greek-bell-tolls.html, accessed January 2012.

8 Chris Edwards, "Public Sector Unions and the Rising Cost of Employee Compensation," *Cato Journal*, Winter 2010, pp. 87–115, http://www.cato.org/ pubs/journal/cj30n1/cj30n1-5.pdf, accessed February 2012.

9 As Eileen Norcross notes, "The parties at the negotiating table share similar goals and benefit from the expansion of public spending, and may do so in a manner that, in the short-run, obscures the full cost of the bill." Norcross, "Public-Sector Unionism: A Review," p. 22.

10 Edwards, "Public Sector Unions and the Rising Cost of Employee Compensation."

11 Arthur Laffer, "The States Are Leading a Pro-Growth Rebellion," *Wall Street Journal*, February 11, 2012, http://online.wsj.com/article/SB100014240529702 03711104577201391354733460.html, accessed April 2012.

12 Randall G. Holcombe and James D. Gwartney, "Unions, Economic Freedom and Growth," *Cato Journal*, Winter 2010, pp. 1–22, http://www.cato.org/pubs/journal/cj30n1/cj30n1-1.pdf, accessed February 2012.

13 Calculated from the national, state, and area employment, hours, and earnings databases on http://www.bls.gov—the U.S. Bureau of Labor Statistics (BLS) website.

14 Steven Malanga, "Yes, There's Bloat in NJ's Schools," *New York Post*, April 9, 2010, http://www.nypost.com/p/news/opinion/opedcolumnists/yes_there _bloat_in_nj_schools_ngZJRi9YViWlhzeHc4nmWP, accessed February 2012.

15 See http://unionstats.com—the Union Membership and Coverage Database, a website maintained by Drs. Barry Hirsch and David Macpherson.

16 This calculation is based on the national, state, and area employment, hours, and earnings databases on http://www.bls.gov—the U.S. Bureau of Labor Statistics (BLS) website.

17 Nicole Gelinas, "New York's Next Fiscal Crisis," *City Journal* (Manhattan Institute), Summer 2008, http://www.city-journal.org/printable.php?id= 2699.

18 Daniel DiSalvo, "The Trouble With Public Sector Unions," *National Affairs*, Fall 2010, http://www.nationalaffairs.com/publications/detail/the-trouble-with -public-sector-unions, accessed December 2011.

19 "A Tale of Two Counties," editorial, *Washington Post*, May 30, 2010, http://www.washingtonpost.com/wp-dyn/content/article/2010/05/29/ AR2010052903132.html, accessed February 2012.

20 "Public Employee State Law Monopoly Bargaining Chart," National Right to Work Committee (2011), on file with the authors.

21 "A Tale of Two Counties."

22 Union Membership and Earnings Database, maintained by labor economists Barry Hirsch and David Macpherson, http://www.unionstats.com. Workers covered by a union contract are workers whose collective bargaining rights have been assigned to a union. Not all of these workers would actually join the union, although in forced-dues states all of these workers will have to pay dues or fees to the union. See NRTW Committee Staff, "Top Union Boss Huffs and Puffs, But Cannot Blow the Facts Down," National Right to Work Committee, June 2010, http://www.nrtwc.org/top-union-boss-huffs-and-puffs-but -cannot-blow-the-facts-down/, accessed February 2012.

23 See the Union Membership and Earnings Database.

24 Right-to-work states provide workers with express right-to-work protections, but some other states don't provide their workers with these express protections but also don't allow forced-dues collection in practice either. Of the twenty-two Free states, eighteen are right-to-work states; Colorado, Kentucky, and Missouri don't allow forced-dues collection from government employees. New Mexico does allow forced-dues provisions under which workers are fired if they don't pay fees or dues to the union that represents them.

25 "Top Union Boss Huffs and Puffs, But Cannot Blow the Facts Down."

26 According to this report, the most likely to default states are: Wisconsin, Massachusetts, Ohio, Nevada, New Jersey, New York, Michigan, California, and Illinois. Gus Lubin, "The 10 States Most Likely to Default," Money Game, *Business Insider*, May 20, 2010, http://www.businessinsider.com/10-states-most-likely-to-default-2010-5, accessed February 2012. Despite its title, the web article listed only nine states, plus New York City, as the gravest default risks in the United States. The determination of which states are most likely to default was based on market data for the credit default swaps for the state, which relates to how much a party would have to pay to insure against a default by the state or locality.

27 "Top Union Boss Huffs and Puffs, But Cannot Blow the Facts Down."

28 However, one of the most-likely-to-default states was Nevada, a right-to-work state.

29 The number of private sector jobs fell in these nine states by about 4 percent over a ten-year period ending 2009; but over the same time period, state and local government jobs increased by 9 percent. Ibid.

30 For example, in the states that have less than 40 percent of government workers unionized, the median per capita state debt in 2007 was more than $2,200. Among states with "between 40 and 60 percent" of government workers unionized, the median debt was more than $3,600. David Freddoso, "Public Sector Unions and State Debt Go Hand in Hand," *Washington Examiner*, April 4, 2010, http://washingtonexaminer.com/blogs/beltway-confidential/public-sector-unions-and-state-debt-go-hand-hand, accessed February 2012.

31 See, for example, "How U.S. Land Use Restrictions Exacerbated the International Finance Crisis," Demographia, April 2008, http://www.demographia.com/db-overhang.pdf, accessed February 2012. Demographia is a website focusing on land-use policies. See also "Reforming Regulation to Reduce New York's Exorbitant Cost of Living," New Yorkers For Growth, http://www.newyorkersforgrowth.com/reforming-regulation.asp, accessed February 2012.

32 Mark Robyn and Gerald Prante, "State-Local Tax Burdens Fall in 2009 as Tax Revenues Shrink Faster Than Income," Special Report, Tax Foundation, February 23, 2011, http://www.taxfoundation.org/news/show/22320.html, accessed February 2012.

33 The Hon. Talmadge Heflin and Katy Hawkins, "Trends in State Government: State Government Spending," Policy Brief, Texas Public Policy Foundation, October 2010, http://www.texaspolicy.com/pdf/2010-10-PB05-StateSpendingTrends-th-kh.pdf, accessed February 2012.

34 Edwards, "Public Sector Unions and the Rising Cost of Employee Compensation."

35 Ibid.

36 Larry Kudlow, "Madison Madness," *National Review Online,* February 18, 2011, http://www.nationalreview.com/articles/260135/madison-madness-larry-kudlow, accessed January 2012.

37 Steven Malanga, "Unions vs. Taxpayers," *Wall Street Journal,* May 14, 2009, available at http://www.manhattan-institute.org/html/miarticle.htm?id=4544, accessed January 2012.

38 Giovanna Fabiano,"Traffic Duty, Overtime Boost Englewood Police Paychecks," *(Hackensack, N.J.) Record,* April 18, 2010, available at http://www.istockanalyst.com/article/viewiStockNews/articleid/4041340, accessed February 2012.

39 Luke Funk, "Audit: NJ Turnpike Wasted Millions on Perks," My Fox New York, October 19, 2010, http://www.myfoxny.com/dpp/traffic/traffic_news/audit-excessive-perks-for-nj-turnpike-employees-20101019-apx, accessed February 2012.

40 Nicole Gelinas, "MTA's Too-Nice Pay," *New York Post,* July 13, 2011, http://www.nypost.com/p/news/opinion/opedcolumnists/mta_too_nice_pay_yaOJpA4zHnVb6YRskNqB3K, accessed January 2012.

41 Frederic U. Dicker, "Andy Rocks the 'Bloat,'" *New York Post,* March 19, 2010, http://www.nypost.com/p/news/local/andy_rocks_the_bloat_pMD64QLibsykw6vhTXJHfO, accessed February 2012.

42 Ibid.

43 Once Cuomo took over as governor of New York, however, he seemed to become less concerned about union featherbedding. In 2011, he nixed an effort to end the Triborough Amendment, a New York law that allows inflated union contracts to be extended beyond their expiration dates. This amendment, which has been on the books in New York for many years, reduces the pressures on unions to give concessions in contract negotiations, because their contract can't lapse if a deal isn't reached. Jacob Gershman, "Triborough Labor Law Likely to Survive," *Wall Street Journal,* January 12, 2012, http://online.wsj.com/article/SB10001424052970204124204577155332171320006.html, accessed January 2012.

44 Herbert London, "New York Is the Ultimate Nanny State," Newsmax, July 2, 2010, http://www.newsmax.com/HerbertLondon/London-unions-public-dependence/2010/07/02/id/363709, accessed January 2012.

45 Jason Grotto, "Watchdog Update: Feds Probe Union Pension Deals," *Chicago Tribune,* December 8, 2011, http://www.chicagotribune.com/news/local/ct-met-union-pension-subpoena-20111208,0,7092967.story, accessed March 2012.

46 Ibid.

47 Ibid.

48 Ray Long and Jason Grotto, "2 Teachers Union Lobbyists Teach for a Day to Qualify for Hefty Pensions," *Chicago Tribune,* October 22, 2011, http://www.chicagotribune.com/news/local/ct-met-pensions-teacher-perk-20111023,0,7187206.story, accessed March 2012.

49 Ibid.

50 DiSalvo, "The Trouble With Public Sector Unions."

51 Mark Steyn, *After America: Get Ready for Armageddon* (Washington, D.C.: Regnery Publishing, 2011), p. 220.

52 Chris Rizo, "Calif. AG Candidate Takes Aim at Public Employee Pensions," LegalNewsline.com, February 8, 2010, http://legalnewsline.com/news/225451-calif.-ag-candidate-takes-aim-at-public-employee-pensions.

53 "The Widening Gap: The Great Recession's Impact on State Pension and Retiree Health Care Costs," Pew Center on the States, April 25, 2011, http://www.pewcenteronthestates.org/uploadedFiles/Pew_pensions_retiree_benefits.pdf, accessed February 2012.

54 Martin Z. Braun and Cristina Alesci, "NYC Actuary Said to Seek Lower Pension-Fund Rate of Return of 7% from 8%," Bloomberg, January 12, 2012, http://www.bloomberg.com/news/2012-01-11/nyc-actuary-said-to-seek-lower-pension-fund-rate-of-return-of-7-from-8-.html, accessed February 2012.

55 The report explains, "There are several reasons for the current crisis. Some states and local governments have lacked fiscal discipline, some have promised overly generous benefits, and many have failed to make the annual contributions necessary to maintain an actuarially sound pension plan. States have not been entirely at fault, as they had no control over the recent precipitous drop in interest rates or the volatile stock market. But regardless of the reason for the current pension crisis, the need for action can no longer be denied." Senate Finance Committee, "State and Local Government Defined Benefit Pension Plans: The Pension Debt Crisis that Threatens America," January 2012, http://finance.senate.gov/newsroom/ranking/release/?id=f9a92142-d190-4bca-a310-b43cb462eb45, accessed February 2012.

56 Edwards, "Public Sector Unions and the Rising Cost of Employee Compensation."

57 David Cho, "Growing Deficits Threaten Pensions," *Washington Post*, May 11, 2008, http://www.washingtonpost.com/wp-dyn/content/article/2008/05/10/AR2008051002883.html?hpid=topnews, accessed February 2012.

58 A 2009 CalPERS chart showing the life expectancies for California male and female police officers and firefighters at age fifty-five is reproduced on page 243 of Steven Greenhut, *Plunder!* (Santa Ana, Calif.: Forum Press, 2009).

59 David Crane, "California's $500-Billion Pension Time Bomb," *Los Angeles Times*, April 6, 2010, http://articles.latimes.com/2010/apr/06/opinion/la-oe-crane6-2010apr06.

60 "State & County QuickFacts: California," U.S. Census Bureau, http://quickfacts.census.gov/qfd/states/06000.html, accessed January 2012.

61 Jon Bruner, "Is your state a debt disaster?" Forbes.com, January 20, 2010, http://www.forbes.com/2010/01/20/states-debt-pensions-interactive-map.html, accessed February 2012.

62 See Bruner.

63 Senate Finance Committee, "State and Local Government Defined Benefit Pension Plans."

64 Ibid.

65 Tax charts are available on the Tax Foundation's website, http://www.taxfoundation.org/research/topic/9.html, accessed February 2012.

66 Bureau of Labor Statistics, "State and Area Employment, Hours, and Earnings," http://data.bls.gov/timeseries/SMS34000009000000001?data_tool= XGtable, accessed April 2012.

67 Cristobal Young, Charles Varner and Douglas S. Massey, "Trends in New Jersey Migration: Housing, Employment and Taxation," Policy Research Institute for the Region, September 2008.

68 Ibid.

69 "Statement by Governor Corzine Regarding the Princeton Migration Study," September 2008, http://www.politickernj.com/governors-press-office/23545/ statement-governor-corzine-regarding-princeton-migration-study, accessed May 2012.

70 The U.S. Treasury Department data cited here were obtained at http://www .mytaxburden.org—the Tax Foundation's State to State Migration database.

71 Shannon Muller, "Leaving New Jersey," *Asbury Park Press*, October 2, 2009, http://www.app.com/article/20091002/NEWS/310020001/Leaving-New-Jersey, accessed February 2012.

72 See "Domestic Net Migration in the United States: 2000 to 2004," table 2, U.S. Census Bureau, April 2006; and "Cumulative Estimates of the Components of Resident Population Change for the United States, Regions, States, and Puerto Rico: April 1, 2000 to July 1, 2009," U.S. Census Bureau, December 2009.

73 "Estimates of the Components of Resident Population Change for the United States, Regions, States, and Puerto Rico: July 1, 2008 to July 1, 2009."

74 Joel Kotkin, "The Golden State's War on Itself," *City Journal* (Manhattan Institute), Summer 2010, http://www.city-journal.org/2010/20_3_california -economy.html, accessed February 2012.

75 See Joseph Vranich's six-part entry for December 6, 2010, at Business Relocatiun Coach, beginning at http://thebusinessrelocationcoach.blogspot.com/ 2010_12_01_archive.html; "California Business Exodus Now Triple Last Year's Rate," *Fox & Hounds Daily*, September 21, 2010, http://www.foxand houndsdaily.com/2010/09/7861-california-business-exodus-now-triple-last -years-rate/, accessed February 2012.

76 "State to State Migration Data," Tax Foundation, http://interactive.taxfounda tion.org/migration/, accessed February 2012.

77 The calculations were made by considering "net migration" for California and North Carolina for the period 1999 to 2009, using the Tax Foundation's State to State Migration calculator, http://interactive.taxfoundation.org/migration/.

78 Laura Ingraham, "The Public Employee Union War against the States," Laura Ingraham's Notes, Facebook, January 4, 2011, http://www.facebook.com/note .php?note_id=482319946394&id=271042954725, accessed January 2012.

79 Michelle Caruso-Cabrera, *You Know I'm Right: More Prosperity, Less Government* (New York: Simon and Schuster, 2010), p. 69.

Chapter 7. Corruption and Conspiracy

1 Joseph A. Loftus, "Meany is Shocked by Racket's Scope," *New York Times*, November 2, 1957, p. 1.

2 Carl F. Horowitz, *Union Corruption in America: Still a Growth Industry*, (Springfield, Va.: National Institute for Labor Relations Research, 2004), http://www.nilrr.org/files/Horowitz.pdf, accessed January 2012.

3 "FBI investigating former SEIU leader Andy Stern," *CBS News*, September 28, 2010, http://www.cbsnews.com/stories/2010/09/28/national/main6907828 .shtml, accessed January 2012; Kris Maher and Evan Perez, "SEIU Probed Over Consulting Pacts," *Wall Street Journal*, September 28, 2010.

4 "About the National Commission on Fiscal Responsibility and Reform," FiscalCommission.gov, http://www.fiscalcommission.gov/about; "Andrew L. Stern," Columbia Business School Directory, http://www4.gsb.columbia.edu/ cbs-directory/detail/7515985/Andrew+Stern.

5 See In the Matter of the Construction & General Laborers' District Council of Chicago & Vicinity Laborers' International Union of North America Independent Hearing Officer, Docket No. 97-30T, February 7, 1998, Order and Memorandum, http://www.ipsn.org/laborers/chicago_district_council/t97-30 .htm, accessed May 2012. John O'Brien, "Corruption Charges Spur Union Council's Takeover," *Chicago Tribune*, February 11, 1998, http://articles .chicagotribune.com/1998-02-11/news/9802110221_1_mob-influence-union -hearing-officer-international-union, accessed January 2012.

6 105 Cong. Rec. 1,727 (1959) (statement of James P. Mitchell, Secretary of Labor, Feb. 4, 1959, before Subcommittee on Labor, Senate Committee on Labor & Public Welfare).

7 "Fighting Union Corruption: The Landrum-Griffin Act," McGraw-Hill Answers.com, http://www.mcgraw-hillanswers.com/fighting-union-corruption -landrum-griffin-act, accessed January 2012. See also "Union Members Bill of Rights," UnionFacts.com, http://www.unionfacts.com/crime-and-corruption/ union-members-bill-of-rights/.

8 "Disclosure and Deterrence," UnionFacts.com, http://www.unionfacts.com/ crime-and-corruption/disclosure-and-deterrence/, accessed February 2012.

9 "Death by 23,000 Cuts and the Failure of Self-Governance," UnionFacts.com, http://www.unionfacts.com/crime-and-corruption/death-by-23000-cuts-and -the-failure-of-self-governance/, accessed February 2012.

10 James B. Jacobs and Dimitri D. Portnoi, "Combating Organized Crime with Union Democracy: A Case Study of the Election Reform in United States v. International Brotherhood of Teamsters," *Loyola of Los Angeles Law Review* 42, no. 2 (Winter 2009), pp. 335–425, http://digitalcommons.lmu.edu/llr/ vol42/iss2/2, accessed February 2012.

11 Steven Greenhouse, "Behind Turmoil For Teamsters, Rush for Cash," *New York Times*, September 21, 1997, http://www.nytimes.com/1997/09/21/us/ behind-turmoil-for-teamsters-rush-for-cash.html?pagewanted=all&src=pm, accessed February 2012.

12 Ibid.

13 United States v. International Brotherhood of Teamsters, 998 F.Supp. 759 (S.D.N.Y. 1997); http://www.leagle.com/xmlResult.aspx?page=7&xmldoc= 19971747988FSupp759_11679.xml&docbase=CSLWAR2-1986-2006& SizeDisp=7, accessed May 2012, affirmed, 156 F.3rd 354 (Second Cir.

1998); Decision of Kenneth Conboy to Disqualify IBT President Ron Carey, (S.D.N.Y. 1997), http://www.ipsn.org/teamsters/carey_decision.htm, accessed May 2012; Steven Greenhouse, "An Overseer Bars Teamster Leader from Re-election," *New York Times*, November 15, 1997, http://www.nytimes .com/1997/11/18/us/an-overseer-bars-teamster-leader-from-re-election.html ?pagewanted=all&src=pm, accessed February 2012.

14 Decision of Teamsters Election Officer Kenneth Conboy to Disqualify Int'l Brotherhood of Teamsters President Ron Carey, p. 11.

15 Brody Mullins and Kris Maher, "Obama Says Teamsters Need Less Oversight," *Wall Street Journal*, May 5, 2008, http://online.wsj.com/article/ SB120994756511766395.html, accessed May 2012.

16 "How to Get an Honest Union Election," Association for Union Democracy, September 2004, http://www.uniondemocracy.org/Legal/honestel.htm, accessed January 2012.

17 Steven Greenhouse, "Ex-officials of City Union Convicted of Rigging Vote," *New York Times*, July 26, 2000, http://www.nytimes.com/2000/07/26/nyregion/ ex-officials-of-city-union-convicted-of-rigging-vote.html?ref=albertadiop, accessed May 2012; Ken Boehm, "The Scandals of AFSCME District Council 37," part 1, Labor Watch, Capital Research Center, September 2002, pp. 1–7.

18 Steven Greenhouse, "Trustee Ends his Oversight of District 37; Chief Chosen," *New York Times*, February 27, 2002, http://www.nytimes.com/2002/02/27/ nyregion/trustee-ends-his-oversight-of-district-37-chief-chosen.html, accessed May 2012.

19 Kevin Killeen, "Possible Fraud Invalidates St. Louis Police Union Election," CBS St. Louis, September 30, 2011, http://stlouis.cbslocal.com/2011/09/30/ possible-fraud-invalidates-st-louis-police-union-election/, accessed January 2012.

20 "Second Election Yields Same Winner for St. Louis Police Officers Association Presidency," *St. Louis Today*, October 26, 2011, http://www .stltoday.com/news/local/crime-and-courts/article_64c9e9ec-0018-11e1 -9a70-0019bb30f31a.html, accessed January 2012.

21 "As Workers Celebrate May Day, Union Officials Attempt to Steal Internal Leadership Election," Occupy UCI! May 1, 2011, http://occupyuci.wordpress .com/2011/05/01/as-workers-celebrate-may-day-union-officials-attempt-to -steal-internal-leadership-election/, accessed January 2012. See also "Elected Officers," uaw2865.org, http://www.uaw2865.org/?page_id=82, accessed January 2012.

22 U.S. Department of Labor, Office of Labor-Management Standards (OLMS), "Civil Enforcement Actions 2011," http://www.dol.gov/olms/regs/compliance/ civil_actions_2011.htm, accessed January 2012.

23 Anna Phillips, "Teachers Union Elections: Who Votes and Who Cares," GothamSchools, March 25, 2010, http://gothamschools.org/2010/03/25/ teachers-union-elections-who-votes-and-who-cares/, accessed January 2012.

24 Anna Phillips, "As Ballots Come In, a Look at the Teachers Union Elections," GothamSchools, March 25, 2010, http://gothamschools.org/2010/03/25/as

-ballots-come-in-a-look-at-the-teachers-union-elections/, accessed January 2012.

25 Elaine L. Chao, "Obama Tries to Stop Union Disclosure," *Wall Street Journal*, May 6, 2009, http://online.wsj.com/article/SB124157604375290453.html, accessed January 2012.

26 A monthly report of certain union embezzlement cases can be found at LaborUnionReport.com, http://www.laborunionreport.com/portal/tag/union-embezzlement/, accessed April 2012.

27 Russ Buettner, "Union's Money Fueled Lavish Lifestyle, Prosecutors Say," *New York Times*, January 4, 2010, http://www.nytimes.com/2010/01/04/nyregion/04sandhog.html?pagewanted=all, accessed February 2012.

28 Carl Horowitz, "Benefits Manager for NYC Sandhogs Pleads Guilty," National Legal and Policy Center, November 4, 2011, http://nlpc.org/stories/2011/11/04/benefits-manager-nyc-sandhogs-union-pleads-guilty, accessed February 2012.

29 "Your Rights & FAQ," UnionFacts.com, http://www.unionfacts.com/ article/union-member-resources/your-rights-faq/, accessed January 2012.

30 Ibid. See also "What rights are guaranteed to me as a union member under the Bill of Rights for members of labor organizations?" Frequently Asked Questions, U.S. Department of Labor, Office of Labor-Management Standards (OLMS), http://www.dol.gov/olms/regs/compliance/LMRDAQandA.htm, accessed February 2012. According to the Department of Labor, the Landrum-Griffin's "Bill of Rights guarantees members a voice in setting the union's rates of dues, fees, and assessments." The Act covers all unions that represent some private sector workers. The Civil Service Reform Act provides a similar bill of rights for federal employees. However, unions representing only state, county, and municipal workers are not bound by this law, and their members are not protected by a bill of rights. Individual states could change this by passing their own state-level laws based on Landrum-Griffin that would not only provide for a bill of rights for union members but would also require financial disclosure for state and municipal workers unions, not currently required under federal law.

31 Representative Darrell Issa, "Follow the Money: ACORN, SEIU and their Political Allies," U.S. House of Representatives, 111th Congress Committee on Oversight and Government Reform, February 18, 2010, Appendices, http://oversight.house.gov/wp-content/uploads/2012/02/20100218followthem oneyacornseiuandtheirpoliticalallies.pdf, accessed January 2012.

32 The Issa report quoted SEIU insiders, who explained, "Wade Rathke was a Board Member of SEIU. Madeleine Talbott and her husband Keith Kelleher served on the boards of both SEIU and ACORN. Zach Polett is the chief of political operations at ACORN. The ACORN Office in St. Louis, Missouri is owned by SEIU 880 and ACORN Housing. Jeff Ordower, the Missouri head organizer for ACORN, works in the SEIU building in St. Louis. Ordower, who works at the SEIU offices, is the field operations director for ACORN." Ibid., pp. 23–24.

33 Adam Schaeffer, "NEA Dues and ACORN," *Cato @ Liberty* (blog), September 15, 2009, http://www.cato-at-liberty.org/nea-dues-and-acorn/, accessed March 2012.

34 "AFSCME Official Admits to Embezzling $180,000 Intended for ACORN Affiliate," *LaborUnionReport* (blog), RedState, June 26, 2010, http://www.redstate.com/laborunionreport/2010/06/26/afscme-official-admits-embezzling-180000-intended-for-acorn-affiliate/, accessed March 2012.

35 "Obama and Acorn," *Wall Street Journal*, October 14, 2008, http://online.wsj.com/article/SB122394051071230749.html, accessed March 2012.

36 John Fund, "An Acorn Whistle-Blower Testifies in Court," *Wall Street Journal*, October 30, 2008, http://online.wsj.com/article/SB122533169940482893.html, accessed April 2012.

37 Issa, "Follow the Money."

38 Ibid., p. 4.

39 Ibid.

40 John Fund, *Stealing Elections* (New York: Encounter Books, 2008), p. 60.

41 "Reid Blocks ACORN Probe," editorial, *Las Vegas-Review Journal*, September 25, 2009 http://www.lvrj.com/opinion/reid-blocks-acorn-probe-61438132.html, accessed January 2012.

42 Ibid.

43 Matthew Vadum, "ACORN Fined Maximum in Nevada Vote Fraud Scheme," *American Spectator*, August 10, 2011, http://spectator.org/blog/2011/08/10/acorn-fined-maximum-in-nevada, accessed January 2012.

44 Ibid.

45 "Reid Blocks ACORN Probe."

46 Matthew Vadum, "New ACORN Groups Join SEIU's Economic Terrorism Campaign," *American Spectator*, July 25, 2011, http://spectator.org/blog/2011/07/25/breaking-new-acorn-groups-join, accessed February 2012.

47 "What is Union Democracy?" Association for Union Democracy, http://www.uniondemocracy.org/Home/whatitis.htm, accessed February 2012.

48 James Sherk, "Labor Department Rolls Back Transparency for Unions," *The Foundry* (blog), Heritage Foundation, October 31, 2011, http://blog.heritage.org/2011/10/31/labor-department-rolls-back-transparency-for-unions/, accessed February 2012.

49 Ibid.

50 Chao, "Obama Tries to Stop Union Disclosure."

Chapter 8. Shadowboss Battle Plan

1 Care workers who are paid by their clients out of funds from government subsidy programs have been unionized, but so have care workers in some states like Washington and New York who are regular care providers under state law but who are not paid out of government subsidies. *Getting Organized: Unionizing Home-Based Child Care Providers—2010 Update* (Washington, D.C.: National Women's Law Center, 2010), p. 9, http://www.nwlc.org/sites/default/files/pdfs/gettingorganizedupdate2010.pdf.

2 Bradford Plumer, "Love's Labor Lost," *New Republic*, April 23, 2008, http://www.tnr.com/article/environment-energy/labors-love-lost, accessed January 2012.

3 Ibid.

4 Matthew Kaminisky, "Let's Share the Wealth: Weekend Interview with Andy Stern," *Wall Street Journal*, December 6, 2008, http://online.wsj.com/article/SB122852244367484311.html, accessed January 2012.

5 Steve Early, "Wither Change to Win?" October 10, 2011, *In These Times*, http://www.inthesetimes.com/working/entry/12074/whither_change_to_win/, accessed January 2012. Early coined the term "Ivy League Amigos" in his book *The Civil Wars in U.S. Labor* (New York: Haymarket Books, 2011).

6 Plumer, "Love's Labor Lost."

7 Ibid.

8 For an interesting discussion of the AFL-CIO anti-raiding policy and current skirmishes, see Steve Early, "The Situational Ethics of Union 'Raiding,'" *Talking Union* (blog), September 19, 2009, http://talkingunion.wordpress.com/2009/09/19/the-situational-ethics-of-union-%E2%80%98raiding%E2%80%99/, accessed March 2012.

9 "About Us", Change to Win, http://www.changetowin.org/about, accessed January 2012.

10 An advocacy group that favors unionization of home child-care providers explains that these workers are "not in traditional employer-employee relationships." The report explains that "home-based providers are not covered by existing labor laws, and unions have had to advocate for new laws to organize these providers." "Home-Based Child Care Providers Finding Strength in Unions," press release, National Women's Law Center, March 6, 2007, http://www.nwlc.org/press-release/home-based-child-care-providers-finding-strength-unions, accessed January 2012.

11 Jonathan Walters, "Solidarity Forgotten," Governing the States and Localities, June 2006, http://www.governing.com/topics/health-human-services/Solidarity-Forgotten.html, accessed January 2012.

12 "Building a Union of Family Child Care and FFN Providers," webinar presentation, National Women's Law Center, http://www.nwlc.org/sites/default/files/pdfs/Oct4WebinarPresentation.pdf, accessed January 2012.

13 *Getting Organized: Unionizing Home-Based Child Care Providers—2010 Update.*

14 Organizing the unorganizable has brought the SEIU and other unions enormous, record-setting increases in membership. In 1999, the SEIU won the right to represent 74,000 home-care workers in California. This was the largest increase in membership won in a single election since 1941. When it brought 49,000 home child-care providers in Illinois into the union in 2005, this represented the second largest membership election since 1941. Peggie R. Smith, "The Publicization of Home-Based Care Work in State Labor Law," *Minnesota Law Review* 92, no. 5 (May 2008), pp. 1390–1423.

15 See Harris v. Quinn, No. 10-3835 (7th Cir. September 1, 2011), http://law.justia.com/cases/federal/appellate-courts/ca7/10-3835/10-3835-2011-09-01

-opinion-2011-09-01.html, accessed April 2012. The counsel for the plaintiffs is William Messenger, a staff attorney for the National Right to Work Legal Defense Foundation.

16 Robert Fitch, *Solidarity for Sale: How Corruption Destroyed the Labor Movement and Undermined America's Promise* (New York: Perseus Books Group, 2006), p. 307.

17 Executive Order 2003-08.

18 In Executive Order 2003-08, Governor Blagojevich set up a legal mechanism that would allow state officials to bargain with the union as if the state were the employer of the personal assistants. This same executive order stated that personal assistants "are not state employees," and that the disabled people who participate in the Rehabilitation Program "control their hiring, in-home supervision, and termination," but the order permitted them to be unionized anyway.

19 William Messenger, attorney for the plaintiffs in Harris v. Quinn, interview with the authors, October 7, 2010.

20 Andy Stern, *A Country That Works: Getting America Back on Track*, paperback ed. (New York: Simon and Schuster, 2006), p. 93.

21 As is true generally when unions are given collective bargaining power over a group of workers in a bargaining unit, the workers did not have to actually join the union. But they were required to either join the union and pay dues, or decline to join the union but pay similar agency fees, as a condition of their employment.

22 *The Rush Limbaugh Show*, Premiere Radio Networks, November 11, 2011.

23 Plaintiffs' brief in Harris v. Quinn. Trevor Burrus, "When Your Representatives Choose Representatives For You," *Cato @ Liberty* (blog), February 29, 2012, http://www.cato-at-liberty.org/when-your-representatives-choose-representatives-for-you/, accessed May 2012.

24 As of March 2012, mandatory union representation and mandatory dues or fees for child- and/or health-care providers are currently authorized or imposed by the state executive in eleven states: California, Illinois, Maine, Maryland, Massachusetts, Michigan, Missouri, New Mexico, New York, Oregon, and Washington. Two right-to-work states, Iowa and Kansas, authorized mandatory representation but did not force providers to pay union dues or fees. Additionally, several counties in Minnesota also have unionized care providers, for a total of fourteen states that have forced unionization of care providers.

25 Fitch, *Solidarity for Sale*, pp. 310–311. In 1998, the Los Angeles County Board of Supervisors, acting at SEIU lobbyists' behest, voted to create a so-called Personal Assistance Services Council (PASC). This was one of those public authorities set up to be the employer of record for the personal assistants and to provide the local union with an identifiable bargaining partner.

26 Michael White, "L.A. Health Workers Vote on Unions," Associated Press, February 26, 1999.

27 Ed White, "Michigan Child-Care Workers Suing to Break Free of UAW Union," *Washington Post*, November 11, 2010, http://www.washingtonpost

.com/wp-dyn/content/article/2010/09/13/AR2010091300088.html, accessed April 2012.

28 Ibid.

29 *Varney and Company,* Fox Business Network, September 20, 2010.

30 Ibid.

31 The settlement with the state of Michigan ensures that the state cannot force home-care workers to financially support a union as a condition of receiving state assistance. "Homecare Providers Win Settlement with State to Permanently Stop Childcare Unionization Scheme," press release, National Right to Work Legal Defense Foundation, http://www.nrtw.org/en/press/2011/05/homecare-providers-win-settlement-st.

32 Eileen Boris and Jennifer Klein, "Organizing Homecare: Low Wage Workers in the Welfare State," *Politics and Society* 34, no. 1 (March 2006), p. 83.

33 Smith, "The Publicization of Home-Based Care Work in State Labor Law."

34 In her testimony to the House Committee on Oversight and Government Reform, Sally Coomer explained how she was forced into a union in Washington State for being a Medicaid care provider to her disabled daughter Becky. Pursuant to an SEIU-supported initiative, she is now her daughter's employee. She explained that while her daughter is considered her employer, "the Governor of the State of Washington is deemed the employer for bargaining purposes only"—in other words, she and other care providers are treated as "government employees" so that they can be forcibly unionized, but they aren't given any of the benefits of government employment. Finally, she noted that not only did care providers have to pay union dues, but the new system meant that the parent providers "were no longer able to contribute to the social security system per IRS tax law..."

Sally explains that she really has no other option than to comply and join the union: "Some may argue that if you don't want to be a union member, then don't be a provider for your own daughter... Thousands of parents and family members are forced to be union members, just for the privilege of taking care of a love one." (We might note here that Sally describes herself as being forced to be a union member, although more correctly, she was forced either to join the union or pay agency fees for representation.) House Committee on Oversight and Government Reform, "The Right to Choose: Protecting Union Workers from Forced Political Contributions," testimony of Sally Coomer, February 8, 2012, http://oversight.house.gov/index.php?option=com_content&view=article&id=1583%3A2-8-2012-qthe-right-to-choose-protecting-union-workers-from-forced-political-contributionsq&catid=12&Itemid=20, accessed February 2012.

35 With this new model, providers would generally be state employees for the limited purpose of collective bargaining.

36 Boris and Klein, p. 93. In some states like California, public authorities were established on a county or district basis, while other states like Oregon established one public authority for the entire state.

37 "Andy Stern's Go-To Guy," *Wall Street Journal*, May 14, 2009, http://online.wsj.com/article/SB124226652880418035.html, accessed February 2012.

38 Wade Rathke, "Becker to the NLRB," *Wade Rathke: Chief Organizer Blog* (blog), April 20, 2009, http://chieforganizer.org/2009/04/30/becker-to-the-nlrb/, accessed January 2012.

39 Ryan O'Donnell, "Craig Becker: Big Labor's Big Ally," *The Foundry* (blog), Heritage Organization, March 26, 2010, http://blog.heritage.org/2010/03/26/craig-becker-big-labor%E2%80%99s-big-ally/, accessed January 2012.

40 Ibid.

41 Matthew Boyle, "Obama Yanks Controversial Pro-Union Appointee from Labor Board," *Daily Caller*, December 15, 2011, http://dailycaller.com/2011/12/15/obama-yanks-controversial-pro-union-appointee-from-labor-board/, accessed January 2012.

42 Becker was the key pro-union member of the NLRB in the Boeing matter, even though some claim he had a financial conflict of interest. W. James Antle III, "Craig Becker and Boeing," *American Spectator*, October 2, 2011, http://spectator.org/archives/2011/10/03/craig-becker-and-boeing, accessed January 2012.

43 Rathke, "Becker to the NLRB."

44 "The Right to Choose: Protecting Union Workers from Forced Political Contributions," testimony of Sally Coomer.

45 *Getting Organized*, p. 10.

46 An executive order in the State of Minnesota took away the rights of providers to vote in a union election even more overtly. The order called for an election to unionize home child-care providers. Providers who were regulated by the state but didn't receive subsidies could be unionized in the election but weren't permitted to vote. Because of publicity surrounding the Minnesota case, the election was put on hold, and its procedures are being challenged in federal court. Rep. Joe Hoppe, "Child Care Union Vote Anything But 'Most Fair,'" *Fergus Falls Journal*, November 28, 2011, http://www.fergusfallsjournal.com/2011/11/28/child-care-union-vote-anything-but-%E2%80%98most-fair%E2%80%99/, accessed December 2011.

47 "Public Sector Decertification Laws (as of 8/2010)," National Right to Work Legal Defense Foundation, http://www.nrtw.org/public-sector-decertification-laws-8-1-2010. Generally, employees would have to file a petition with the state with the support of at least 30 percent of the employees stating that the union is no longer supported by a majority of the workers. Then, the state will hold another election to determine whether the union should be decertified. Often there are narrow time periods during which decertification petitions may be filed.

48 Tom Gantert, "Union Lawyer Admits in Court That Stealth Unionization Is a 'Slippery Slope,'" *Michigan Capitol Confidential* (blog), Mackinac Center For Public Policy, July 14, 2010, http://www.michigancapitolconfidential.com/13177.

49 Ibid.

50 Don Loos, "21.1 Million Reasons Big Labor Pours Money into Obama-Care," BigGovernment.com, January 7, 2010, http://biggovernment.com/dloos/2010/01/07/21-1-million-reasons-big-labor-pours-money-into-obamacare/, accessed December 2011.

51 Caralyn Davis, "Union Membership Grows among Healthcare Workers," FierceHealthcare, http://www.fiercehealthcare.com/story/union-membership-grows-among-healthcare-workers/2010-02-22, accessed March 2012.

52 William Messinger, "Does the First Amendment Allow States to Compel Recipients of Government Monies to Support State-Designated Representatives?" *Engage* 11, no. 2 (September 2010), pp. 88–91, available at http://www.fed-soc.org/publications/detail/does-the-first-amendment-allow-states-to-compel-recipients-of-government-monies-to-support-state-designated-representatives.

53 Ibid., p. 90.

54 Executive Order 07-21 issued by Governor Kathleen Sebelius, July 18, 2007, Kansas State Library, http://www.kslib.info/executive/documents/EO%2007-21.pdf.

55 Messenger, "Does the First Amendment Allow States to Compel Recipients of Government Monies to Support State-Designated Representatives?"

56 The First Amendment provides, "Congress shall make no law respecting an establishment of religion, or prohibiting the free exercise thereof; or abridging the freedom of speech, or of the press; or the right of the people peaceably to assemble, and *to petition the Government for a* redress *of grievances*." (Emphasis added.)

57 Illinois EO 2003-08 (app. 46s); EL 2009-15 (App. 49a); see Writ of Certiorari, Harris v. Quinn, Messenger, November 29, 2011, p. 10.

Chapter 9. Insurrection

1 See U.S. Department of Commerce, Bureau of Economic Analysis, "Compensation of Employees by Industry" (database SA06N), http://www.bea.gov/iTable/iTable.cfm?reqid=70&step=1&isuri=1&acrdn=4.

2 Clay Barbour, "State Unions Fume over Betrayal, Prepare for Future Negotiations," *LaCrosse Tribune*, December 17, 2010, http://lacrossetribune.com/news/state-and-regional/wi/6dc723c4-09d9-11e0-976f-001cc4c03286.html, accessed January 2012.

3 Patrick McIlheran, "A Progressive Fight to Rein in Unions," *New York Post*, January 5, 2011, http://www.nypost.com/p/news/opinion/opedcolumnists/progressive_fight_to_rein_in_unions_bKH3ZTRwbtQYRYJko5VFnL, accessed January 2012.

4 Ibid.

5 Ibid.

6 Chris Tomlinson, "Wisconsin Governor Scott Walker Gives Speech to Conservatives at Legislative Forum in Texas," Associated Press, January 12, 2012, available at http://host.madison.com/news/local/govt-and-politics/elections/walker-gives-speech-to-conservative-group-in-texas/article_5f59cef0-3d3a-11e1-9db6-001871e3ce6c.html, accessed February 2012.

7 Mike Johnson, "Wisconsin AFL-CIO Ads Attack Walker Plan on Collective Bargaining," *Milwaukee Journal Sentinel*, February 13, 2011, http://www.jsonline.com/news/statepolitics/116114284.html, accessed January 2012; Scott Bauer, "Wisconsin Governor to Outline Ultimate Intentions in Budget,"

Associated Press, February 28, 2011, available at http://abcnews.go.com/US/wireStory?id=13017077, accessed January 2012.

8 One report explained, "The governor said he could not risk public safety by potential strikes from law enforcement. But the governor said that he was prepared, should other state workers strike in protest." Clay Barbour and Mary Spicuzza, "Walker Takes Broad Swipe at Public Employee Unions," *Wisconsin Elections and Politics*, February 12, 2011, http://host.madison.com/news/local/govt-and-politics/walker-takes-broad-swipe-at-public-employee-unions/article_c814c77a-3600-11e0-b9e0-001cc4c03286.html, accessed January 2012. Another report suggested that the reason Walker left public safety workers' contracts intact was "the unions for state troopers, Milwaukee police officers and Milwaukee firefighters all endorsed Walker, while most other unions endorsed his Democratic opponent, Milwaukee Mayor Tom Barrett." Johnson, "Wisconsin AFL-CIO Ads Attack Walker Plan on Collective Bargaining."

9 Dee Hall, "More Than 80 Threats Made against Walker, Lawmakers and Others, Records Show," *Wisconsin State Journal*, May 13, 2011, http://host.madison.com/wsj/news/local/govt-and-politics/article_884e3352-7cf4-11e0-98ed-001cc4c03286.html, accessed January 2012.

10 Mike Johnson and Jason Stein, "Justice Department Investigating Death Threats against Republican Senators, Representatives," *Milwaukee Journal Sentinel*, March 10, 2011, http://www.jsonline.com/blogs/news/117738098.html, accessed January 2012.

11 Bill Glauber, "Woman Charged with Email Threats," *Milwaukee Journal Sentinel*, March 31, 2011, http://www.jsonline.com/blogs/news/119023079.html, accessed January 2012.

12 Ed Treleven, "Woman Placed in First-Offenders Program for Bomb Threat to GOP State Senators," *Wisconsin State Journal*, December 16, 2011, http://host.madison.com/news/local/crime_and_courts/article_e8322b18-27e7-11e1-b21f-0019bb2963f4.html, accessed January 2012.

13 Richard Moore, "Union Boycotts against Walker Supporters Sputtering, Fragmenting," *Lakeland (Wisc.) Times*, April 15, 2011, http://www.lakelandtimes.com/main.asp?SectionID=9&SubSectionID=9&ArticleID=13036&TM=55897.49, accessed January 2012.

14 Mary Bruce, "Wisconsin Teachers Protest Ed Budget, Union Cuts," *ABC News*, February 17, 2011, http://abcnews.go.com/Politics/wisconsin-protests-news-wisconsin-governor-scott-walkers-proposal/story?id=12942012, accessed February 2012; Adam Rodewald, "Sick Leave, Disciplinary Records Reveal Teachers' Split Over Union Law Fight," *(Oshkosh, Wisc.) Northwestern*, April 17, 2011; Stephen Stromberg, "Wisconsin's Governor Is Not Hitler," *PostPartisan* (blog), *Washington Post*, February 18, 2011, http://voices.washingtonpost.com/postpartisan/2011/02/wisconsins_governor_is_not_hit.html, accessed January 2012.

15 David A. Keene, "A New Day for Wisconsin," *The Hill*, February 28, 2011, http://thehill.com/opinion/columnists/david-keene/146555-a-new-day-for-wisconsin-, accessed January 2012.

16 Bill O'Reilly, "Is Liberal America Going to Win Union Controversy?" video and transcript, *The O'Reilly Factor*, http://www.foxnews.com/on-air/oreilly/transcript/bill-oreilly-liberal-america-going-win-union-controversy#ixzz1j5oFG63r, accessed January 12, 2012.

17 "The Dick Morris Poll: American Voters Back Governors against Public Employee Unions," PR Newswire, March 18, 2011, available at http://www.thefreelibrary.com/The+Dick+Morris+Poll%3A+American+Voters+Back+Governors+Against+Public...-a0251806124, accessed January 2012.

18 *The Savage Nation*, Talk Radio Network, February 18, 2011.

19 Andrew Breitbart, "I Repeat to the Trumka Obama Class War Cult: Go to Hell," BigGovernment.com, April 16, 2011, http://biggovernment.com/abreitbart/2011/04/16/repeat-to-the-trumkaobama-class-war-cult-go-to-hell/, accessed January 2012.

20 Charles Krauthammer, "Union Owned and Operated," *Chicago Tribune*, June 20, 2011, http://articles.chicagotribune.com/2011-06-20/news/ct-oped-0620-krauthammer-20110620-8_1_president-barack-obama-exports-union-address, accessed January 2012.

21 See Stephen Hayes and John McCormack, "On Wisconsin! How Republicans Won the Battle of Madison," *Weekly Standard*, March 21, 2011, http://www.weeklystandard.com/articles/wisconsin_554095.html, accessed February 2012.

22 "In Wisconsin, Big Labor Politicians Help Make Right-to-Work Case," *Daily Caller*, March 30, 2011 http://dailycaller.com/2011/03/30/in-wisconsin-big-labor-politicians-help-make-right-to-work-case/, accessed February 2012.

23 "Wisconsin's Battle Supreme," editorial, *Wall Street Journal*, March 25, 2011, http://online.wsj.com/article/SB10001424052748704050204576218793987334696.html, accessed January 2012.

24 Patrick Marley and Don Walker, "Supreme Court Reinstates Collective Bargaining Law," *Milwaukee Journal Sentinel*, June 14, 2011, http://www.jsonline.com/news/statepolitics/123859034.html, accessed February 2012.

25 George Will, "Liberals' Wisconsin Waterloo," *Washington Post*, August 24, 2011, http://www.washingtonpost.com/opinions/liberals-wisconsin-waterloo/2011/08/23/gIQArm5GcJ_story.html, accessed January 2012.

26 Larry Sandler, "Milwaukee to See Net Gain from State Budget," *Milwaukee Journal Sentinel*, August 8, 2011, http://www.jsonline.com/news/statepolitics/127269673.html, accessed January 2012.

27 Moe Lane, "Wisconsin Labor Union Reform: Saving Jobs, Money, Schools," RedState, July 26, 2011, http://www.redstate.com/moe_lane/2011/07/26/wisconsin-labor-union-reform-saving-jobs-money-schools/, accessed January 2012.

28 Steven Moore, "The Most Important Non-Presidential Election of the Decade," *Wall Street Journal*, January 28, 2012, http://online.wsj.com/article/SB10001424052970204573704577186830049178636.html?KEYWORDS=wisconsin+budget+reform, accessed February 2012.

29 Moore, "The Most Important Non-Presidential Election of the Decade."

30 George Will, "Liberals' Wisconsin Waterloo," *Washington Post*, August 24, 2011, http://www.washingtonpost.com/opinions/liberals-wisconsin-waterloo/2011/08/23/gIQArm5GcJ_story.html, accessed February 2012.

31 Moore, "The Most Important Non-Presidential Election of the Decade."

32 "A Wisconsin Vindication," *Wall Street Journal*, April 16, 2012, http://online.wsj.com/article/SB10001424052702304432704577348080124322186.html?mod=WSJ_hp_mostpop_read, accessed April 2012.

33 Mark Walsh, "Mixed Court Decision for Wisconsin Anti-Union Law," *School Law* (blog), *Education Week*, April 2, 2012, http://blogs.edweek.org/edweek/school_law/2012/04/mixed_court_decision_for_wisco.html, accessed April 2012; Wisconsin Education Association Council v. Walker, No. 3:2011cv00428 (W.D. Wisc. March 30, 2012), available at the Wisconsin Department of Justice website, http://www.doj.state.wi.us/news/files/opinion-order-20120330.pdf, accessed April 2012.

34 "Ohio Gov. Kasich Signs Controversial Union Bill," Newsmax, March 31, 2011, http://www.newsmax.com/InsideCover/Ohio-union-bill-JohnKasich/2011/03/31/id/391365, accessed February 2012.

35 "A Wisconsin Vindication."

36 Christian Schneider, "Why Ohio Is Not Wisconsin," *The Corner* (blog), *National Review Outline*, November 9, 2011, http://www.nationalreview.com/corner/282720/why-ohio-not-wisconsin-christian-schneider, accessed January 2012.

37 Sam Hananel, "Unions Gearing Up to Spend Big in 2012 Elections," *Huffington Post*, February 22, 2012, http://www.huffingtonpost.com/2012/02/22/labor-unions-obama-elections-2012_n_1293173.html, accessed February 2012.

38 Ibid.

39 Jason Hart, "Ohio Workers Keep Losing Thanks to Big Labor's Win," RedState, January 17, 2012, http://www.redstate.com/jasonahart/2012/01/17/ohio-workers-losing-thanks-to-big-labor/, accessed January 2012.

40 *Squawk Box*, CNBC, May 27, 2010.

41 Athena Merritt, "Christie Signs N.J. Budget That's 9% Lower Than Last Year," *Philadelphia Business Journal*, June 29, 2010, http://www.bizjournals.com/philadelphia/stories/2010/06/28/daily14.html?page=all, accessed February 2012.

42 Lisa Fleisher, "Gov. Christie Outlines Cuts to N.J. Workers' Pension, Benefits," *(Newark, N.J.) Star-Ledger*, September 15, 2010, http://www.nj.com/news/index.ssf/2010/09/gov_christie_outlines_cuts_to.html, accessed January 2012.

43 Bob Luebke, "House Votes to End Dues Check Off Benefit for NCAE," John W. Pope Civitas Institute, January 5, 2012, http://www.nccivitas.org/2012/house-votes-to-end-dues-check-off-benefit-for-ncae/, accessed January 2012.

44 John Frank, "GOP overrides veto of bill to weaken teachers group," *CharlotteObserver.com*, January 5, 2012, http://www.charlotteobserver.com/2012/01/05/2899853/gop-passes-late-night-bill-to.html, accessed January 2012.

45 Kyle Olson, "Tennessee Trumps Wisconsin: Kills Teacher Collective Bargaining. Dead." Biggovernment.com, June 5, 2011, http://biggovernment.com/kolson/2011/06/05/tennessee-trumps-wisconsin-kills-teacher-collective-bargaining-dead/, accessed February 2012.

46 "Fallin Signs Municipal Collective Bargaining Repeal," Capitol Beat OK, April 29, 2011, http://capitolbeatok.com/_webapp_3887193/Fallin_signs _municipal_collective_bargaining_repeal, accessed February 2012.

47 Abby Goodnough, "Massachusetts House seeks to limit collective bargaining," *New York Times*, April 4, 2011, http://www.nytimes.com/2011/04/30/ business/economy/30massachusetts.html, accessed February 2012.

48 Kimberley Strassel, "Union busting, Massachusetts Style," *Wall Street Journal*, April 29, 2011, http://online.wsj.com/article/SB10001424052748704463804576291240909536676.html, accessed February 2012; Jennifer Levitz, "Massachusetts curbs bargaining," *Wall Street Journal*, July 2, 2011, http://online.wsj.com/article/SB10001424052702303763404576420294248965916.html, accessed February 2012.

49 Letter from President Robert J. Haynes, Massachusetts AFL-CIO, April 15, 2011, http://www.massaflcio.org/node/196671, accessed February 2012.

50 Hillary Chalbot, "Governor Patrick Signs $30.6 Billion State Budget," *Boston Herald*, July, 11, 2011, http://bostonherald.com/news/regional/view/2011 _0711gov_patrick_signs_306b_state_budget, accessed February 2012.

51 Ivan Osorio and Trey Kovacs, "Labor Unions and the Democratic Party," Labor Watch, Capital Research Center, July 2011, http://www.capitalresearch.org/pubs/pdf/v1309465576.pdf, accessed January 2012.

52 Osorio and Kovacs, "Labor Unions and the Democratic Party."

53 Jon Ward, "Democrat Caddell rips White House for obeisance to organized labor," *Daily Caller*, February 17, 2010, http://dailycaller.com/2010/02/17/ democrat-caddell-rips-white-house-for-obeisance-to-organized-labor/, accessed January 2012.

54 "WCBS 880 Interview: NJ St. Sen. Pres. Stephen Sweeney Talks Politics, Credit, And More," CBS New York, June 29, 2011, http://newyork.cbslocal.com/2011/06/29/wcbs-880-interview-nj-st-sen-pres-stephen-sweeney-talks -politics-credit-and-more/, accessed January 2012. See Associated Press, "Chris Christie, Stephen Sweeney Are New Jersey's Odd Couple," *Politico*, May 21, 2011, http://www.politico.com/news/stories/0511/55416.html, accessed January 2012.

55 Daniel Massey, "Union Membership in New York Slips to New Low," *Crain's New York Business*, February 22, 2012, http://www.crainsnewyork.com/ article/20120222/LABOR_UNIONS/120229975#ixzz1nDbn4oAa, accessed February 2012.

56 Lachlan Markay, "Unions Defend Keystone Opposition: We Have to Support Obama!" *The Foundry* (blog), Heritage Foundation, January 24, 2012, http:// blog.heritage.org/2012/01/24/unions-defend-keystone-opposition-we-have -to-support-obama/, accessed January 2012.

57 Ibid.

58 Indiana's new right-to-work statute applies only to private sector workers—not to any state or local government workers, although some public sector employees already had right-to-work protection. For example, collective bargaining was already prohibited for most state employees by a law enacted in 2011. That law also contained specific right-to-work protection, even though state workers

who don't have forced union representation can't have forced dues. But that law specifically does not cover state police, state educational institutions, and local government workers. Indiana has had right-to-work protections for teachers on the books for many years—but not for other public school employees or for other local government employees. So this means that all government workers in Indiana already had right-to-work protections except: state police, state educational institution employees, and (nonteacher) local government employees such as police, firefighters, school employees, and others, who still do not have such protections.

Conclusion

1 Liberty Chick, "Union Bosses Target 86-Yr Old Volunteer Crossing Guard," BigGovernment.com, February 11, 2010, http://biggovernment.com/libertychick/2010/02/11/union-bosses-target-86-yr-old-volunteer-crossing-guard/, accessed January 2012.

2 Ibid.

3 Labor Union Report, "AFSCME Bosses still want 86 year old volunteer crossing guard fired," Redstate.com, February 8, 2010, http://www.redstate.com/laborunionreport/2010/02/08/afscme-bosses-still-want-86-year-old-volunteer-crossing-guard-fired/, accessed April 2012.

4 Pete Peterson, "No Volunteers, Please, We're Unionized," *City Journal*, November 30, 2011, http://www.city-journal.org/2010/eon1130pp.html, accessed January 2012.

5 "Pennsylvania Union Leader Resigns Amid Criticism for Threatening Legal Action over Boy Scout's Volunteerism," *Fox News*, November 23, 2009, http://www.foxnews.com/story/0,2933,576438,00.html, accessed January 2012.

6 U.S. v. Enmons, 410 U.S. 396 (1973).

7 Ronald Reagan, "Remarks and a Question-and-Answer Session With Reporters on the Air Traffic Controllers Strike, August 3, 1981," The American Presidency Project, http://www.presidency.ucsb.edu/ws/index.php?pid=44138#axzz1shzndo8C, accessed April 2012.

Index

About the Authors

Mallory Factor is the John C. West Professor of International Politics and American Government at The Citadel. He is a *Forbes* columnist, the senior editor of money and politics for TheStreet.com, a political commentator, and a businessman. Mallory Factor is the co-founder of The Monday Meeting, an influential group of conservative political leaders, journalists, donors, think tank heads, and grassroots leaders in New York City—the largest meeting of its type in America.

Elizabeth Factor is an attorney and consultant.